Introduction
to the
Play

In the Theater of the Mind

HAYDEN SERIES IN LITERATURE

Robert W. Boynton, Consulting Editor

Former Principal, Senior High School
and Chairman, English Department
Germantown Friends School

Introduction to the Play

In the Theater of the Mind

Revised Second Edition

ROBERT W. BOYNTON
and
MAYNARD MACK
Yale University

HAYDEN BOOK COMPANY, INC.
Rochelle Park, New Jersey

ACKNOWLEDGMENTS

The Devil's Disciple by George Bernard Shaw is used by permission of the Society of Authors.

Botticelli. From *Sweet Eros, Next, and Other Plays*, by Terrence McNally, copyright © 1969 by Terrence McNally. Reprinted by permission of Random House, Inc.

Day of Absence. © Copyright 1966, by Douglas Turner Ward. Reprinted by permission of the author and of Dramatists Play Service, Inc. CAUTION: *Day of Absence*, being duly copyrighted, is subject to a royalty. The amateur acting rights in the play are controlled exclusively by the Dramatists Play Service, Inc., 440 Park Avenue South, New York, NY 10016. No amateur production of the play may be given without obtaining in advance the written permission of the Dramatists Play Service, Inc., and paying the requisite fee.

The Glass Menagerie. Copyright 1945 by Tennessee Williams and Edwina D. Williams and renewed 1973 by Tennessee Williams. Reprinted by permission of Random House, Inc.

The Infernal Machine by Jean Cocteau is reprinted with the permission of Editions Bernard Grasset and the translator, Carl Widman, who holds coyright on this version. *The Infernal Machine and Other Plays*, copyright © 1963 by New Directions. Reprinted by permission of New Directions Publishing Corporation and Albert Bermel.

Library of Congress Cataloging in Publication Data

Boynton, Robert W.   comp.
    Introduction to the play.

    (Hayden series in literature)
    Includes complete texts of The devil's disciple,
by G. B. Shaw; Botticelli, by T. McNally; Day of
absence, by D. T. Ward; The glass menagerie, by
T. Williams; and The infernal machine, by J.
Cocteau.
    1. Drama — 20th century. I. Mack, Maynard,
1909-   II. Title.
PN6112.B65   1976   808.82'51   75-45199
ISBN 0-8104-5731-8

The First Edition of this volume was published under the title *Introduction to the Play.*

Printed in the United States of America

5   6   7   8   9   PRINTING

83 84   YEAR

Preface

The study of plays has long been a normal part of the high school English program, but too often the content has been limited to a few Shakespearean tragedies and perhaps a modern play or two, sometimes presented rather apologetically as poor substitutes for the real thing on a stage. With the increasing interest in good movies, both American and foreign, and in the occasional excellent drama on television, the reading and study of plays might well drift further into the wings.

Young people seldom see good plays, either professional or amateur, for a variety of reasons, some simply unfortunate, some deplorable. Unfortunate is the fact that unless students live near a very large city or a university town, good theater is simply not available except at excessive cost of money and time. Deplorable is the fact that many high schools make no attempt to put on serious adult plays: dramatic productions are characteristically limited to springtime performances of potboilers written to make everyone happy except those in the cast and audience who are offended by being treated like nincompoops.

The thesis of this book is that the study of serious drama is of central importance in any English curriculum and that while students should be encouraged and enabled to see as many productions of good plays as possible (and to produce them for themselves), the reading of plays has its own distinct value and is in no sense a "poor substitute" for seeing a performance. The theater of the mind is an exciting place if it's open for business. Any group of actors preparing to put on a play will read it through a number of times, silently and aloud, and spend a good deal of time talking about what goes on and why—what various lines mean and how they mght be handled. It's a group process, with people feeding insights to each other. When you read a play, you should try to go through this process with yourself.

Teachers familiar with the average high school drama textbook or anthology will find a quite different approach in this book. The usual technical terminology is missing, not because it is useless or wrong, but because it can get in the way of a focus on the essential nature of drama: a continuously unfolding, direct head-to-head acting out of some human conflict set in motion and seeking a resolution in the presence of a seen or unseen audience, themselves, as observers, also directly involved and yet removed at the same time.

We also pay considerable attention to the conventions of the drama as an art form and the theater as its arena, something generally ignored in textbooks, yet of crucial importance to an understanding of dramatic form and practice. We have chosen plays that are reasonably familiar and also representative of the best of early and recent twentieth century theater: Bernard Shaw's *The Devil's Disciple*, Jean Cocteau's *The Infernal Machine*, Tennessee Williams's *The Glass Menagerie*, Douglas Turner Ward's *Day of Absence*, and Terrence McNally's *Botticelli*.

The first part of the book is organized for intensive analysis and discussion of the nature of drama, with constant reference to specific scenes and acts. The opening lines of a scene from *Hamlet* and the whole of *The Devil's Disciple* are analyzed in great detail, with further questions for student consideration. A careful initial study of the Table of Contents will give a clear picture of how we have proceeded. The second part of the book consists of the remaining four plays, with introductory comments and detailed questions at the end relating each play to the concerns raised in the first part and to each other.

Contents

Introduction
to the
Play

In the Theater of the Mind

What is a play?

Plays are more exciting when acted than when read, but we learn more about them from reading them. And when we take what we have learned from reading back to the theater or the movie house or the television set, we suddenly find them still more exciting than they were before. Knowing about plays, like knowing about baseball, intensifies our interest. What then is a play? To answer that question, let's look at a small part of a very famous one, *Hamlet.*

POLONIUS.　'A° will come straight.° Look you lay° home to him.
　　　Tell him his pranks have been too broad° to bear with,
　　　And that your grace hath screened and stood between
　　　Much heat° and him. I'll silence° me even here.
5　　　Pray you be round° with him.
　　[HAMLET.　(*within*) Mother, mother, mother!]
　　QUEEN.　I'll warrant you; fear me not.° Withdraw; I hear him
　　　coming. [*Polonius hides behind the arras.*]
　　　　　　　　　Enter Hamlet
　　HAMLET.　Now, mother, what's the matter?
10　QUEEN.　Hamlet, thou hast thy father° much offended.
　　HAMLET.　Mother, you have my father° much offended.
　　QUEEN.　Come, come, you answer with an idle° tongue.
　　HAMLET.　Go, go, you question with a wicked tongue.
　　QUEEN.　Why, how now, Hamlet?
　　HAMLET.　What's the matter now?
　　QUEEN.　Have you forgot me?°
15　HAMLET.　No, by the rood,° not so!
　　　You are the queen, your husband's brother's wife,
　　　And (would it were not so) you are my mother.
　　QUEEN.　Nay, then I'll set those ° to you that can speak.

° **'A':** he.
° **straight:** at once.
° **lay:** thrust.
° **broad:** free.
° **heat:** i.e., the King's anger.
° **silence:** hide (in silence).
° **round:** blunt.
° **I'll ... not:** I guarantee it; don't worry.
° **father:** i.e., the King.
° **father:** the former King, Hamlet's natural father.
° **Idle:** foolish.
° **me:** i.e., who I am.
° **rood:** cross.
° **those:** i.e., the King, Polonius, etc.

HAMLET.   Come, come, and sit you down. You shall not budge.
20   You go not till I set you up a glass °
           Where you may see the inmost part of you.
QUEEN.   What wilt thou do? Thou wilt not murther me?
           Help ho!
POLONIUS.   [*behind*] What, ho! help!
25   HAMLET.   [*draws*] How now? a rat? ° Dead for a ducat,° dead!
           [*Makes a pass through the arras and kills Polonius*]
POLONIUS.   [*behind*] O, I am slain!
QUEEN.   O me, what hast thou done?
HAMLET.   Nay, I know not. Is it the king?
QUEEN.   O, what a rash and bloody deed is this!
HAMLET.   A bloody deed—almost as bad, good mother,
30   As kill a king, and marry with his brother.
QUEEN.   As kill a king?
HAMLET.   Ay, lady, it was my word.
           [*Lifts up the arras and sees Polonius*]
           Thou wretched, rash, intruding fool, farewell!
           I took thee for thy better. Take thy fortune.
           Thou find'st to be too busy ° is some danger.—
35   Leave wringing of your hands. Peace, sit you down
           And let me wring your heart, for so I shall
           If it be made of penetrable stuff,
           If damned custom have not brazed it so
           That it is proof and bulwark against sense.

Here is a piece of dialogue that has roused spectators for three hundred and fifty years. What does it tell us about the nature of a play?

(a) A play is an action involving some form of conflict or struggle.

In *Hamlet* the conflict is multiple and complex. At the center the conflict is between and within the two "mighty opposites," Hamlet and his uncle. Hamlet's uncle has usurped Hamlet's father's throne after murdering him, and still earlier had seduced Hamlet's mother, now his wife and queen. In the opening act Hamlet's father's ghost swears him to revenge the murder. From then on the conflict is drawn in specific terms. Hamlet must verify the ghost's disclosure and carry out the punishment; the King must discover what intentions underlie his nephew's odd and sometimes ominous behavior. In general terms, the conflict between the unworldly, reflective, irresolute Prince and the self-seeking, crafty, decisive King is the conflict between virtue and corruption, openness and deceit, being and seeming to be.

Around this central conflict revolve numerous secondary

° **glass:** mirror.

° **rat:** Hamlet supposes the victim to be the king.

° **for a ducat:** I'll bet a ducat (a gold coin).

° **busy:** i.e., in other people's affairs.

interlocking ones, such as that between Hamlet and his mother, which comes to a head in the scene whose opening lines appear above. He had thought her a loving and virtuous wife and mother, but has learned that she is just the opposite. In their meeting in this scene, she struggles to blunt the barbs of his disgust and live in peace with the bargain she has made; he struggles to make her *be* what she has seemed to be. The mother-son clash echoes the central conflict.

(b) The conflict of a play, though it will find expression in some sort of physical behavior, lies essentially in the human mind and feeling.

There is considerable physical action in this brief exchange. Polonius bids the Queen be firm and hides himself behind the wall hangings so that he can hear what goes on. The Queen is left alone and Hamlet enters. Very quickly she loses control of the situation and tries to leave, but is detained physically and forced to sit. When she cries for help, her cry is repeated by Polonius, and Hamlet springs up, drawing his sword as he does, and drives it into the arras. He withdraws it covered with blood and knows that he has hit home. His mother, who has followed him to the arras, looks down with him at the slain Polonius as he flings back the curtain. He drops it again, turns to her with his "leave wringing of your hands," and bids her sit. She retreats to the chair—no need for force now—her eyes steadily upon him.

The raw stage movement is simple, but exciting. Equally exciting is the action we sense going on inside the two principals. As the scene opens, she intends to upbraid him for his insulting behavior to his uncle and to her. She will be firm and blunt; she will demand a change. He, in turn, intends to chastise her for the indecency of her hasty remarriage and her wantonness. As he has said to himself, just before going to her chamber,

> Let me be cruel, not unnatural;
> I will speak daggers to her, but use none.

From the very first, his spoken "daggers" blunt her resolve; the bitterness of his verbal attack turns her firmness to fear. She cries out in terror, and her cry is echoed by the hidden Polonius.

Hamlet's anger, up to this point barely held in check, now bursts into extreme physical expression as he plunges his sword into the arras. The sight of it bloodied increases his mother's terror, and she can only hope that in his madness he will not turn it on her. This is not what he came to do, however. His violence cools, and he turns again to anguished denunciation. He intends to "wring her heart" so that some semblance of the virtue that once seemed to be hers may actually return to her. She has lost her struggle to make him ignore what is and accept what seems to be. The conflict between them is not over, but its resolution is foretold.

(c) In reading a play, we follow the action of mind and feelings through the language.

How do we know that what we have said above about the physical action and the internal action has any sort of accuracy? We know because the language of the dialogue tells us. If we look again at the exchange between Hamlet and his mother, this time line by line, we can see how the language works to tell us what the characters do and what they are feeling.

Polonius's simple if earnest counsel (". . . lay home to him. . . . be round with him") and his easy insistence that she has borne great trial in defending him to his stepfather the King ("your grace has screened and stood between/Much heat and him") is more appropriate to the proposed handling of an unruly boy than of an incensed man. Her reply sounds resolute enough ("I'll warrant you; fear me not"), but it is mocked by what happens within moments after Hamlet's arrival.

She signals that arrival with her "withdraw; I hear him coming." Polonius "silences" himself behind the arras, as he says he will in line 4. The Queen is left alone, tensely waiting. There is a brave show in her pose, and in the brief moment between Polonius's hiding and Hamlet's entrance she believes she will do what she has said she will. We may imagine her—on the stage we would see her—gathering her energies for the onset, preparing to assume an attitude of indignation, and imagining that he will already be shamefaced for his shocking behavior in the preceding scene. His defiant entrance and blunt question, "Now, mother, what's the matter?" take her by surprise.

The double meaning of "what's the matter?" (*1*—what's the matter with you? what's bothering you? and *2*—what's the "matter" —the subject—you want to see me about? what's on your mind?) suggests a calculated belligerency and lack of respect, with not even a suggestion of mannered formality preceding it. She tries to maintain her composure and answers him, ignoring his rudeness. But he throws back her stiff accusation ("Hamlet, thou hast thy father much offended") and her vexed rebuke ("Come, come, you answer with an idle tongue") with counteraccusations that mimic hers. When she refers to "thy father" (meaning Hamlet's uncle, her new husband), he slashes back with "my father" (meaning the murdered King), and it is perfectly clear what he thinks of the change. These replies are not what she has bargained for. They are angry, and they are riddling: why should he call her questions "wicked"?

She then tries to put him in the wrong, first with a surprised and hurt, "Why, how now, Hamlet?" (i.e., what's the matter with *you*? why are you acting so strangely? why do you do this to your mother?). But he sticks insolently to the "matter" in hand: "What's the matter now?" Rather pathetically, she asserts her position and her dignity: "Have you forgot me?" Have you forgotten that I am your mother and the Queen? But each shifting of her ground leaves her more defenseless. "Have you forgot me?" What a question to ask! He has thought of little else, for she has come to represent to him—ever since the Ghost divulged the adultery and the murder (in which, for anything he knows, she probably had a part)—all that is most degraded in the world: treachery, dishonor, faithlessness. He pours out his disillusionment in his reply; derides her position as Queen simply by mentioning it with scorn; refuses to apply the word "husband" to the man she is married to now (as he had refused to apply the word "father" to him in line 11); and finally, cruelest of all, deplores the very fact that she is his mother.

Her desired recourse is to break off the encounter entirely, to let the King or Polonius intervene: "Nay, then I'll set those to you that can speak." It is her last hope, but it fails. As she tries to run from the room, he seizes her by the arm and roughly forces her to the chair: "Come, come, and sit you down. You shall not budge. You go not till . . .". The violence that accompanies these words and the pent-up violence seething in them communicates itself immediately to her. We sense her dread in the fact that her almost involuntary response to being forced to sit is to blurt out, "What wilt thou do? Thou wilt not murther me? Help, ho!" This is no simple outcry of pain at rough handling. She is terrified, and we must read the preceding lines in the context of this response. The gestures that all along accompany her loss of control will clearly indicate her growing awareness of violence hanging in the air and about to break out.

The same note is struck in Hamlet's reaction to the echo of the Queen's cry from behind the arras. In a moment of instantaneous action completely unlike anything in his previous behavior in the play, he plunges his sword through the arras with a mixture of contempt and exaltation, conveyed in the lines he speaks: "How now? a rat? Dead for a ducat, dead!" He believes it is the King ("a rat"), and the elation of possibly having carried out the Ghost's charge brings the cry of triumph, "Dead for a ducat, dead!" (I'll bet a ducat he's dead!) The flashing finality of the act contrasts with his previous behavior only minutes before when, on his way to his mother's chamber, he passed the King at his prayers, and could easily have killed him but did not. (Of course, a moment's thought would have told him that this could hardly be the King, whom he had just left; but the Hamlet of this moment is not a man of thought.)

When he withdraws the sword from Polonius, the Queen stands rooted, aghast at what has happened: "O me, what hast thou done? . . . O, what a rash and bloody deed is this!" His sword is still bared; and for all she knows, in what she has just seen of his sudden mad fury, he may bury it in her. The "rash and bloody deed" has relaxed the pressure, however, and now the seething within comes out, not in further physical action, but in his dagger-like retort. He vents now what is uppermost in his mind, what really is "the matter":

> A bloody deed—almost as bad, good mother,
> As kill a king, and marry with his brother.

As she repeats with unfeigned horror the deadly phrase, ". . . kill a king," she suddenly understands that it is not simply her hasty remarriage which has been rankling in him, but a bloodier and more calculating deed by far than the killing of an intruder. Perhaps she had never faced the possibility, in the heat of her desire, that her new husband might have murdered her old for his crown and his wife. Perhaps she knew—yet did not feelingly know till forced to contemplate it now in the light of another's knowledge. The play does not tell us what we are to think on this score. What it does tell us is that the phrase lands with crushing weight. After it there is silence on her part, a silence which shows how thoroughly the meaning of "as kill a king" sinks into her consciousness.

We have seen how each line builds carefully on the one before it. The Queen's comments and questions bring replies she does not expect and cannot handle, but they build clearly, if ironically, on what she has said. Line 10 tells Hamlet exactly "what's the matter" so far as she is concerned; line 11 twists the sense to reveal "what's the matter" so far as Hamlet is concerned; line 12 chides him for playing on her words with an "idle tongue"; line 13 plays on her chiding and accuses her of a "wickedness" not yet defined. So it continues throughout. The statements and retorts come in rapid order, and the wordplay imitates a grossly one-sided, but deadly fencing match (the conception of a duel—of wits, of words, of stratagems, of rapiers—dominates the play throughout). The climax of the verbal combat comes in lines 28–31 where the repeated phrasing and unexpected rhyme slow the pace and underline the enormity of the two murders, particularly that of Hamlet's father. First Hamlet echoes his mother's "a . . . bloody deed," another utterance of hers which, like "have offended" and "Have you forgot me?" arouses answers she had not foreseen. On his mind it flashes the image of another "bloody deed," and he drives home his final thrust: ". . . almost as bad, good mother,/As kill a king, and marry with his brother." For the first time, in her reply, the echo of a phrase comes from her and not from him, and for the first time it is not a parry: it is the receiving of a finishing blow. There is no elation at this success, just a blunt "Ay, lady, it was my word"—not even the sarcasm of "good mother," just "lady."

He then, as the stage direction unnecessarily says, lifts the arras, sees that it is Polonius he has killed, and, in words as alien to the Hamlet we see in Act I as the slaughter itself, he dismisses the old man (and, therefore, the slaughter) curtly, almost coldly. That done, he drops the arras, turns again to his mother, and sits her down once more—this time by simply commanding her to sit.

(d) At any given point in a play the conflict will be expressed through confrontation—either that of two characters or that of two states of mind in the same character.

Implicit in even the most casual of real conversations is the principle of one-to-one opposition: a conversation is essentially a give-and-take between two people at any one time, no matter how many others may be around listening. Dialogue imitates this behavior; but like all art, it brings order and direction to what is naturally, in the "real" world, casual and rambling. Any normal conversation, even a very serious one, is full of false starts, side comments, meaningless remarks made to fill the air; and there is a randomness to its direction that would strangle a good play. Dialogue (stage conversation) is as different from real conversation as a modern dance recital is from a stroll in the park: one is art, the other is raw material. Just as dance has its roots in normal, everyday bodily movements, so dialogue finds its roots in the fact that human beings rarely use language simply to get and give information, but rather to confront one another, "foreheads together" (which is what "confront" means), in matters both sober and trifling, important and unimportant.

In a play, the verbal action is a carefully ordered series of confrontations between characters, usually two at any given point. Scene divisions, whether designated by the playwright, as in a modern play, or by an editor, as with most of Shakespeare's, usually come where there is a specific change of place involved, or perhaps a change of time. More accurately, they should come with a change of one-to-one confrontations, but it would be a distortion of a play's movement to cut up the text in such a way. The confrontations flow smoothly one into the next. The editor's act and scene divisions in Shakespeare's plays, for instance, are helpful enough for reference purposes, but it is essential to produce or read the plays as if they were not there. It is extremely doubtful that Shakespeare ever saw *Hamlet* in his imagination as a five-act, twenty-scene, stop-and-go play. Rather he must have seen it as a closely woven series of fully three times as many "scenes" growing inevitably out of, and into, each other without much regard for place or time, but only for the multiple working out of the central conflict. As we shall see in detail later, Shaw indicates no change of scene in Act I of *The Devil's Disciple*, although there are at least eight clearly differentiated "scenes," each essentially a one-to-one confrontation.

In any scene so defined, several people may be present, but the "action" will almost always take place between two. The others, either participating occasionally, or simply listening, or, sometimes, overhearing, are, in a very real sense, audience. Yet the meaning of the conflict may be sought in their silent involvement as well as in the reactions of the principals of the moment. We are not to let ourselves be distracted by them, but their presence serves to focus our attention on the main action of the scene.

The meeting between Hamlet and his mother well illustrates this point. Primarily the struggle is played out between them, but it also includes the silent listener, Polonius, perfectly aware behind the arras (where we know he is) that the game is going against the Queen. Panic grows in him too, so much that it takes only the shouted alarm from the Queen to set off his echoing cry. That cry and Hamlet's bloody response shift the focus momentarily to this audience-behind-the-arras, now truly "silenced"; but only momentarily, for the action of the scene is still between Hamlet and his mother.

As Polonius lies dead while Hamlet carries out his promise to "wring [her] heart," a still wider audience—ourselves—is sharply aware of his presence: aware that he will never "tell . . . what I know" to the King, as he had promised; aware that Hamlet must do something with the body before the scene ends; aware, most importantly, that Polonius's presence as silenced audience is as much a commentary on the conflict unfolding as if he were still alive and hidden.

Central to any scene, then, is the dialogue between the two principals of the moment. Surrounding them in many scenes will be a first circle of listeners—the other characters, participants in the scene because in some way involved in the working out of the conflict. Surrounding these we take our own seats—readers of the play or playgoers in the theater: the "real" audience. We are drawn into the drama more surely and more understandingly because the attention of the stage-audience is also focused on the confrontation, and their silent invitation is to us to join them.

The Devil's Disciple

We have looked in great detail at part of a scene from *Hamlet* to bring out the fact that the essential element of drama lies in confrontation, most often one-to-one. Now it is time to turn to the first of five plays in this book, *The Devil's Disciple*, by George Bernard Shaw, to examine act by act the structuring to which these confrontations contribute and the other elements of dramatic form with which they are normally entwined. At the end of each act we shall therefore have a good deal to say about how it is put together.

George Bernard Shaw is one of the masters of the modern theater. Born in Dublin, he lived the last sixty or so years of his life in England and brought to the English stage a brilliant wit, an incisive critical mind, and a consuming interest in theater craftsmanship. In a sense he used the stage as a soapbox from which to harangue his fellow man about all manner of human foolishness, stupidity, and ignorance; but he never let the preacher in him smother the playwright. Most of his fifty-odd plays have lost little of their sting or their delight, largely because the man who wrote them learned his trade remarkably well.

(Although the play is printed with discussion and questions following the individual act, read the *entire* play through before turning to them. Act I starts on page 11, Act II on page 43, and Act III on page 71. The remaining four plays will be printed without interruption, with headnotes preceding and questions at the very end.)

The Devil's Disciple

GEORGE BERNARD SHAW
(1856–1950)

CHARACTERS
(*in order of appearance*)

MRS. TIMOTHY DUDGEON, *mother of Christy and Richard*

ESSIE, *daughter of Peter Dudgeon*

CHRISTY DUDGEON, *youngest son of Mrs. Dudgeon*

ANTHONY ANDERSON, *Westerbridge's minister*

JUDITH ANDERSON, *wife of Anthony*

LAWYER HAWKINS

WILLIAM DUDGEON *and wife*

TITUS DUDGEON *and wife*

RICHARD DUDGEON, *oldest son of Mrs. Dudgeon*

An ENGLISH SERGEANT *and soldiers of the British army*

MAJOR SWINDON, *an officer of the British army*

GENERAL BURGOYNE

MR. BRUDENELL, *chaplain to the British troops*

ACT I

At the most wretched hour between a black night and a wintry morning in the year 1777, Mrs. Dudgeon, of New Hampshire, is sitting up in the kitchen and general dwelling room of her farmhouse on the outskirts of the town of Websterbridge. She is not a prepossessing woman. No woman looks her best after sitting up all night; and Mrs. Dudgeon's face, even at its best, is grimly trenched by the channels into which the barren forms and observances of a dead Puritanism can pen a bitter temper and a fierce pride. She is an elderly matron who has worked hard and got nothing by it except dominion and detestation in her sordid home, and an unquestioned reputation for piety and respectability among her neighbors, to whom drink and debauchery are still so much more tempting than religion and rectitude, that they conceive goodness simply as self-denial. This conception is easily extended to others-denial, and finally generalized as covering anything disagreeable. So Mrs. Dudgeon, being exceedingly disagreeable, is *held to be exceedingly good. Short of flat felony, she enjoys complete license except for amiable weaknesses of any sort, and is consequently, without knowing it, the most licentious woman in the parish on the strength of never having broken the seventh commandment or missed a Sunday at the Presbyterian church.*

The year 1777 is the one in which the passions roused by the breaking-off of the American colonies from England, more by their own weight than by their own will, boiled up to shooting point, the shooting being idealized to the English mind as suppression of rebellion and maintenance of British dominion, and to the American as defense of liberty, resistance to tyranny, and self-sacrifice on the altar of the Rights of Man. Into the merits of these idealizations it is not here necessary to inquire; suffice it to say, without prejudice, that they have convinced both Americans and English that the most highminded course for them to pursue is to kill as many of one another as possible, and that military operations to that end are in full swing, morally supported by confident requests from the clergy of both sides for the blessing of God on their arms.

Under such circumstances many other women besides this disagreeable Mrs. Dudgeon find themselves sitting up all night waiting for news. Like her, too, they fall asleep towards morning at the risk of nodding themselves into the kitchen fire. Mrs. Dudgeon sleeps with a shawl over her head, and her feet on a broad fender of iron laths, the step of the domestic altar of the fireplace, with its huge hobs and boiler, and its hinged arm above the smoky mantelshelf for roasting. The plain kitchen table is opposite the fire, at her elbow, with a candle on it in a tin sconce. Her chair, like all the others in the room, is uncushioned and unpainted; but as it has a round railed back and a seat conventionally molded to the sitter's curves, it is comparatively a chair of state. The room has three doors, one on the same side as the fireplace, near the corner, leading to the best bedroom; one, at the opposite end of the opposite wall, leading to the scullery and washhouse; and the housedoor, with its latch, heavy lock, and clumsy wooden bar, in the front wall, between the window in its middle and the corner next the bedroom door. Between the door and the window a rack of pegs suggests to the deductive observer that the men of the house are all away, as there are no hats or coats on them. On the other side of the window the clock hangs on a nail, with its white wooden dial, black iron weights, and brass pendulum. Between the clock and the corner, a big cupboard, locked, stands on a dwarf dresser full of common crockery.

On the side opposite the fireplace, between the door and the corner, a shamelessly ugly black horsehair sofa stands against the wall. An inspection of its stridulous surface shows that Mrs. Dudgeon is not alone. A girl of sixteen or seventeen has fallen asleep on it. She is a wild, timid looking creature with black hair and tanned skin. Her frock, a scanty garment, is rent, weatherstained, berry-

stained, and by no means scrupulously clean. It hangs on her with
a freedom which, taken with her brown legs and bare feet, suggests
no great stock of underclothing.

Suddenly there comes a tapping at the door, not loud enough to
wake the sleepers. Then knocking, which disturbs Mrs. Dudgeon a
little. Finally the latch is tried, whereupon she springs up at once.

MRS. DUDGEON. (*Threateningly.*) Well, why don't you open the
door? (*She sees that the girl is asleep, and immediately raises a
clamor of heartfelt vexation.*) Well, dear, dear me! Now this is—
(*shaking her*) wake up, wake up: do you hear?

THE GIRL. (*Sitting up.*) What is it?

MRS. DUDGEON. Wake up; and be ashamed of yourself, you unfeeling sinful girl, falling asleep like that, and your father hardly cold
in his grave.

THE GIRL. (*Half asleep still.*) I didn't mean to. I dropped off—

MRS. DUDGEON. (*Cutting her short.*) Oh yes, you've plenty of excuses, I daresay. Dropped off! (*Fiercely, as the knocking recom-
mences.*) Why don't you get up and let your uncle in? after me
waiting up all night for him! (*She pushes her rudely off the sofa.*)
There: I'll open the door: much good you are to wait up. Go and
mend that fire a bit.

The girl, cowed and wretched, goes to the fire and puts a log on.
MRS. DUDGEON unbars the door and opens it, letting into the
stuffy kitchen a little of the freshness and a great deal of the chill
of the dawn, also her second son CHRISTY, a fattish, stupid, fair-
haired, roundfaced man of about 22, muffled in a plaid shawl and
gray overcoat. He hurries, shivering, to the fire, leaving MRS.
DUDGEON to shut the door.

CHRISTY. (*At the fire.*) F—f—f! but it is cold. (*Seeing the girl, and
staring lumpishly at her.*) Why, who are you?

THE GIRL. (*Shyly.*) Essie.

MRS. DUDGEON. Oh, you may well ask. (*To* ESSIE.) Go to your
room, child, and lie down, since you haven't feeling enough to keep
you awake. Your history isn't fit for your own ears to hear.

ESSIE. I—

MRS. DUDGEON. (*Peremptorily.*) Don't answer me, Miss; but show
your obedience by doing what I tell you. (ESSIE, *almost in tears,
crosses the room to the door near the sofa.*) And don't forget your
prayers. (ESSIE *goes out.*) She'd have gone to bed last night just
as if nothing had happened if I'd let her.

CHRISTY. (*Phlegmatically.*) Well, she can't be expected to feel Uncle
Peter's death like one of the family.

MRS. DUDGEON. What are you talking about, child? Isn't she his
daughter—the punishment of his wickedness and shame? (*She
assaults her chair by sitting down.*)

CHRISTY.   (*Staring.*) Uncle Peter's daughter!

MRS. DUDGEON.   Why else should she be here? D'ye think I've not had enough trouble and care put upon me bringing up my own girls, let alone you and your good-for-nothing brother, without having your uncle's bastards—

CHRISTY.   (*Interrupting her with an apprehensive glance at the door by which Essie went out.*) Sh! She may hear you.

MRS. DUDGEON.   (*Raising her voice.*) Let her hear me. People who fear God don't fear to give the devil's work its right name. (CHRISTY, *soullessly indifferent to the strife of Good and Evil, stares at the fire, warming himself.*) Well, how long are you going to stare there like a stuck pig? What news have you for me?

CHRISTY.   (*Taking off his hat and shawl and going to the rack to hang them up.*) The minister is to break the news to you. He'll be here presently.

MRS. DUDGEON.   Break what news?

CHRISTY.   (*Standing on tiptoe, from boyish habit, to hang his hat up, though he is quite tall enough to reach the peg, and speaking with callous placidity, considering the nature of the announcement.*) Father's dead too.

MRS. DUDGEON.   (*Stupent.*) Your father!

CHRISTY.   (*Sulkily, coming back to the fire and warming himself again, attending much more to the fire than to his mother.*) Well, it's not my fault. When we got to Nevinstown we found him ill in bed. He didn't know us at first. The minister sat up with him and sent me away. He died in the night.

MRS. DUDGEON.   (*Bursting into dry angry tears.*) Well, I do think this is hard on me—very hard on me. His brother, that was a disgrace to us all his life, gets hanged on the public gallows as a rebel; and your father, instead of staying at home where his duty was, with his own family, goes after him and dies, leaving everything on my shoulders. After sending this girl to me to take care of, too! (*She plucks her shawl vexedly over her ears.*) It's sinful, so it is: downright sinful.

CHRISTY.   (*With a slow, bovine cheerfulness, after a pause.*) I think it's going to be a fine morning, after all.

MRS. DUDGEON.   (*Railing at him.*) A fine morning! And your father newly dead! Where's your feelings, child?

CHRISTY.   (*Obstinately.*) Well, I didn't mean any harm. I suppose a man may make a remark about the weather even if his father's dead.

MRS. DUDGEON.   (*Bitterly.*) A nice comfort my children are to me! One son a fool, and the other a lost sinner that's left his home to live with smugglers and gypsies and villains, the scum of the earth!

Someone knocks.

CHRISTY.   (*Without moving.*) That's the minister.

MRS. DUDGEON. (*Sharply.*) Well, aren't you going to let Mr. Anderson in?

CHRISTY *goes sheepishly to the door.* MRS. DUDGEON *buries her face in her hands, as it is her duty as a widow to be overcome with grief.* CHRISTY *opens the door, and admits the minister,* ANTHONY ANDERSON, *a shrewd, genial, ready Presbyterian divine of about 50, with something of the authority of his profession in his bearing. But it is an altogether secular authority, sweetened by a conciliatory, sensible manner not at all suggestive of a quite thoroughgoing other-worldliness. He is a strong, healthy man too, with a thick sanguine neck; and his keen, cheerful mouth cuts into somewhat fleshy corners. No doubt an excellent parson, but still a man capable of making the most of this world, and perhaps a little apologetically conscious of getting on better with it than a sound Presbyterian ought.*

ANDERSON. (*To* CHRISTY, *at the door, looking at* MRS. DUDGEON *whilst he takes off his cloak.*) Have you told her?

CHRISTY. She made me. (*He shuts the door; yawns; and loafs across to the sofa, where he sits down and presently drops off to sleep.*)

ANDERSON *looks compassionately at* MRS. DUDGEON. *Then he hangs his cloak and hat on the rack.* MRS. DUDGEON *dries her eyes and looks up at him.*

ANDERSON. Sister: the Lord has laid his hand very heavily upon you.

MRS. DUDGEON. (*With intensely recalcitrant resignation.*) It's His will, I suppose; and I must bow to it. But I do think it hard. What call had Timothy to go to Springtown, and remind everybody that he belonged to a man that was being hanged?—and (*spitefully*) that deserved it, if ever a man did.

ANDERSON. (*Gently.*) They were brothers, Mrs. Dudgeon.

MRS. DUDGEON. Timothy never acknowledged him as his brother after we were married: he had too much respect for me to insult me with such a brother. Would such a selfish wretch as Peter have come thirty miles to see Timothy hanged, do you think? Not thirty yards, not he. However, I must bear my cross as best I may: least said is soonest mended.

ANDERSON. (*Very grave, coming down to the fire to stand with his back to it.*) Your eldest son was present at the execution, Mrs. Dudgeon.

MRS. DUDGEON. (*Disagreeably surprised.*) Richard?

ANDERSON. (*Nodding.*) Yes.

MRS. DUDGEON. (*Vindictively.*) Let it be a warning to him. He may end that way himself, the wicked, dissolute, godless—(*She suddenly stops; her voice fails; and she asks, with evident dread*) Did Timothy see him?

ANDERSON. Yes.

MRS. DUDGEON. (*Holding her breath.*) Well?

ANDERSON.   He only saw him in the crowd: they did not speak. (MRS. DUDGEON, *greatly relieved, exhales the pent up breath and sits at her ease again.*) Your husband was greatly touched and impressed by his brother's awful death. (MRS. DUDGEON *sneers. ANDERSON breaks off to demand with some indignation*) Well, wasn't it only natural, Mrs. Dudgeon? He softened towards his prodigal son in that moment. He sent for him to come to see him.

MRS. DUDGEON.   (*Her alarm renewed.*) Sent for Richard!

ANDERSON.   Yes; but Richard would not come. He sent his father a message; but I'm sorry to say it was a wicked message—an awful message.

MRS. DUDGEON.   What was it?

ANDERSON.   That he would stand by his wicked uncle and stand against his good parents, in this world and the next.

MRS. DUDGEON.   (*Implacably.*) He will be punished for it. He will be punished for it—in both worlds.

ANDERSON.   That is not in our hands, Mrs. Dudgeon.

MRS. DUDGEON.   Did I say it was, Mr. Anderson? We are told that the wicked shall be punished. Why should we do our duty and keep God's law if there is to be no difference made between us and those who follow their own likings and dislikings, and make a jest of us and of their Maker's word?

ANDERSON.   Well, Richard's earthly father has been merciful to him; and his heavenly judge is the father of us all.

MRS. DUDGEON.   (*Forgetting herself.*) Richard's earthly father was a softheaded—

ANDERSON.   (*Shocked.*) Oh!

MRS. DUDGEON.   (*With a touch of shame.*) Well, I am Richard's mother. If I am against him who has any right to be for him? (*Trying to conciliate him.*) Won't you sit down, Mr. Anderson? I should have asked you before; but I'm so troubled.

ANDERSON.   Thank you. (*He takes a chair from beside the fireplace, and turns it so that he can sit comfortably at the fire. When he is seated he adds, in the tone of a man who knows that he is opening a difficult subject.*) Has Christy told you about the new will?

MRS. DUDGEON.   (*All her fears returning.*) The new will! Did Timothy—? (*She breaks off, gasping, unable to complete the question.*)

ANDERSON.   Yes. In his last hours he changed his mind.

MRS. DUDGEON.   (*White with intense rage.*) And you let him rob me?

ANDERSON.   I had no power to prevent him giving what was his to his own son.

MRS. DUDGEON.   He had nothing of his own. His money was the money I brought him as my marriage portion. It was for me to deal with my own money and my own son. He dare not have done it if I had been with him; and well he knew it. That was why he stole away like a thief to take advantage of the law to rob me by making a new will behind my back. The more shame on you, Mr. Anderson,

—you, a minister of the gospel—to act as his accomplice in such a crime.

ANDERSON. (*Rising.*) I will take no offense at what you say in the first bitterness of your grief.

MRS. DUDGEON. (*Contemptuously.*) Grief!

ANDERSON. Well, of your disappointment, if you can find it in your heart to think that the better word.

MRS. DUDGEON. My heart! My heart! And since when, pray, have you begun to hold up our hearts as trustworthy guides for us?

ANDERSON. (*Rather guiltily.*) I—er—

MRS. DUDGEON. (*Vehemently.*) Don't lie, Mr. Anderson. We are told that the heart of man is deceitful above all things, and desperately wicked. My heart belonged, not to Timothy, but to that poor wretched brother of his that has just ended his days with a rope round his neck—aye, to Peter Dudgeon. You know it: old Eli Hawkins, the man to whose pulpit you succeeded, though you are not worthy to loose his shoe latchet,° told it you when he gave over our souls into your charge. He warned me and strengthened me against my heart, and made me marry a Godfearing man—as he thought. What else but that discipline has made me the woman I am? And you, you, who followed your heart in your marriage, you talk to me of what I find in my heart. Go home to your pretty wife, man; and leave me to my prayers. (*She turns from him and leans with her elbows on the table, brooding over her wrongs and taking no further notice of him.*)

ANDERSON. (*Willing enough to escape.*) The Lord forbid that I should come between you and the source of all comfort! (*He goes to the rack for his coat and hat.*)

MRS. DUDGEON. (*Without looking at him.*) The Lord will know what to forbid and what to allow without your help.

ANDERSON. And whom to forgive, I hope—Eli Hawkins and myself, if we have ever set up our preaching against His law. (*He fastens his cloak, and is now ready to go.*) Just one word—on necessary business, Mrs. Dudgeon. There is the reading of the will to be gone through; and Richard has a right to be present. He is in the town; but he has the grace to say that he does not want to force himself in here.

MRS. DUDGEON. He shall come here. Does he expect us to leave his father's house for his convenience? Let them all come, and come quickly, and go quickly. They shall not make the will an excuse to shirk half their day's work. I shall be ready, never fear.

ANDERSON. (*Coming back a step or two.*) Mrs. Dudgeon: I used to have some little influence with you. When did I lose it?

MRS. DUDGEON. (*Still without turning to him.*) When you married for love. Now you're answered.

ANDERSON. Yes: I am answered. (*He goes out, musing.*)

° **latchet:** a leather shoelace.

MRS. DUDGEON.   (*To herself, thinking of her husband.*) Thief! Thief!
(*She shakes herself angrily out of her chair; throws back the shawl
from her head; and sets to work to prepare the room for the reading of the will, beginning by replacing Anderson's chair against the
wall and pushing back her own to the window. Then she calls, in
her hard, driving, wrathful way.*) Christy. (*No answer; he is fast
asleep.*) Christy. (*She shakes him roughly.*) Get up out of that;
and be ashamed of yourself—sleeping, and your father dead! (*She
returns to the table; puts the candle on the mantelshelf; and takes
from the table drawer a red table cloth which she spreads.*)

CHRISTY.   (*Rising reluctantly.*) Well, do you suppose we are never
going to sleep until we are out of mourning?

MRS. DUDGEON.   I want none of your sulks. Here: help me to set
this table. (*They place the table in the middle of the room, with
Christy's end towards the fireplace and Mrs. Dudgeon's towards
the sofa. CHRISTY drops the table as soon as possible, and goes to
the fire, leaving his mother to make the final adjustment of its
position.*) We shall have the minister back here with the lawyer
and all the family to read the will before you have done toasting
yourself. Go and wake that girl; and then light the stove in the
shed: you can't have your breakfast here. And mind you wash
yourself, and make yourself fit to receive the company. (*She punc-
tuates these orders by going to the cupboard; unlocking it; and
producing a decanter of wine, which has no doubt stood there
untouched since the last state occasion in the family, and some
glasses, which she sets on the table. Also two green ware plates,
on one of which she puts a barnbrack° with a knife beside it. On
the other she shakes some biscuits out of a tin, putting back one
or two, and counting the rest.*) Now mind: there are ten biscuits
there: let there be ten there when I come back after dressing
myself. And keep your fingers off the raisins in that cake. And tell
Essie the same. I suppose I can trust you to bring in the case of
stuffed birds without breaking the glass? (*She replaces the tin in
the cupboard, which she locks, pocketing the key carefully.*)

CHRISTY.   (*Lingering at the fire.*) You'd better put the inkstand instead, for the lawyer.

MRS. DUDGEON.   That's no answer to make to me, sir. Go and do as
you're told. (*CHRISTY turns sullenly to obey.*) Stop: take down
that shutter before you go, and let the daylight in: you can't expect
me to do all the heavy work of the house with a great lout like you
idling about.

CHRISTY *takes the window bar out of its clamps, and puts it aside;
then opens the shutter, showing the grey morning.* MRS. DUD-
GEON *takes the sconce from the mantelshelf; blows out the candle;
extinguishes the snuff by pinching it with her fingers, first licking
them for the purpose; and replaces the sconce on the shelf.*

° **barnbrack:** a bun, usually made with currants or raisins.

CHRISTY. (*Looking through the window.*) Here's the minister's wife.

MRS. DUDGEON. (*Displeased.*) What! Is she coming here?

CHRISTY. Yes.

MRS. DUDGEON. What does she want troubling me at this hour, before I am properly dressed to receive people?

CHRISTY. You'd better ask her.

MRS. DUDGEON. (*Threateningly.*) You'd better keep a civil tongue in your head. (*He goes sulkily towards the door. She comes after him, plying him with instructions.*) Tell that girl to come to me as soon as she's had her breakfast. And tell her to make herself fit to be seen before the people. (CHRISTY *goes out and slams the door in her face.*) Nice manners, that! (*Someone knocks at the house door: she turns and cries inhospitably*) Come in. (JUDITH ANDERSON, *the Minister's wife, comes in. Judith is more than twenty years younger than her husband, though she will never be as young as he in vitality. She is pretty and proper and ladylike, and has been admired and petted into an opinion of herself sufficiently favorable to give her a self-assurance which serves her instead of strength. She has a pretty taste in dress, and in her face the pretty lines of a sentimental character formed by dreams. Even her little self-complacency is pretty, like a child's vanity. Rather a pathetic creature to any sympathetic observer who knows how rough a place the world is. One feels, on the whole, that Anderson might have chosen worse, and that she, needing protection, could not have chosen better.*) Oh, it's you, is it, Mrs. Anderson?

JUDITH. (*Very politely—almost patronizingly.*) Yes. Can I do anything for you, Mrs. Dudgeon? Can I help to get the place ready before they come to read the will?

MRS. DUDGEON. (*Stiffly.*) Thank you, Mrs. Anderson, my house is always ready for anyone to come into.

MRS. ANDERSON. (*With complacent amiability.*) Yes, indeed it is. Perhaps you had rather I did not intrude on you just now.

MRS. DUDGEON. Oh, one more or less will make no difference this morning, Mrs. Anderson. Now that you're here, you'd better stay. If you wouldn't mind shutting the door! (JUDITH *smiles, implying* "How stupid of me!" *and shuts it with an exasperating air of doing something pretty and becoming.*) That's better. I must go and tidy myself a bit. I suppose you don't mind stopping here to receive anyone that comes until I'm ready.

JUDITH. (*Graciously giving her leave.*) Oh yes, certainly. Leave that to me, Mrs. Dudgeon; and take your time. (*She hangs her cloak and bonnet on the rack.*)

MRS. DUDGEON. (*Half sneering.*) I thought that would be more in your way than getting the house ready. (ESSIE *comes back.*) Oh, here you are! (*Severely.*) Come here: let me see you. (ESSIE *timidly goes to her.* MRS. DUDGEON *takes her roughly by the arm*

*and pulls her round to inspect the results of her attempt to clean
and tidy herself—results which show little practice and less conviction.*) Mm! That's what you call doing your hair properly, I
suppose. It's easy to see what you are, and how you were brought
up. (*She throws her arm away, and goes on, peremptorily.*) Now
you listen to me and do as you're told. You sit down there in the
corner by the fire; and when the company comes don't dare to
speak until you're spoken to. (ESSIE *creeps away to the fireplace.*)
Your father's people had better see you and know you're there:
they're as much bound to keep you from starvation as I am. At any
rate they might help. But let me have no chattering and making
free with them, as if you were their equal. Do you hear?

ESSIE.   Yes.

MRS. DUDGEON.   Well, then go and do as you're told. (ESSIE *sits
down miserably on the corner of the fender furthest from the
door.*) Never mind her, Mrs. Anderson: you know who she is and
what she is. If she gives you any trouble, just tell me; and I'll
settle accounts with her. (MRS. DUDGEON *goes into the bedroom,
shutting the door sharply behind her as if even it had to be made
do its duty with a ruthless hand.*)

JUDITH.   (*Patronizing Essie, and arranging the cake and wine on the
table more becomingly.*) You must not mind if your aunt is strict
with you. She is a very good woman, and desires your good too.

ESSIE.   (*In listless misery.*) Yes.

JUDITH.   (*Annoyed with Essie for her failure to be consoled and edi-
fied, and to appreciate the kindly condescension of the remark.*)
You are not going to be sullen, I hope, Essie.

ESSIE.   No.

JUDITH.   That's a good girl! (*She places a couple of chairs at the table
with their backs to the window, with a pleasant sense of being a
more thoughtful housekeeper than Mrs. Dudgeon.*) Do you know
any of your father's relatives?

ESSIE.   No. They wouldn't have anything to do with him: they were
too religious. Father used to talk about Dick Dudgeon; but I never
saw him.

JUDITH.   (*Ostentatiously shocked.*) Dick Dudgeon! Essie: do you wish
to be a really respectable and grateful girl, and to make a place for
yourself here by steady good conduct?

ESSIE.   (*Very half-heartedly.*) Yes.

JUDITH.   Then you must never mention the name of Richard Dudgeon
—never even think about him. He is a bad man.

ESSIE.   What has he done?

JUDITH.   You must not ask questions about him, Essie. You are too
young to know what it is to be a bad man. But he is a smuggler;
and he lives with gypsies; and he has no love for his mother and
his family; and he wrestles and plays games on Sunday instead of

going to church. Never let him into your presence, if you can help it, Essie; and try to keep yourself and all womanhood unspotted by contact with such men.

ESSIE.   Yes.

JUDITH.   (*Again displeased.*) I am afraid you say Yes and No without thinking very deeply.

ESSIE.   Yes. At least I mean—

JUDITH.   (*Severely.*) What do you mean?

ESSIE.   (*Almost crying.*) Only—my father was a smuggler; and— (*Someone knocks.*)

JUDITH.   They are beginning to come. Now remember your aunt's directions, Essie; and be a good girl. (CHRISTY *comes back with the stand of stuffed birds under a glass case, and an inkstand, which he places on the table.*) Good morning, Mr. Dudgeon. Will you open the door, please: the people have come.

CHRISTY.   Good morning. (*He opens the house door.*)

The morning is now fairly bright and warm; and ANDERSON, *who is the first to enter, has left his cloak at home. He is accompanied by* LAWYER HAWKINS, *a brisk, middleaged man in brown riding gaiters and yellow breeches, looking as much squire as solicitor. He and Anderson are allowed precedence as representing the learned professions. After them comes the family, headed by the senior uncle,* WILLIAM DUDGEON, *a large, shapeless man, bottle-nosed and evidently no ascetic at table. His clothes are not the clothes, nor his anxious wife the wife, of a prosperous man. The junior uncle,* TITUS DUDGEON, *is a wiry little terrier of a man, with an immense and visibly purse-proud wife, both free from the cares of the William household.*

HAWKINS at once goes briskly to the table and takes the chair nearest the sofa, Christy having left the inkstand there. He puts his hat on the floor beside him, and produces the will. UNCLE WILLIAM *comes to the fire and stands on the hearth warming his coattails, leaving* MRS. WILLIAM *derelict near the door.* UNCLE TITUS, *who is the lady's man of the family, rescues her by giving her his disengaged arm and bringing her to the sofa, where he sits down warmly between his own lady and his brother's.* ANDERSON *hangs up his hat and waits for a word with* JUDITH.

JUDITH.   She will be here in a moment. Ask them to wait. (*She taps at the bedroom door. Receiving an answer from within, she opens it and passes through.*)

ANDERSON.   (*Taking his place at the table at the opposite end to Hawkins.*) Our poor afflicted sister will be with us in a moment. Are we all here?

CHRISTY.   (*At the house door, which he has just shut.*) All except Dick.

The callousness with which Christy names the reprobate jars on the moral sense of the family. UNCLE WILLIAM *shakes his head slowly and repeatedly.* MRS. TITUS *catches her breath convulsively through her nose. Her husband speaks.*

UNCLE TITUS.   Well, I hope he will have the grace not to come. I hope so.

The Dudgeons all murmur assent, except CHRISTY, *who goes to the window and posts himself there, looking out.* HAWKINS *smiles secretively as if he knew something that would change their tune if they knew it.* ANDERSON *is uneasy: the love of solemn family councils, especially funeral ones, is not in his nature.* JUDITH *appears at the bedroom door.*

JUDITH.   (*With gentle impressiveness.*) Friends, Mrs. Dudgeon. (*She takes the chair from beside the fireplace; and places it for* MRS. DUDGEON, *who comes from the bedroom in black, with a clean handkerchief to her eyes. All rise, except* ESSIE. MRS. TITUS *and* MRS. WILLIAM *produce equally clean handkerchiefs and weep. It is an affecting moment.*)

UNCLE WILLIAM.   Would it comfort you, sister, if we were to offer up a prayer?

UNCLE TITUS.   Or sing a hymn?

ANDERSON.   (*Rather hastily.*) I have been with our sister this morning already, friends. In our hearts we ask a blessing.

ALL.   (*Except* ESSIE.) Amen.

They all sit down, except JUDITH, *who stands behind Mrs. Dudgeon's chair.*

JUDITH.   (*To* ESSIE.) Essie: did you say Amen?

ESSIE.   (*Scaredly.*) No.

JUDITH.   Then say it, like a good girl.

ESSIE.   Amen.

UNCLE WILLIAM.   (*Encouragingly.*) That's right: that's right. We know who you are: but we are willing to be kind to you if you are a good girl and deserve it. We are all equal before the Throne.

This republican sentiment does not please the women, who are convinced that the Throne is precisely the place where their superiority, often questioned in this world, will be recognized and rewarded.

CHRISTY.   (*At the window.*) Here's Dick.

ANDERSON *and* HAWKINS *look round sociably.* ESSIE, *with a gleam of interest breaking through her misery, looks up.* CHRISTY *grins and gapes expectantly at the door. The rest are petrified with the intensity of their sense of Virtue menaced with outrage by the approach of flaunting Vice. The reprobate appears in the doorway, graced beyond his alleged merits by the morning sunlight. He is certainly the best looking member of the family; but his expression is reckless and sardonic, his manner defiant and satirical, his dress picturesquely careless. Only, his forehead and mouth betray an extraordinary steadfastness; and his eyes are the eyes of a fanatic.*

RICHARD. (*On the threshold, taking off his hat.*) Ladies and gentlemen: your servant, your very humble servant. (*With this comprehensive insult, he throws his hat to* CHRISTY *with a suddenness that makes him jump like a negligent wicket keeper,° and comes into the middle of the room, where he turns and deliberately surveys the company.*) How happy you all look! how glad to see me! (*He turns towards Mrs. Dudgeon's chair; and his lip rolls up horribly from his dog tooth as he meets her look of undisguised hatred.*) Well, mother: keeping up appearances as usual? that's right, that's right. (JUDITH *pointedly moves away from his neighborhood to the other side of the kitchen, holding her skirt instinctively as if to save it from contamination.* UNCLE TITUS *promptly marks his approval of her action by rising from the sofa, and placing a chair for her to sit down upon.*) What! Uncle William! I haven't seen you since you gave up drinking. (*Poor* UNCLE WILLIAM, *shamed, would protest; but* RICHARD *claps him heartily on his shoulder, adding*) you have given it up, haven't you? (*releasing him with a playful push*) of course you have: quite right too: you overdid it. (*He turns away from* UNCLE WILLIAM *and makes for the sofa.*) And now, where is that upright horsedealer Uncle Titus? Uncle Titus; come forth. (*He comes upon him holding the chair as* JUDITH *sits down.*) As usual, looking after the ladies!

UNCLE TITUS. (*Indignantly.*) Be ashamed of yourself, sir—

RICHARD. (*Interrupting him and shaking his hand in spite of him.*) I am: I am; but I am proud of my uncle—proud of all my relatives—(*again surveying them*) who could look at them and not be proud and joyful? (UNCLE TITUS, *overborne, resumes his seat on the sofa.* RICHARD *turns to the table.*) Ah, Mr. Anderson, still at the good work, still shepherding them. Keep them up to the mark, minister, keep them up to the mark. Come! (*with a spring he seats himself on the table and takes up the decanter*) clink a glass with me, Pastor, for the sake of old times.

ANDERSON. You know, I think, Mr. Dudgeon, that I do not drink before dinner.

RICHARD. You will, some day, Pastor: Uncle William used to drink before breakfast. Come: it will give your sermons unction. (*He smells the wine and makes a wry face.*) But do not begin on my mother's company sherry. I stole some when I was six years old; and I have been a temperate man ever since. (*He puts the decanter down and changes the subject.*) So I hear you are married, Pastor, and that your wife has a most ungodly allowance of good looks.

ANDERSON. (*Quietly indicating* JUDITH.) Sir: you are in the presence of my wife. (JUDITH *rises and stands with stony propriety.*)

° **negligent . . . keeper:** reference to the game of cricket; the batsman must keep alert to defend the wicket.

RICHARD.   (*Quickly slipping down from the table with instinctive good manners.*) Your servant, madam: no offense. (*He looks at her earnestly.*) You deserve your reputation; but I'm sorry to see by your expression that you're a good woman. (*She looks shocked, and sits down amid a murmur of indignant sympathy from his relatives.* ANDERSON, *sensible enough to know that these demonstrations can only gratify and encourage a man who is deliberately trying to provoke them, remains perfectly goodhumored.*) All the same, Pastor, I respect you more than I did before. By the way, did I hear, or did I not, that our late lamented Uncle Peter, though unmarried, was a father?

UNCLE TITUS.   He had only one irregular child, sir.

RICHARD.   Only one! He thinks one a mere trifle! I blush for you, Uncle Titus.

ANDERSON.   Mr. Dudgeon: you are in the presence of your mother and her grief.

RICHARD.   It touches me profoundly, Pastor. By the way, what has become of the irregular child?

ANDERSON.   (*Pointing to* ESSIE.) There, sir, listening to you.

RICHARD.   (*Shocked into sincerity.*) What! Why the devil didn't you tell me that before? Children suffer enough in this house without —(*He hurries remorsefully to* ESSIE.) Come, little cousin! never mind me: it was not meant to hurt you. (*She looks up gratefully at him. Her tearstained face affects him violently; and he bursts out, in a transport of wrath.*) Who has been making her cry? Who has been ill-treating her? By God—

MRS. DUDGEON.   (*Rising and confronting him.*) Silence your blasphemous tongue. I will bear no more of this. Leave my house.

RICHARD.   How do you know it's your house until the will is read? (*They look at one another for a moment with intense hatred; and then she sinks, checkmated, into her chair.* RICHARD *goes boldly up past* ANDERSON *to the window, where he takes the railed chair in his hand.*) Ladies and gentlemen: as the eldest son of my late father, and the unworthy head of this household, I bid you welcome. By your leave, Minister Anderson: by your leave, Lawyer Hawkins. The head of the table for the head of the family. (*He places the chair at the table between the minister and the attorney; sits down between them; and addresses the assembly with a presidential air.*) We meet on a melancholy occasion: a father dead! an uncle actually hanged, and probably damned. (*He shakes his head deploringly. The relatives freeze with horror.*) That's right: pull your longest faces (*his voice suddenly sweetens gravely as his glance lights on* ESSIE) provided only there is hope in the eyes of the child. (*Briskly.*) Now then, Lawyer Hawkins: business, business. Get on with the will, man.

TITUS.   Do not let yourself be ordered or hurried, Mr. Hawkins.

HAWKINS.   (*Very politely and willingly.*) Mr. Dudgeon means no offense, I feel sure. I will not keep you one second, Mr. Dudgeon.

Just while I get my glasses—(*He fumbles for them. The Dudgeons look at one another with misgiving.*)

RICHARD.   Aha! They notice your civility, Mr. Hawkins. They are prepared for the worst. A glass of wine to clear your voice before you begin. (*He pours out one for him and hands it; then pours one for himself.*)

HAWKINS.   Thank you, Mr. Dudgeon. Your good health, sir.

RICHARD.   Yours, sir. (*With the glass half way to his lips, he checks himself, giving a dubious glance at the wine, and adds, with quaint intensity*) Will anyone oblige me with a glass of water?

ESSIE, *who has been hanging on his every word and movement, rises stealthily and slips out behind* MRS. DUDGEON *through the bedroom door, returning presently with a jug and going out of the house as quietly as possible.*

HAWKINS.   The will is not exactly in proper legal phraseology.

RICHARD.   No: my father died without the consolations of the law.

HAWKINS.   Good again, Mr. Dudgeon, good again. (*Preparing to read.*) Are you ready, sir?

RICHARD.   Ready, aye ready. For what we are about to receive, may the Lord make us truly thankful. Go ahead.

HAWKINS.   (*Reading.*) "This is the last will and testament of me Timothy Dudgeon on my deathbed at Nevinstown on the road from Springtown to Websterbridge on this twenty-fourth day of September, one thousand seven hundred and seventy seven. I hereby revoke all former wills made by me and declare that I am of sound mind and know well what I am doing and that this is my real will according to my own wish and affections."

RICHARD.   (*Glancing at his mother.*) Aha!

HAWKINS.   (*Shaking his head.*) Bad phraseology, sir, wrong phraseology. "I give and bequeath a hundred pounds to my younger son Christopher Dudgeon, fifty pounds to be paid to him on the day of his marriage to Sarah Wilkins if she will have him, and ten pounds on the birth of each of his children up to the number of five."

RICHARD.   How if she won't have him?

CHRISTY.   She will if I have fifty pounds.

RICHARD.   Good, my brother. Proceed.

HAWKINS.   "I give and bequeath to my wife Annie Dudgeon, born Annie Primrose"—you see he did not know the law, Mr. Dudgeon: your mother was not born Annie: she was christened so—"an annuity of fifty-two pounds a year for life (MRS. DUDGEON, *with all eyes on her, holds herself convulsively rigid*) to be paid out of the interest on her own money"—there's a way to put it, Mr. Dudgeon! Her own money!

MRS. DUDGEON.   A very good way to put God's truth. It was every penny my own. Fifty-two pounds a year!

HAWKINS.   "And I recommend her for her goodness and piety to the forgiving care of her children, having stood between them and her as far as I could to the best of my ability."

MRS. DUDGEON.   And this is my reward! (*Raging inwardly.*) You know what I think, Mr. Anderson: you know the word I gave to it.

ANDERSON.   It cannot be helped, Mrs. Dudgeon. We must take what comes to us. (*To* HAWKINS.) Go on, sir.

HAWKINS.   "I give and bequeath my house at Websterbridge with the land belonging to it and all the rest of my property soever to my eldest son and heir, Richard Dudgeon.

RICHARD.   Oho! The fatted calf, Minister, the fatted calf.

HAWKINS.   "On these conditions—"

RICHARD.   The devil! Are there conditions?

HAWKINS.   "To wit: first, that he shall not let my brother Peter's natural child starve or be driven by want to an evil life."

RICHARD.   (*Emphatically, striking his fist on the table.*) Agreed.

MRS. DUDGEON, *turning to look malignantly at* ESSIE, *misses her and looks quickly round to see where she has moved to; then, seeing that she has left the room without leave, closes her lips vengefully.*

HAWKINS.   "Second, that he shall be a good friend to my old horse Jim"—(*again shaking his' head*) he should have written James, sir.

RICHARD.   James shall live in clover. Go on.

HAWKINS.   "—and keep my deaf farm laborer Prodger Feston in his service."

RICHARD.   Prodger Feston shall get drunk every Saturday.

HAWKINS.   "Third, that he make Christy a present on his marriage out of the ornaments in the best room."

RICHARD.   (*Holding up the stuffed birds.*) Here you are, Christy.

CHRISTY.   (*Disappointed.*) I'd rather have the china peacocks.

RICHARD.   You shall have both. (CHRISTY *is greatly pleased.*) Go on.

HAWKINS.   "Fourthly and lastly, that he try to live at peace with his mother as far as she will consent to it."

RICHARD.   (*Dubiously.*) Hm! Anything more, Mr. Hawkins?

HAWKINS.   (*Solemnly.*) "Finally I give and bequeath my soul into my Maker's hands, humbly asking forgiveness for all my sins and mistakes, and hoping that He will so guide my son that it may not be said that I have done wrong in trusting to him rather than to others in the perplexity of my last hour in this strange place."

ANDERSON.   Amen.

THE UNCLES AND AUNTS.   Amen.

RICHARD.   My mother does not say Amen.

MRS. DUDGEON.   (*Rising, unable to give up her property without a struggle.*) Mr. Hawkins: is that a proper will? Remember, I have his rightful, legal will, drawn up by yourself, leaving all to me.

HAWKINS.   This is a very wrongly and irregularly worded will, Mrs. Dudgeon: though (*turning politely to* RICHARD) it contains in my judgment an excellent disposal of his property.

ANDERSON.   (*Interposing before* MRS. DUDGEON *can retort.*) That is not what you are asked, Mr. Hawkins. Is it a legal will?

HAWKINS.   The courts will sustain it against the other.

ANDERSON.   But why, if the other is more lawfully worded?

HAWKINS.   Because, sir, the courts sustain the claim of a man—and that man the eldest son—against any woman, if they can. I warned you, Mrs. Dudgeon, when you got me to draw that other will, that it was not a wise will, and that though you might make him sign it, he would never be easy until he revoked it. But you wouldn't take advice; and now Mr. Richard is cock of the walk. (*He takes his hat from the floor; rises; and begins pocketing his papers and spectacles.*)

This is the signal for the breaking-up of the party. ANDERSON takes his hat from the rack and joins UNCLE WILLIAM at the fire. TITUS fetches JUDITH her things from the rack. The three on the sofa rise and chat with HAWKINS. MRS. DUDGEON, now an intruder in her own house, stands inert, crushed by the weight of the law on women, accepting it, as she has been trained to accept all monstrous calamities, as proofs of the greatness of the power that inflicts them, and of her own wormlike insignificance. For at this time, remember, Mary Wollstonecraft° is as yet only a girl of eighteen, and her Vindication of the Rights of Women is still fourteen years off. MRS. DUDGEON is rescued from her apathy by ESSIE, who comes back with the jug full of water. She is taking it to RICHARD when MRS. DUDGEON stops her.

MRS. DUDGEON.   (*Threatening her.*) Where have you been? (*ESSIE, appalled, tries to answer, but cannot.*) How dare you go out by yourself after the orders I gave you?

ESSIE.   He asked for a drink—(*She stops, her tongue cleaving to her palate with terror.*)

JUDITH.   (*With gentler severity.*) Who asked for a drink? (*ESSIE, speechless, points to RICHARD.*)

RICHARD.   What! I!

JUDITH.   (*Shocked.*) Oh Essie, Essie!

RICHARD.   I believe I did. (*He takes a glass and holds it to ESSIE to be filled. Her hand shakes.*) What! afraid of me?

ESSIE.   (*Quickly.*) No. I—(*She pours out the water.*)

RICHARD.   (*Tasting it.*) Ah, you've been up the street to the market gate spring to get that. (*He takes a draught.*) Delicious! Thank you. (*Unfortunately, at this moment he chances to catch sight of Judith's face, which expresses the most prudish disapproval of his evident attraction for Essie, who is devouring him with her grateful eyes. His mocking expression returns instantly. He puts down the glass; deliberately winds his arm round Essie's shoulders; and brings her into the middle of the company. Mrs. Dudgeon being in Essie's way as they come past the table, he says*) By your leave, mother. (*and compels her to make way for them*) What do they call you? Bessie?

° **Mary Wollstonecraft:** English writer, best known for the book mentioned, published in 1792.

ESSIE.   Essie.

RICHARD.   Essie, to be sure. Are you a good girl, Essie?

ESSIE.   (*Greatly disappointed that he, of all people, should begin at her in this way.*) Yes. (*She looks doubtfully at JUDITH.*) I think so. I mean I—I hope so.

RICHARD.   Essie: did you ever hear of a person called the devil?

ANDERSON.   (*Revolted.*) Shame on you, sir, with a mere child—

RICHARD.   By your leave, Minister: I do not interfere with your sermons: do not you interrupt mine. (*To ESSIE.*) Do you know what they call me, Essie?

ESSIE.   Dick.

RICHARD.   (*Amused: patting her on the shoulder.*) Yes, Dick; but something else too. They call me the Devil's Disciple.

ESSIE.   Why do you let them?

RICHARD.   (*Seriously.*) Because it's true. I was brought up in the other service; but I knew from the first that the Devil was my natural master and captain and friend. I saw that he was in the right, and that the world cringed to his conqueror only through fear. I prayed secretly to him; and he comforted me, and saved me from having my spirit broken in this house of children's tears. I promised him my soul, and swore an oath that I would stand up for him in this world and stand by him in the next. (*Solemnly.*) That promise and that oath made a man of me. From this day this house is his home; and no child shall cry in it: this hearth is his altar; and no soul shall ever cower over it in the dark evenings and be afraid. Now (*turning forcibly on the rest*) which of you good men will take this child and rescue her from the house of the devil?

JUDITH.   (*Coming to ESSIE and throwing a protecting arm about her.*) I will. You should be burnt alive.

ESSIE.   But I don't want to. (*She shrinks back, leaving RICHARD and JUDITH face to face.*)

RICHARD.   (*To JUDITH.*) Actually doesn't want to, most virtuous lady!

UNCLE TITUS.   Have a care, Richard Dudgeon. The law—

RICHARD.   (*Turning threateningly on him.*) Have a care, you. In an hour from this there will be no law here but martial law. I passed the soldiers within six miles on my way here: before noon Major Swindon's gallows for rebels will be up in the market place.

ANDERSON.   (*Calmly.*) What have we to fear from that, sir?

RICHARD.   More than you think. He hanged the wrong man at Springtown: he thought Uncle Peter was respectable, because the Dudgeons had a good name. But his next example will be the best man in the town to whom he can bring home a rebellious word. Well, we're all rebels; and you know it.

ALL THE MEN.   (*Except ANDERSON.*) No, no, no!

RICHARD.   Yes, you are. You haven't damned King George up hill and down dale as I have; but you've prayed for his defeat; and you,

Anthony Anderson, have conducted the service, and sold your family bible to buy a pair of pistols. They mayn't hang me, perhaps; because the moral effect of the Devil's Disciple dancing on nothing wouldn't help them. But a minister! (JUDITH, *dismayed, clings to* ANDERSON) or a lawyer! (HAWKINS *smiles like a man able to take care of himself*) or an upright horsedealer! (UNCLE TITUS *snarls at him in rage and terror*) or a reformed drunkard! (UNCLE WILLIAM, *utterly unnerved, moans and wobbles with fear*) eh? Would that show that King George meant business—ha?

ANDERSON. (*Perfectly self-possessed.*) Come, my dear: he is only trying to frighten you. There is no danger. (*He takes her out of the house. The rest crowd to the door to follow him, except* ESSIE, *who remains near* RICHARD.)

RICHARD. (*Boisterously derisive.*) Now then: how many of you will stay with me; run up the American flag on the devil's house; and make a fight for freedom? (*They scramble out,* CHRISTY *among them, hustling one another in their haste.*) Ha ha! Long live the devil! (*To* MRS. DUDGEON, *who is following them.*) What, mother! Are you off too?

MRS. DUDGEON. (*Deadly pale, with her hand on her heart as if she received a deathblow.*) My curse on you! My dying curse! (*She goes out.*)

RICHARD. (*Calling after her.*) It will bring me luck. Ha ha ha!

ESSIE. (*Anxiously.*) Mayn't I stay?

RICHARD. (*Turning to her.*) What! Have they forgotten to save your soul in their anxiety about their own bodies? Oh yes: you may stay. (*He turns excitedly away again and shakes his fist after them. His left fist, also clenched, hangs down.* ESSIE *seizes it and kisses it, her tears falling on it. He starts and looks at it.*) Tears! The devil's baptism! (*She falls on her knees, sobbing. He stoops goodnaturedly to raise her, saying*) Oh yes, you may cry that way, Essie, if you like.

END OF ACT I

The Devil's Disciple, Act I: Discussion

We can divide Act I into eight separate "scenes" (using the term as we defined it in the general introduction). Some are only a few lines long; one takes almost half the act. Seven of them center in simple confrontation of two persons, where Shaw carefully keeps third characters out of the way. In the eighth, the main scene of the act, a series of incidents within incidents enables Dick Dudgeon to confront first one, then another, of his antagonists.

The first brief scene, between Mrs. Dudgeon and Essie, opens with them both fast asleep in the semidarkness, the fire burning low and the candle flickering on the table. Mrs. Dudgeon sits, of course, in the best chair, her feet on the fender of the fireplace; Essie is across the room on the sofa. The tapping on the door, and then the knocking, fail to wake either, but the trying of the latch brings Mrs. Dudgeon to her feet. We can catch her exasperation in having come out of an undutifully deep sleep in her short opening question to Essie, who, for all Mrs. Dudgeon knows, may have kept dutifully awake. For "the sake of appearances" in front of Essie, she has to act as if she had not fallen asleep, and the question serves the purpose perfectly. When she finds Essie asleep, she eases further into her self-righteousness, shakes the poor girl, scolding all the while, berates her for not having the decency to stay awake with her father "hardly cold in the grave," belittles her mumbled excuse, and finally opens the door herself.

Several things have been revealed besides Mrs. Dudgeon's shrewish nature and Essie's misery: they both had unintentionally fallen asleep; Essie's father is lately dead; and they had been "waiting up all night" for Essie's uncle. We don't know why they were waiting up, and we don't know what connection Essie and her father have with Mrs. Dudgeon; but we suspect a close one. We're immediately in the middle of mystery: a browbeaten child, a father dead, an all-night vigil, a bringer of answers (and perhaps more mystery) on the other side of the door. The important thing is the forward movement, carrying with it relevant information about the past.

The next scene, between Mrs. Dudgeon and Christy, answers some questions and raises others. Christy, obviously not the expected uncle, hastens to the fireplace to warm himself. He sees Essie and asks her who she is. Neither her answer nor Mrs. Dudgeon's helps him very much, but his delightfully ironic remark about her not being "expected to feel Uncle Peter's death like one of the family" brings a full explanation of all the relationships, not in any wooden way as a simple answer to a simple question, but obliquely through the normal disposition of Mrs. Dudgeon to scold and preach. We wonder why it wasn't the expected "uncle" who appeared at the door, and our wonder increases the more Mrs. Dudgeon fails to mention the fact or comment on Christy's unexpected appearance (or, perhaps, his coming alone).

Essie is dismissed on the acceptable but not very convincing pretext that her "history isn't fit for [her] own ears to hear" (several lines later, Mrs. Dudgeon answers Christy's "Sh" with a caustic "Let her hear me" when she speaks of that very "history"). Shaw doesn't want Essie in the kitchen when the minister arrives (she would mean unnecessary clutter at that point), so he gets her offstage at an opportune moment. She has served well as feeble opposition for Mrs. Dudgeon; now Christy and the minister can take over that function.

Just as we begin to wonder what Christy is doing on the scene (he wasn't expected, and he's done little but warm himself and half-listen to his mother's ranting), Mrs. Dudgeon asks him bluntly, "What news have you for me?" and gets his boorish reply, "Father's dead too." By this time we know that Christy's father and Essie's uncle are the same person. One piece of mystery is solved, but another takes its place: what happened to Mr. Dudgeon, and what connection has this death with the prior one? Each clarification poses a new question, and the interweaving of the two is perfectly illustrated several lines further on in Mrs. Dudgeon's response to Christy's grimly amusing, "Well, it's not my fault," and his dry account of what happened, in language appropriate to instructions for shoeing a horse. In her outburst of self-pity, she fills in some missing details, still leaving the basic questions unanswered: what "public gallows"? why a "rebel"? why did Mr. Dudgeon want to go to his brother?

At this point the minister's knock might well come, because the next few lines seem to add nothing new. If any lines appear superfluous, these do. The only new information is that the other son has "left his home," but Shaw doesn't need all this to say that. Christy has already shown himself to be an insensible clod (who, ironically, often makes unintended sense, as he does here); Mrs. Dudgeon has already had her opportunity to castigate an "unfeeling" child about lack of respect for a dead father, and she has unburdened herself about her worthless sons. The seemingly superfluous lines reinforce our impressions of Christy and his mother; but, more important, they reinforce our insight into the world of the Dudgeons, and therefore into "dead Puritanism": it is a world where "appearances" substitute for "feelings," where conventional, expected behavior, however calloused, substitutes for genuine human responses. The central conflict of the play lies in just this opposition, and each scene before Dick's entrance reveals some aspect of the unchristian "Christian" behavior he is leagued with the devil against.

The third scene centers in the confrontation of Mrs. Dudgeon and Minister Anderson. Seated again in her chair, she "buries her face in her hands, as it is her duty as a widow to be overcome with grief," and Christy opens the door. After letting the minister in and telling him that he has broken the news, he eliminates himself from the scene by going to the sofa and conveniently falling asleep. Anderson, as duty-bound in his own way as Mrs. Dudgeon is in hers, looks on Mrs. Dudgeon "compassionately" and attempts a consoling remark. He gets a hard, self-pitying answer for his pains, and the rest of the scene proceeds in the same vein: Anderson tries to uphold the value of Christian charity toward a "brother" and a "prodigal son"; Mrs. Dudgeon will have none of it and justifies her bitterness with her warped understanding of "punishment" and "duty" and "denial of the heart." Anderson's kind of gentle, detached, self-possessed forgiving spirit is no match for Mrs. Dudgeon's vindictive, cocksure brand of self-denying Puritanism. As Dick Dudgeon proves when he confronts his mother and his self-righteous relatives, only the so-called Devil's Disciple can handle the devil.

In the course of the third confrontation, we find that a reconciliation of sorts has occurred between Richard and his father, largely on his father's part (Anderson says that "Richard's earthly father has been merciful to him"), that a new will has been written, and that there is obviously some connection between the two. We also learn that Mrs. Dudgeon knows full well what her stake will be in the new will and that she long ago embraced self-denial—or heart-denial—as a way of life when she married Timothy Dudgeon instead of his brother Peter. Dick's eventual entrance is prepared for by Anderson's comment that the will has to be read to the whole family, and by Mrs. Dudgeon's insistence that it shall be done at the family's convenience, in her house, even if Dick has had the "grace" to say that he "does not want to force himself" on them.

Scene four, between Christy and his mother, gets the room prepared for the reading of the will without necessitating a break in the act. The minister leaves and she wakes Christy, complaining all the while. In the process of preparation we get further insights into her character: she "unlocks" the cupboard to get the wine decanter ("untouched since the last state occasion") and a tin of biscuits; puts the biscuits (carefully counted) and one currant bun on plates, and relocks the cupboard, afterwards "pocketing the key carefully." And when Christy opens the shutter to reveal the "grey morning," she carefully blows out the candle. (Notice in Act II how differently all the details dealing with food, light, and locking-up are handled in the Anderson household.)

Mrs. Dudgeon sends Christy to wake Essie, have breakfast, and wash up. Just as he leaves, the minister's wife arrives, and scene five gives Mrs. Dudgeon a chance to react against Mrs. Anderson's self-satisfied sweetness, again no match for Mrs. Dudgeon's acidity. Essie returns as scene five moves into scene six and gets tongue-lashed by Mrs. Dudgeon, who then leaves the stage to Mrs. Anderson and the unhappy girl. The confrontation in scene six gives us a picture of another side of self-righteousness, one we see more of in Act II: Mrs. Anderson's pious fretting about the supposed wickedness (hardly convincing as she outlines it) of Dick Dudgeon and her smug advice to Essie to "be a good girl."

All six scenes, most of them providing Mrs. Dudgeon with various targets for her bitterness and self-pity, prepare the way for Dick Dudgeon's entrance as the Devil's Disciple. Scene seven is his scene, and it is built as a series of confrontations as he badgers and bullies and blasphemes with complete success and obvious delight. His mother has little to say: she can only sputter occasionally in outraged defiance, and finally quit her house (and the play) with the prophetic words, "My curse on you! My dying curse!" She has served Shaw's purpose as the embodiment of most that is wrong with "dead Puritanism," and she slinks off in defeat, "her hand on her heart as if she had received a deathblow," which she had.

In a brief eighth scene, after they all "scramble out" when Dick calls on them to stay "in the devil's house; and make a fight for freedom," Essie's baptism of tears crowns the victory of the true disciple.

Before asking you to consider other details of Act I through questions, we must make a further observation. We have so far looked quite soberly at Act I, with little indication that it is all delightfully amusing. Shaw called the play a "threadbare popular melodrama," and while we may agree that he had his tongue in cheek in calling it "threadbare," it certainly has most of the trappings of soap opera: the cruel mother gets her due, the abandoned orphan finds her knight, the rakish hero makes sport of humbug, the somber family gathers for the Reading of the Will, true virtue is rewarded, etc. All this is so handled as to be funny. Yet at the same time it asks to be taken seriously as comment on true and false religion.

QUESTIONS

1. What is ironic about Mrs. Dudgeon's comment to Essie when she dismisses her from the room: "And don't forget your prayers. . . . She'd have gone to bed last night just as if nothing had happened if I'd let her"? Consider Mrs. Dudgeon's own behavior.
2. What is the implication of Shaw's stage direction about Christy just before he says, "Father's dead too": "standing on tiptoe, from boyish habit, to hang his hat up, though he is quite tall enough to reach the peg"?
3. In the scene between Mrs. Dudgeon and Anderson, why is Mrs. Dudgeon "surprised" about the fact that Richard was at the execution of his uncle, and "greatly relieved" when the minister says

that "they did not speak"? What in the rest of Anderson's speech shows that he very well knows what her real concern is, although he has momentarily not answered her truthfully?

4. In the same scene, show how Mrs. Dudgeon, in using the same kind of Christian terminology that Anderson would use (such as "do our duty and keep God's law"), unconsciously reveals how different from his is her interpretation of its meaning. In particular, how does she pick up his word "heart" (when he says, ". . . if you can find it in your heart to think that the better word") and distort his own teaching?

5. Judith announces Mrs. Dudgeon's entrance from the bedroom in solemn tones, as if she were introducing royalty. How does Dick's entrance a few moments later contrast satirically with his mother's?

6. Mrs. Anderson forces Essie to say "Amen" when the minister says, "In our hearts we ask a blessing." How does this contrast with Mrs. Dudgeon's failure to say "Amen" when Lawyer Hawkins finishes reading the will? Who calls attention to her failure? Why is that significant?

7. Why is Dick Dudgeon able to get a rise out of his mother, his uncles, and Judith so easily? (Consider what he says to them.) What kind of response does he get from Anderson when he tries for the same result? What does this suggest about Anderson?

8. What does Dick's immediate sympathy for Essie show about him? What is Essie's role in Act I? Why is she needed in the opening scene? In the scene with Dick? Why is it significant that she leaves the house and goes "to the market gate spring" to get Dick some water?

9. Notice how the scene when Dick enters is set so that the "opposition" is carefully arranged around the periphery of the room. Dick takes the center of the stage immediately and turns first to one side, then to the other. He is in constant movement, while the rest move stiffly or remain rigid. What inner psychological difference between him and them does this dramatize in visual terms? Finally he settles in the "chair of state" at the middle of the table. Anderson and Hawkins sit at either end, halfway between him and the "enemy"—not quite with him, but not against him either. Trace the broad stage movement through the rest of the scene. paying particular attention to when and how Mrs. Dudgeon is isolated, and when and why Essie is brought "into the middle of the company." Can it be said that Timothy Dudgeon and his brother, though dead, also occupy positions in the room? Where?

10. In the same scene Shaw manages the confrontations so that he keeps Dick at the center of attention. Dick directs the conversation and initiates most of the changes of subject. When someone else takes the offensive, he promptly squelches him. For instance, when Uncle Titus says, "Be ashamed of yourself, sir . . ." he twists his meaning with, "I am: I am; but I'm proud of my uncle—proud of all my relatives. . . ." When his mother rises from the chair and

says, "Silence your blasphemous tongue. I will bear no more of this. Leave my house," he checkmates her with, "How do you know it's your house until the will is read?" Show how, through the rest of the scene, Dick controls each confrontation, forcing people to deal with him. How is he made to remain the center of attention even when Mrs. Dudgeon asks Lawyer Hawkins if the will is "proper"?

11. What function does Hawkins have besides that of will-reader? What is his attitude toward the form of the will? the content? toward the other characters?

12. What is Dick mocking in his two comments to Hawkins: 1—"my father died without the consolation of the law" and 2—"For what we are about to receive, may the Lord make us truly thankful"? How does their use in this context sum up his attitude toward all that his relatives stand for? Why are these references particularly appropriate at this time in this place?

13. Considering the play as a whole, why does Shaw have the Andersons leave before Dick says, "Now then: how many of you will stay with me; run up the American flag on the devil's house; and make a fight for freedom?"

14. We have seen that Mrs. Dudgeon's name fits her personality. What else does "dudgeon" mean that can be said to fit Dick's personality? Why is it significant that Mrs. Dudgeon's maiden name was "Annie Primrose"?

15. What is meant by saying that "tears" are "the devil's baptism"?

16. Shaw makes extensive use of various forms of irony. The simplest kind occurs when a character says or does something whose meaning is opposite from what it appears to be on the surface. Sometimes it is intended by the speaker, as when Dick enters the Dudgeon gathering and says, "Ladies and gentlemen: your servant, your very humble servant," or when Mrs. Dudgeon says to Christy, "A nice comfort my children are to me!" Sometimes it is unintended, as when Mrs. Dudgeon says to Anderson: "He [Eli Hawkins] warned me and strengthened me against my heart, and made me marry a Godfearing man—as he thought. What else but that discipline has made me the woman I am?" Slightly different is dramatic irony, in which what is said means something different to the spectator than it does to the characters. Mrs. Dudgeon says to her son as she leaves the house, "My curse on you! My dying curse." She does not expect the dying to be imminent, but it is. Also different are ironic reversals, in which what happens is the opposite of what is intended or might be expected: Annie *Primrose* becomes Annie *Dudgeon* through a distorted understanding of what Christian self-denial means. The Devil's Disciple explains his "conversion" in terms that spell out what Christian charity is. Point out other instances of these three forms of irony in Act I. (Dick's comments are loaded with intended irony; Mrs. Dudgeon's with unintended. The will-reading scene is built on ironic reversals.)

The world of a play:
Characters

(a) A play is performed on a stage, or printed in a book; in other words, it is a created thing: it is art.

The world of a play mirrors the world we know only in the sense that the observations made about the human condition are observations we recognize as pertinent to it. That is the only reality it has. The play world may be recognizable and reasonable in everyday terms, but it does not need to be. In Greek plays, gods and furies are made to appear on the stage; in Shakespeare, we meet with ghosts, witches, and fairies; Samuel Beckett's *Happy Days*, to mention only one of dozens of nonrealistic twentieth-century plays, gives us protagonists who are buried up to their necks in sand. For that matter, the most realistic playwright is often essentially asking us: What is the *real world*, and how do we know? The world of the play is in the playwright's head and the audience's head, and it has both nothing at all—and also everything—to do with the real world outside and inside them both. A play helps us see what we are, but it does not necessarily do so by showing us the actions of any particular people or place or time.

Even if there had been historically a Prince of Denmark named Hamlet, with all of the relatives and acquaintances that appear in Shakespeare's play, and even if he had lost a father and mother the way this play-Hamlet has lost both, the real Hamlet and the play-Hamlet would be the same in name only. Shakespeare's Hamlet exists only in the play—in the fascinating complexity of his personality. We know that what he does to his mother in the brief section of a scene we have studied is humanly comprehensible, given the sense of betrayal her degraded behavior has brought to him. At the same time, we see the human comprehensibility of the Queen's pathetic attempts to deny to herself what she has become. The play is played on the stage, but it exists in our minds and on our senses, and it is by our minds and senses that we judge of its truth, not by its historical factuality or lack of it.

Since a play is art, not life, it is purified of all randomness and miscellaneousness. We have seen how the opening 39 lines of Act III iv of *Hamlet* and the whole of Act I of *The Devil's Disciple* form an intricate pattern of personal and verbal confrontation. Every word works; nothing is wasted, nothing is irrelevant. If the scene from *Hamlet* had been a copy of a real encounter, taken in shorthand by a real Polonius behind the arras, how different it would be! No normal exchange would—or could—start at such a pitch and maintain it. Even the quickest of wits would fail of the verbal dexterity that makes Hamlet's rejoinders so telling.

Moreover, if this were a "slice of life," we would expect a more fumbling, less strictly sequential action. Polonius would not necessarily cry out at the precise moment he does. Hamlet's mother, seeing his sword out, would not necessarily stay in the room. The blow through the arras would not necessarily be fatal. Even Hamlet's calling out, "Mother, mother, mother!" as he approaches the chamber does not necessarily reflect reality; we do not usually announce our coming by calling out names and are less likely to if we have been summoned and are expected. Yet the repeated "mother" has a very plain *artistic* purpose: it puts everyone, including ourselves, on the alert for Hamlet's arrival on stage, and perhaps tells us too, in its crescendo of repetition, of the energy and agitation of his mood. In short, nobody talks or acts exactly the way characters do in a play, and yet a play is an imitation of the way people talk and act. Art selects and foreshortens, patterns confusion, reveals more by telling less.

(b) The characters in a play have both uniqueness and universality.

Although a character is a product of art, not nature, we should insist that he be more than a mouthpiece for an idea or a point of view. He should suggest a personality, not a mechanism; he should suggest that if he gets a pin stuck in him, he will bleed. At the same time, any character is both a person and more than a person, because he represents, symbolically, some human attribute or bundle of attributes. Mrs. Dudgeon is undoubtedly a very credible person; it is not difficult to imagine her kind in action in our ordinary world. Yet, just as important, she embodies many traits of Shaw's "dead Puritanism"—self-righteous priggery, self-serving insistence on proper appearances, self-satisfied condemnation of anything that smacks of pleasure—with enough exaggeration to be seen as emblem, as even caricature, as well as character.

Thus, we recognize *The Devil's Disciple* as a play not to be taken wholly seriously on the personal level and do not feel a deep involvement in Mrs. Dudgeon's elimination from the scene any more than we sense a loss in Peter Dudgeon's hanging. On the contrary, we take pleasure in the irony of her "dying curse" threat and in her son's easy victory over her warped view of religion. Had the play not been structured as a comedy, we should probably have been teased into greater concern when she receives her come-uppance. In either case, we are to recognize her value to the play both as individual and as symbol.

The same can be said of any character in Act I of *The Devil's Disciple*, although some are more validly understood as individuals and some as representations. Essie and Christy and the whole

Dudgeon clan in attendance at the reading of the will seem blood-less indeed if viewed as distinct and complex personalities. As representatives of types and attitudes they are admirably clear-cut and useful. Mrs. Anderson is not much more in Act I than a counterpart of the "bad" Mrs. Dudgeon: she is the "good" woman who is just as self-righteous, self-serving, and self-satisfied as Mrs. Dudgeon, just as much of a prig, but one who has not yet gone sour. There is not much blood in her in either Acts I or II, but we see signs of it in her reaction to Essie in Act II, and we see her come to life in Act III as she realizes what a fool she has been making of herself. Her husband plays the stock role of gentle and self-contained minister to the flock in Act I; but as Act II progresses he becomes more complex and closer to being a full-fledged person. Dick, of course, functions symbolically as the embodiment of Christian charity, simple human decency, and common sense. At the same time he is thoroughly alive, precisely because his sense of the ridiculous allows him to see himself and others with understanding. Both simple and complex in Shaw's conception, he clearly sees through the hypocrisy of his world, and thoroughly enjoys himself observing it; but he does not remain apart from the world and he is perfectly willing to give up living in it for the sake of affirming his own involvement.

The playgoer's—and playreader's—job is to keep in mind the double function every character has in his uniqueness and in his universality, not for the purpose of separating these dimensions out, as if to say "Now he's being unique, very much a distinct individual" and "Now he's being universal, so take what he says in that light," but simply for the purpose of seeing the continual interaction in drama of the particular individual (or incident or image or word) with the general patterns that enclose him (or it).

(c) Close attention to the language of a play will reveal the subtle interaction of uniqueness and universality.

If there is admittedly a loss in not seeing an actual production, there is a corresponding gain in reading with care. A performance, or a handful of performances, will not necessarily reveal all the meaning that a play contains. The mind's eye of a reader can serve in some ways for a better stage. It allows us to observe more closely than we can in the theater, to "turn back" and ponder; and it allows us to entertain all the possible ways of understanding a character or scene at the same time.

To illustrate, look again at the language of the Hamlet-Queen confrontation. For one thing, the individuality of mother and son comes across clearly and powerfully. In the uneven match, the Queen's words flap feebly against his. The brave show of her opening rebuke descends to scolding, then to bewilderment, then to a pathetic play for sympathy, and finally to a helpless attempt to break off entirely. In contrast, Hamlet moves to the attack: brutal in his mockery of her meaning and phraseology; almost childishly insolent in his "What's the matter now?" and "Dead for a ducat, dead!" and contemptuous in his comments over the body of the dead Polonius. This is not the language, as earlier in the play, of a sensitive young courtier filled with disgust for the corruption in the world; it is the language of an embittered, self-despising, cornered soul lashing out at that world.

More is communicated, however, than any character can intend on any normal occasion of verbal interchange—nuances or extensions of meaning that the spectator in the theater, or the reader who is simply plunging forward in chase of the story line, will certainly miss. For instance, Polonius advises the Queen "to lay (thrust) home to" Hamlet, and to "be round (blunt) with" him. The words describe perfectly the exchange we see evolve, but ironically the thrusts and bluntness come from Hamlet, not from the Queen. More ironic is the fact that the major thrust is the one through the arras which kills Polonius, who had spoken more truly than he knew when he said, "I'll silence me even here." His being "too busy" minding other people's business led him to silence (hide) himself behind the arras, thus setting the stage for his being silenced (killed) once and for all. Similarly, the rather obvious ironic twist that Hamlet gives to the meaning of "father" is followed directly by the more penetrating irony of the twist given the word "offended." His mother can only mean by it, "insulted or affronted"; Hamlet means "sinned against" in its deepest moral sense; and the gulf between what he has done and what she has done is summed up in that difference of meaning.

We can see a similar kind of language function in Act I of *The Devil's Disciple*. While each character plays out his individual role in the plot, Shaw so manipulates the language as to give each one a representative function that makes him or her in a real sense larger than life. Almost every time Mrs. Dudgeon speaks, Shaw labels her manner unflatteringly: "threateningly," "fiercely," "sharply," "bitterly," etc. Even her name is used to comment on her personality: "dudgeon"—i.e., "ill humor, resentment." How well are the labels supported by the dialogue? So well that they are not at all necessary. Her sentences are clipped and hard, those of the common scold ("Oh yes, you've plenty of excuses, I daresay. Dropped off! . . . Why don't you get up and let your uncle in? after me waiting up all night for him! . . . There: I'll open the door: much good you are to wait up. Go and mend that fire a bit."). Her favorite sentence forms are the *imperative* ("Wake up; and be ashamed of yourself . . ." "Don't answer me, Miss; but show your obedience. . . ."); the *rhetorical question* (a question in form, but really a statement, since no answer is expected: "Well, I am Richard's mother. If I am against him who has any right to be for him?"); and the *exclamation* ("A nice comfort my children are to me! One son a fool, and the other a lost sinner that's left his home to live with smugglers and gypsies and villains, the scum of the earth!"). The three forms dominate her speech, and all lend themselves beautifully to the "I"-centered, self-pitying, long-suffering, negative, domineering individual.

Within the sentence forms, her choice of words reveals what is uppermost in her mind. Her sentences are larded with words like "sinful," "wicked," "duty," "shame," "punishment," "unfeeling," and "godless." Put together, the clipped phrasing, the sentence form, and the word choices set up a harsh and grating tune, and it would be difficult for an actress to speak the lines without the kind of gestures and movements Shaw has indicated in his stage directions. Her language creates a distinct individual, at the same time that it etches all the worst of "dead Puritanism."

The others also are simultaneously characterized and universalized by their language. Anderson speaks in beautifully rounded, sometimes prayer-like sentences ("Well, Richard's earthly father has been merciful to him; and his heavenly judge is the father of us all." "The Lord forbid that I should come between you and the source of all comfort.") There are almost no contractions in his speech, and very few partial sentences. The vocabulary is simple and unprepossessing: it does not call attention to itself, as does Mrs. Dudgeon's (and Dick's). No matter what the subject of discussion, he speaks with polite and formal phrasing, dignified but not pompous or self-conscious. ("I will take no offense at what you say in the first bitterness of your grief." "In our hearts we ask a blessing." "You know, I think, Mr. Dudgeon, that I do not drink before dinner." "Mr. Dudgeon, you are in the presence of your mother and her grief." "Come, my dear; he is only trying to frighten you. There is no danger.").

Contrast the calm, judicious tone of these sentences with what he says at the end of Act II when he finds out that the British meant to hang him and he knows instinctively what to do about it: "Going to him! What good would that do! I'll go to them, so I will. Get me the pistols: I want them. And money, money: I want money—all the money in the house. A great satisfaction it would be to him to have my company on the gallows." At the end of Act III, when he has saved Dick's life, he speaks still differently, befitting his new role as officer and gentleman: "So I am starting life at fifty as Captain Anthony Anderson of the Springtown militia; and the Devil's Disciple here will start presently as the Reverend Richard Dudgeon, and wag his pow in my old pulpit, and give good advice to this silly sentimental little wife of mine." Minister Anderson, it may occur to us, was not formerly the sort of man to have used "wag his pow," or even "my old pulpit," or "silly sentimental little wife of mine."

Dick Dudgeon is largely defined before he appears by what people say about him. We are prepared to find him a rather refreshing contrast to the "disagreeableness" of Mrs. Dudgeon, the "pathetic . . . self-complacency" of Mrs. Anderson, and even the "conciliatory, sensible manner" of Minister Anderson. These phrases define a world that needs fresh air, and we look for it from the Devil's Disciple, no matter how overbearing or cocksure he may prove to be. We are not disappointed: "Ladies and gentlemen: your servant, your very humble servant."—the hyper-polite form of address used with complete contempt. "How happy you all look! how glad to see me!" The sarcasm chills the Dudgeons and shocks Mrs. Anderson, but since it doesn't seem to bother the minister or the lawyer, we feel that the rest may be getting about what they deserve. Once his opening fusillade is absorbed, his manner loses all of its harshness. He proves, in fact, to be a virtuoso with his tongue. He can be successively *convivial* ("Come! clink a glass with me, Pastor, for the sake of old times."), *witty* (". . . do not begin on my mother's company sherry. I stole some when I was six years old; and I have been a temperate man ever since.") *tart* (in response to Uncle Titus's assurance that Peter Dudgeon "had only one irregular child, sir," he says, "Only one! He thinks one a mere trifle! I blush for you, Uncle Titus."), *tender* ("Come, little cousin; never mind me: it was not meant to hurt you."), *indignant* ("Who has been making her cry? Who has been ill-treating her? By God—"), *hearty* ("Now then, Lawyer Hawkins: business, business. Get on with the will, man."), *gracious* ("Ah, you've been up the street to the market gate spring to get that. Delicious! Thank you."), *sober* ("Have a care, you. In an hour from this there will no law here but martial law."). Above all he can be *lyrical* (and most "universal") as we see perhaps most compellingly in his explanation to Essie of why he is the Devil's Disciple:

". . . I prayed secretly to him; and he comforted me, and saved me from having my spirit broken in this house of children's tears. I promised him my soul and swore an oath that I would stand up for him in this world and stand by him in the next. That promise and that oath made a man of me. From this day this house is his home; and no child shall cry in it: this hearth is his altar; and no soul shall ever cower over it in the dark evenings and be afraid."

What kind of man is individualized and universalized by this kind of language? Obviously, he is no "reprobate," not the embodiment of "flaunting Vice," not "wicked, dissolute, godless." On the contrary, a charmer, a man of wit and decency, a sensitive, good-natured, razor-tongued iconoclast, whose enemy is the hypocrisy of a self-serving "dead Puritanism." He is only the Devil's Disciple in the self-denying world of the Dudgeons or the self-deceiving world of the Andersons. Clearly, he is the man of religion; they are of the devil.

Now reread Act II of *The Devil's Disciple.* At the end we will discuss its scene structure and make some observations on the use of characters as both individuals and universals. After that there are questions for further study and then additional considerations of the world of the play.

ACT II

Minister Anderson's house is in the main street of Websterbridge, not far from the town hall. To the eye of the eighteenth century New Englander, it is much grander than the plain farmhouse of the Dudgeons; but it is so plain itself that a modern house agent would let both at about the same rent. The chief dwelling room has the same sort of kitchen fireplace, with boiler, toaster hanging on the bars, movable iron griddle socketed to the hob, hook above for roasting, and broad fender, on which stand a kettle and a plate of buttered toast. The door, between the fireplace and the corner, has neither panels, fingerplates nor handles: it is made of plain boards, and fastens with a latch. The table is a kitchen table, with a treacle colored cover of American cloth,° chapped at the corners by draping. The tea service on it consists of two thick cups and saucers of the plainest ware, with milk jug and bowl to match, each large enough to contain nearly a quart, on a black japanned tray, and, in the middle of the table, a wooden trencher with a big loaf upon it, and a square half pound block of butter in a crock. The big oak press facing the fire from the opposite side of the room, is for use and storage, not for ornament; and the minister's house coat hangs on a peg from its door, showing that he is out; for when he is in, it is his best coat that hangs there. His big riding boots stand beside the press, evidently in their usual place, and rather proud of themselves. In fact, the evolution of the minister's kitchen, dining room and drawing room into three separate apartments has not yet taken place; and so, from the point of view of our pampered period, he is no better off than the Dudgeons.

But there is a difference, for all that. To begin with, Mrs. Anderson is a pleasanter person to live with than Mrs. Dudgeon. To which Mrs. Dudgeon would at once reply, with reason, that Mrs. Anderson has no children to look after; no poultry, pigs nor cattle; a steady and sufficient income not directly dependent on harvests and prices at fairs; an affectionate husband who is a tower of strength to her: in short, that life is as easy at the minister's house as it is hard at the farm. This is true; but to explain a fact is not to alter it; and however little credit Mrs. Anderson may deserve for making her home happier, she has certainly succeeded in doing it. The outward and visible signs of her superior social pretensions are, a drugget° on the floor, a plaster ceiling between the timbers, and chairs which, though not upholstered, are stained and polished. The fine arts are represented by a mezzotint portrait of some Presbyterian divine, a copperplate

---

° **American cloth:** oilcloth.
° **drugget:** a coarse cotton and woolen rug.

of Raphael's St. Paul preaching at Athens, a rococo presentation clock on the mantelshelf, flanked by a couple of miniatures, a pair of crockery dogs with baskets in their mouths, and, at the corners, two large cowrie shells. A pretty feature of the room is the low wide latticed window, nearly its whole width, with little red curtains running on a rod half way up it to serve as a blind. There is no sofa; but one of the seats, standing near the press, has a railed back and is long enough to accommodate two people easily. On the whole, it is rather the sort of room that the nineteenth century has ended in struggling to get back to under the leadership of Mr. Philip Webb and his disciples in domestic architecture, though no genteel clergyman would have tolerated it fifty years ago.

The evening has closed in; and the room is dark except for the cozy firelight and the dim oil lamps seen through the window in the wet street, where there is a quiet, steady, warm, windless downpour of rain. As the town clock strikes the quarter, JUDITH comes in with a couple of candles in earthenware candlesticks, and sets them on the table. Her self-conscious airs of the morning are gone: she is anxious and frightened. She goes to the window and peers into the street. The first thing she sees there is her husband, hurrying home through the rain. She gives a little gasp of relief, not very far removed from a sob, and turns to the door. ANDERSON comes in, wrapped in a very wet cloak.

JUDITH. (*Running to him.*) Oh, here you are at last, at last! (*She attempts to embrace him.*)

ANDERSON. (*Keeping her off.*) Take care, my love: I'm wet. Wait till I get my cloak off. (*He places a chair with its back to the fire; hangs his cloak on it to dry; shakes the rain from his hat and puts it on the fender; and at last turns with his hands outstretched to* JUDITH.) Now! (*She flies into his arms.*) I am not late, am I? The town clock struck the quarter as I came in at the front door. And the town clock is always fast.

JUDITH. I'm sure it's slow this evening. I'm so glad you're back.

ANDERSON. (*Taking her more closely in his arms.*) Anxious, my dear?

JUDITH. A little.

ANDERSON. Why, you've been crying.

JUDITH. Only a little. Never mind: it's all over now. (*A bugle call is heard in the distance. She starts in terror and retreats to the long seat, listening.*) What's that?

ANDERSON. (*Following her tenderly to the seat and making her sit down with him.*) Only King George, my dear. He's returning to barracks, or having his roll called, or getting ready for tea, or booting or saddling or something. Soldiers don't ring the bell or call over the banisters when they want anything: they send a boy out with a bugle to disturb the whole town.

JUDITH. Do you think there is really any danger?

ANDERSON. Not the least in the world.

JUDITH. You say that to comfort me, not because you believe it.

ANDERSON. My dear: in this world there is always danger for those who are afraid of it. There's danger that the house will catch fire in the night; but we shan't sleep any the less soundly for that.

JUDITH. Yes, I know what you always say; and you're quite right. Oh, quite right: I know it. But—I suppose I'm not brave: that's all. My heart shrinks every time I think of the soldiers.

ANDERSON. Never mind that, dear: bravery is none the worse for costing a little pain.

JUDITH. Yes, I suppose so. (*Embracing him again.*) Oh how brave you are, my dear! (*With tears in her eyes.*) Well, I'll be brave too: you shan't be ashamed of your wife.

ANDERSON. That's right. Now you make me happy. Well, well! (*He rises and goes cheerily to the fire to dry his shoes.*) I called on Richard Dudgeon on my way back; but he wasn't in.

JUDITH. (*Rising in consternation.*) You called on that man!

ANDERSON. (*Reassuring her.*) Oh, nothing happened, dearie. He was out.

JUDITH. (*Almost in tears, as if the visit were a personal humiliation to her.*) But why did you go there?

ANDERSON. (*Gravely.*) Well, it is all the talk that Major Swindon is going to do what he did in Springtown—make an example of some notorious rebel, as he calls us. He pounced on Peter Dudgeon as the worst character there; and it is the general belief that he will pounce on Richard as the worst here.

JUDITH. But Richard said—

ANDERSON. (*Goodhumoredly cutting her short.*) Pooh! Richard said! He said what he thought would frighten you and frighten me, my dear. He said what perhaps (God forgive him!) he would like to believe. It's a terrible thing to think of what death must mean for a man like that. I felt that I must warn him. I left a message for him.

JUDITH. (*Querulously.*) What message?

ANDERSON. Only that I should be glad to see him for a moment on a matter of importance to himself, and that if he would look in here when he was passing he would be welcome.

JUDITH. (*Aghast.*) You asked that man to come here!

ANDERSON. I did.

JUDITH. (*Sinking on the seat and clasping her hands.*) I hope he won't come! Oh, I pray that he may not come!

ANDERSON. Why? Don't you want him to be warned?

JUDITH. He must know his danger. Oh, Tony, is it wrong to hate a blasphemer and a villain? I do hate him. I can't get him out of my mind; I know he will bring harm with him. He insulted you: he insulted me: he insulted his mother.

ANDERSON. (*Quaintly.*) Well, dear, let's forgive him; and then it won't matter.

JUDITH.   Oh, I know it's wrong to hate anybody; but—

ANDERSON. (*Going over to her with humorous tenderness.*) Come, dear, you're not so wicked as you think. The worst sin towards our fellow creatures is not to hate them, but to be indifferent to them; that's the essence of inhumanity. After all, my dear, if you watch people carefully, you'll be surprised to find how like hate is to love. (*She starts, strangely touched—even appalled. He is amused at her.*) Yes: I'm quite in earnest. Think of how some of our married friends worry one another, tax one another, are jealous of one another, can't bear to let one another out of sight for a day, are more like jailers and slaveowners than lovers. Think of those very same people with their enemies, scrupulous, lofty, self-respecting, determined to be independent of one another, careful of how they speak of one another—pooh! haven't you often thought that if they only knew it, they were better friends to their enemies than to their own husbands and wives? Come: depend on it, my dear, you are really fonder of Richard than you are of me, if you only knew it. Eh!

JUDITH.   Oh, don't say that: don't say that, Tony, even in jest. You don't know what a horrible feeling it gives me.

ANDERSON. (*Laughing.*) Well, well: never mind, pet. He's a bad man; and you hate him as he deserves. And you're going to make the tea, aren't you?

JUDITH.   (*Remorsefully.*) Oh yes, I forgot. I've been keeping you waiting all this time. (*She goes to the fire and puts on the kettle.*)

ANDERSON. (*Going to the press and taking his coat off.*) Have you stitched up the shoulder of my old coat?

JUDITH.   Yes, dear. (*She goes to the table, and sets about putting the tea into the teapot from the caddy.*)

ANDERSON. (*As he changes his coat for the older one hanging on the press, and replaces it by the one he has just taken off.*) Did anyone call when I was out?

JUDITH.   No, only— (*Someone knocks at the door. With a start which betrays her intense nervousness, she retreats to the further end of the table with the tea caddy and spoon in her hands, exclaiming*) Who's that?

ANDERSON. (*Going to her and patting her encouragingly on the shoulder.*) All right, pet, all right. He won't eat you, whoever he is. (*She tries to smile, and nearly makes herself cry. He goes to the door and opens it.* RICHARD *is there, without overcoat or cloak.*) You might have raised the latch and come in, Mr. Dudgeon. Nobody stands on much ceremony with us. (*Hospitably.*) Come in. (RICHARD *comes in carelessly and stands at the table, looking round the room with a slight pucker of his nose at the mezzotinted divine on the wall.* JUDITH *keeps her eyes on the tea caddy.*) Is it still raining? (*He shuts the door.*)

RICHARD. Raining like the very (*his eye catches Judith's as she looks quickly and haughtily up*)—I beg your pardon; but (*showing that his coat is wet*) you see—!

ANDERSON. Take it off, sir; and let it hang before the fire a while: my wife will excuse your shirtsleeves. Judith: put in another spoonful of tea for Mr. Dudgeon.

RICHARD. (*Eyeing him cynically.*) The magic of property, Pastor! Are even you civil to me now that I have succeeded to my father's estate?

JUDITH *throws down the spoon indignantly.*

ANDERSON. (*Quite unruffled, and helping* RICHARD *off with his coat.*) I think, sir, that since you accept my hospitality, you cannot have so bad an opinion of it. Sit down. (*With the coat in his hand, he points to the railed seat.* RICHARD, *in his shirtsleeves, looks at him half quarrelsomely for a moment; then, with a nod, acknowledges that the minister has got the better of him, and sits down on the seat.* ANDERSON *pushes his cloak into a heap on the seat of the chair at the fire, and hangs Richard's coat on the back in its place.*)

RICHARD. I come, sir, on your own invitation. You left word you had something important to tell me.

ANDERSON. I have a warning which it is my duty to give you.

RICHARD. (*Quickly rising.*) You want to preach to me. Excuse me: I prefer a walk in the rain. (*He makes for his coat.*)

ANDERSON. (*Stopping him.*) Don't be alarmed, sir: I am no great preacher. You are quite safe. (RICHARD *smiles in spite of himself. His glance softens: he even makes a gesture of excuse.* ANDERSON, *seeing that he has tamed him, now addresses him earnestly.*) Mr. Dudgeon: you are in danger in this town.

RICHARD. What danger?

ANDERSON. Your uncle's danger. Major Swindon's gallows.

RICHARD. It is you who are in danger. I warned you—

ANDERSON. (*Interrupting him goodhumoredly but authoritatively.*) Yes, yes, Mr. Dudgeon; but they do not think so in the town. And even if I were in danger, I have duties here which I must not forsake. But you are a free man. Why should you run any risk?

RICHARD. Do you think I should be any great loss, Minister?

ANDERSON. I think that a man's life is worth saving, whoever it belongs to. (RICHARD *makes him an ironical bow.* ANDERSON *returns the bow humorously.*) Come: you'll have a cup of tea, to prevent catching cold?

RICHARD. I observe that Mrs. Anderson is not quite so pressing as you are, Pastor.

JUDITH. (*Almost stifled with resentment, which she has been expecting her husband to share and express for her at every insult of Richard's.*) You are welcome for my husband's sake. (*She brings the teapot to the fireplace and sets it on the hob.*)

RICHARD.   I know I am not welcome for my own, madam. (*He rises.*)
But I think I will not break bread here, Minister.

ANDERSON.   (*Cheerily.*) Give me a good reason for that.

RICHARD.   Because there is something in you that I respect, and that
makes me desire to have you for my enemy.

ANDERSON.   That's well said. On those terms, sir, I will accept your
enmity or any man's. Judith: Mr. Dudgeon will stay to tea. Sit
down: it will take a few minutes to draw by the fire. (RICHARD
*glances at him with a troubled face; then sits down with his head
bent, to hide a convulsive swelling of his throat.*) I was just saying
to my wife, Mr. Dudgeon, that enmity— (*She grasps his hand and
looks imploringly at him, doing both with an intensity that checks
him at once.*) Well, well, I mustn't tell you, I see; but it was
nothing that need leave us worse friend—enemies, I mean. Judith
is a great enemy of yours.

RICHARD.   If all my enemies were like Mrs. Anderson, I should be the
best Christian in America.

ANDERSON.   (*Gratified, patting her hand.*) You hear that, Judith? Mr.
Dudgeon knows how to turn a compliment.

The latch is lifted from without.

JUDITH.   (*Starting.*) Who is that?

CHRISTY *comes in.*

CHRISTY.   (*Stopping and staring at* RICHARD.) Oh, are you here?

RICHARD.   Yes. Begone, you fool: Mrs. Anderson doesn't want the
whole family to tea at once.

CHRISTY.   (*Coming further in.*) Mother's very ill.

RICHARD.   Well, does she want to see me?

CHRISTY.   No.

RICHARD.   I thought not.

CHRISTY.   She wants to see the minister—at once.

JUDITH.   (*To ANDERSON.*) Oh, not before you've had some tea.

ANDERSON.   I shall enjoy it more when I come back, dear. (*He is
about to take up his cloak.*)

CHRISTY.   The rain's over.

ANDERSON.   (*Dropping the cloak and picking up his hat from the
fender.*) Where is your mother, Christy?

CHRISTY.   At Uncle Titus's.

ANDERSON.   Have you fetched the doctor?

CHRISTY.   No: she didn't tell me to.

ANDERSON.   Go on there at once: I'll overtake you on his doorstep.
(CHRISTY *turns to go.*) Wait a moment. Your brother must be
anxious to know the particulars.

RICHARD.   Psha! not I: he doesn't know; and I don't care. (*Violently.*)
Be off, you oaf. (CHRISTY *runs out.* RICHARD *adds, a little
shamefacedly*) We shall know soon enough.

ANDERSON.   Well, perhaps you will let me bring you the news myself.
Judith: will you give Mr. Dudgeon his tea, and keep him here
until I return.

JUDITH. (*White and trembling.*) Must I—

ANDERSON. (*Taking her hands and interrupting her to cover her agitation.*) My dear: I can depend on you?

JUDITH. (*With a piteous effort to be worthy of his trust.*) Yes.

ANDERSON. (*Pressing her hand against his cheek.*) You will not mind two old people like us, Mr. Dudgeon. (*Going.*) I shall not say good evening: you will be here when I come back. (*He goes out.*)

They watch him pass the window, and then look at each other dumbly, quite disconcerted. RICHARD, noting the quiver of her lips, is the first to pull himself together.

RICHARD. Mrs. Anderson: I am perfectly aware of the nature of your sentiments towards me. I shall not intrude on you. Good evening. (*Again he starts for the fireplace to get his coat.*)

JUDITH. (*Getting between him and the coat.*) No, no. Don't go: please don't go.

RICHARD. (*Roughly.*) Why? You don't want me here.

JUDITH. Yes, I— (*Wringing her hands in despair.*) Oh, if I tell you the truth, you will use it to torment me.

RICHARD. (*Indignantly.*) Torment! What right have you to say that? Do you expect me to stay after that?

JUDITH. I want you to stay; but (*suddenly raging at him like an angry child*) it is not because I like you.

RICHARD. Indeed!

JUDITH. Yes: I had rather you did go than mistake me about that. I hate and dread you; and my husband knows it. If you are not here when he comes back, he will believe that I disobeyed him and drove you away.

RICHARD. (*Ironically.*) Whereas, of course, you have really been so kind and hospitable and charming to me that I only want to go away out of mere contrariness, eh?

JUDITH, *unable to bear it, sinks on the chair and bursts into tears.*

RICHARD. Stop, stop, stop, I tell you. Don't do that. (*Putting his hand on his breast as if to a wound.*) He wrung my heart by being a man. Need you tear it by being a woman? Has he not raised you above my insults, like himself? (*She stops crying, and recovers herself somewhat, looking at him with a scared curiosity.*) There: that's right. (*Sympathetically.*) You're better now, aren't you? (*He puts his hand encouragingly on her shoulder. She instantly rises haughtily, and stares at him defiantly. He at once drops into his usual sardonic tone.*) Ah, that's better. You are yourself again: so is Richard. Well, shall we go to tea like a quiet respectable couple, and wait for your husband's return?

JUDITH. (*Rather ashamed of herself.*) If you please. I—I am sorry to have been so foolish. (*She stoops to take up the plate of toast from the fender.*)

RICHARD. I am sorry, for your sake, that I am—what I am. Allow me. (*He takes the plate from her and goes with it to the table.*)

JUDITH.   (*Following with the teapot.*) Will you sit down? (*He sits down at the end of the table nearest the press. There is a plate and knife laid there. The other plate is laid near it: but* JUDITH *stays at the opposite end of the table, next the fire, and takes her place there, drawing the tray towards her.*) Do you take sugar?

RICHARD.   No: but plenty of milk. Let me give you some toast. (*He puts some on the second plate, and hands it to her, with the knife. The action shows quickly how well he knows that she has avoided her usual place so as to be as far from him as possible.*)

JUDITH.   (*Consciously.*) Thanks. (*She gives him his tea.*) Won't you help yourself?

RICHARD.   Thanks. (*He puts a piece of toast on his own plate; and she pours out tea for herself.*)

JUDITH.   (*Observing that he tastes nothing.*) Don't you like it? You are not eating anything.

RICHARD.   Neither are you.

JUDITH.   (*Nervously.*) I never care much for my tea. Please don't mind me.

RICHARD.   (*Looking dreamily round.*) I am thinking. It is all so strange to me. I can see the beauty and peace of this home: I think I have never been more at rest in my life than at this moment; and yet I know quite well I could never live here. It's not in my nature, I suppose, to be domesticated. But it's very beautiful; it's almost holy. (*He muses a moment, and then laughs softly.*)

JUDITH.   (*Quickly.*) Why do you laugh?

RICHARD.   I was thinking that if any stranger came in here now, he would take us for man and wife.

JUDITH.   (*Taking offense.*) You mean, I suppose, that you are more my age than he is.

RICHARD.   (*Starting at this unexpected turn.*) I never thought of such a thing. (*Sardonic again.*) I see there is another side to domestic joy.

JUDITH.   (*Angrily.*) I would rather have a husband whom everybody respects than—than—

RICHARD.   Than the devil's disciple. You are right; but I daresay your love helps him to be a good man, just as your hate helps me to be a bad one.

JUDITH.   My husband has been very good to you. He has forgiven you for insulting him, and is trying to save you. Can you not forgive him for being so much better than you are? How dare you belittle him by putting yourself in his place?

RICHARD.   Did I?

JUDITH.   Yes, you did. You said that if anybody came in they would take us for man and— (*She stops, terror-stricken, as a squad of soldiers tramps past the window.*) The English soldiers! Oh, what do they—

RICHARD.   (*Listening.*) Sh!

A VOICE.   (*Outside.*) Halt! Four outside: two in with me.

JUDITH *half rises, listening and looking with dilated eyes at* RICHARD, *who takes up his cup prosaically, and is drinking his tea when the latch goes up with a sharp click, and an English sergeant walks into the room with two privates, who post themselves at the door. He comes promptly to the table between them.*

THE SERGEANT. Sorry to disturb you, mum. Duty! Anthony Anderson: I arrest you in King George's name as a rebel.

JUDITH. (*Pointing at* RICHARD.) But that is not— (*He looks up quickly at her, with a face of iron. She stops her mouth hastily with the hand she has raised to indicate him, and stands staring affrightedly.*)

THE SERGEANT. Come, parson: put your coat on and come along.

RICHARD. Yes: I'll come. (*He rises and takes a step towards his own coat; then recollects himself, and, with his back to the sergeant, moves his gaze slowly round the room without turning his head until he sees Anderson's black coat hanging up on the press. He goes composedly to it; takes it down; and puts it on. The idea of himself as a parson tickles him: he looks down at the black sleeve on his arm, and then smiles slyly at* JUDITH, *whose white face shows him that what she is painfully struggling to grasp is not the humor of the situation but its horror. He turns to the sergeant, who is approaching him with a pair of handcuffs hidden behind him, and says lightly*) Did you ever arrest a man of my cloth before, Sergeant?

THE SERGEANT. (*Instinctively respectful, half to the black coat, and to Richard's good breeding.*) Well, no sir. At least, only an army chaplain. (*Showing the handcuffs.*) I'm sorry sir; but duty—

RICHARD. Just so, Sergeant. Well, I'm not ashamed of them: thank you kindly for the apology. (*He holds out his hands.*)

SERGEANT. (*Not availing himself of the offer.*) One gentleman to another, sir. Wouldn't you like to say a word to your missis, sir, before you go?

RICHARD. (*Smiling.*) Oh, we shall meet again before—eh? (*Meaning "before you hang me."*)

SERGEANT. (*Loudly, with ostentatious cheerfulness.*) Oh, of course, of course. No call for the lady to distress herself. Still— (*in a lower voice, intended for Richard alone*) your last chance, sir. *They look at one another significantly for a moment. Then* RICHARD *exhales a deep breath and turns towards* JUDITH.

RICHARD. (*Very distinctly.*) My love. (*She looks at him, pitiably pale, and tries to answer, but cannot—tries also to come to him, but cannot trust herself to stand without the support of the table.*) This gallant gentleman is good enough to allow us a moment of leave-taking. (*The* SERGEANT *retires delicately and joins his men near the door.*) He is trying to spare you the truth; but you had better know it. Are you listening to me? (*She signifies assent.*) Do you understand that I am going to my death? (*She signifies that she understands.*) Remember, you must find our friend who was with us just now. Do you understand? (*She signifies yes.*) See that you get him safely out of harm's way. Don't for your life let him know of my danger; but if he finds it out, tell him that he cannot save me: they would hang him; and they would not spare me. And tell him that I am steadfast in my religion as he is in his, and that he may depend on me to the death. (*He turns to go, and meets the eyes of the* SERGEANT, *who looks a little suspicious. He considers a moment, and then, turning roguishly to* JUDITH *with something of a smile breaking through his earnestness, says.*) And now, my dear, I am afraid the Sergeant will not believe that you love me like a wife unless you give one kiss before I go.

He approaches her and holds out his arms. She quits the table and almost falls into them.

JUDITH.   (*The words choking her.*) I ought to—it's murder—

RICHARD.   No: only a kiss (*softly to her*) for his sake.

JUDITH.   I can't. You must—

RICHARD.   (*Folding her in his arms with an impulse of compassion for her distress.*) My poor girl!

JUDITH, *with a sudden effort, throws her arms round him; kisses him; and swoons away, dropping from his arms to the ground as if the kiss had killed her.*

RICHARD.   (*Going quickly to the* SERGEANT.) Now, Sergeant: quick, before she comes to. The handcuffs. (*He puts out his hands.*)

SERGEANT.   (*Pocketing them.*) Never mind, sir: I'll trust you. You're a game one. You ought to a bin a soldier, sir. Between them two, please. (*The soldiers place themselves one before* RICHARD *and one behind him. The* SERGEANT *opens the door.*)

RICHARD.   (*Taking a last look round him.*) Goodbye, wife: goodbye, home. Muffle the drums, and quick march!

The SERGEANT *signs to the leading soldier to march. They file out quickly.* ***************** *When* ANDERSON *returns from Mrs. Dudgeon's, he is astonished to find the room apparently empty and almost in darkness except for the glow from the fire; for one of the candles has burnt out, and the other is at its last flicker.*

ANDERSON.   Why, what on earth—? (*Calling.*) Judith, Judith! (*He listens: there is no answer.*) Hm! (*He goes to the cupboard; takes a candle from the drawer; lights it at the flicker of the expiring one on the table; and looks wonderingly at the untasted meal by its light. Then he sticks it in the candlestick; takes off his hat; and scratches his head, much puzzled. This action causes him to look at the floor for the first time; and there he sees* JUDITH *lying motionless with her eyes closed. He runs to her and stoops beside her, lifting her head.*) Judith.

JUDITH.   (*Waking; for her swoon has passed into the sleep of exhaustion after suffering.*) Yes. Did you call? What's the matter?

ANDERSON. I've just come in and found you lying here with the candles burnt out and the tea poured out and cold. What has happened?

JUDITH. (*Still astray.*) I don't know. Have I been asleep? I suppose— (*she stops blankly*) I don't know.

ANDERSON. (*Groaning.*) Heaven forgive me, I left you alone with that scoundrel. (JUDITH *remembers. With an agonized cry, she clutches his shoulders and drags herself to her feet as he rises with her. He clasps her tenderly in his arms.*) My poor pet!

JUDITH. (*Frantically clinging to him.*) What shall I do? Oh my God, what shall I do?

ANDERSON. Never mind, never mind, my dearest dear; it was my fault. Come: you're safe now; and you're not hurt, are you? (*He takes his arms from her to see whether she can stand.*) There: that's right, that's right. If only you are not hurt, nothing else matters.

JUDITH. No, no, no: I'm not hurt.

ANDERSON. Thank Heaven for that! Come now: (*leading her to the railed seat and making her sit down beside him*) sit down and rest: you can tell me about it tomorrow. Or (*misunderstanding her distress*) you shall not tell me at all if it worries you. There, there! (*Cheerfully.*) I'll make you some fresh tea: that will set you up again. (*He goes to the table, and empties the teapot into the slop bowl.*)

JUDITH. (*In a strained tone.*) Tony.

ANDERSON. Yes, dear?

JUDITH. Do you think we are only in a dream now?

ANDERSON. (*Glancing round at her for a moment with a pang of anxiety, though he goes on steadily and cheerfully putting fresh tea into the pot.*) Perhaps so, pet. But you may as well dream a cup of tea when you're about it.

JUDITH. Oh stop, stop. You don't know— (*Distracted she buries her face in her knotted hands.*)

ANDERSON. (*Breaking down and coming to her.*) My dear, what is it? I can't bear it any longer; you must tell me. It was my fault: I was mad to trust him.

JUDITH. No: don't say that. You mustn't say that. He—oh no, no: I can't. Tony: don't speak to me. Take my hands—both my hands. (*He takes them, wondering.*) Make me think of you, not of him. There's danger, frightful danger; but it is your danger; and I can't keep thinking of it: I can't, I can't: my mind goes back to your danger. He must be saved—no: you must be saved: you, you, you. (*She springs up as if to do something or go somewhere, exclaiming.*) Oh, Heaven help me!

ANDERSON. (*Keeping his seat and holding her hands with resolute composure.*) Calmly, calmly, my pet. You're quite distracted.

JUDITH. I may well be. I don't know what to do. I don't know what to do. (*Tearing her hands away.*) I must save him. (ANDERSON *rises in alarm as she runs wildly to the door. It is opened in her face by* ESSIE, *who hurries in full of anxiety. The surprise is so disagreeable to* JUDITH *that it brings her to her senses. Her tone is sharp and angry as she demands*) What do you want?

ESSIE.   I was to come to you.

ANDERSON.   Who told you to?

ESSIE.   (*Staring at him, as if his presence astonished her.*) Are you here?

JUDITH.   Of course. Don't be foolish, child.

ANDERSON.   Gently, dearest: you'll frighten her. (*Going between them.*) Come here, Essie. (*She comes to him.*) Who sent you?

ESSIE.   Dick. He sent me word by a soldier. I was to come here at once and do whatever Mrs. Anderson told me.

ANDERSON.   (*Enlightened.*) A soldier! Ah, I see it all now! They have arrested Richard. (JUDITH *makes a gesture of despair.*)

ESSIE.   No. I asked the soldier. Dick's safe. But the soldier said you had been taken.

ANDERSON.   I! (*Bewildered, he turns to* JUDITH *for an explanation.*)

JUDITH.   (*Coaxingly.*) All right, dear: I understand. (*To* ESSIE.) Thank you, Essie, for coming: but I don't need you now. You can go home.

ESSIE.   (*Suspicious.*) Are you sure Dick has not been touched? Perhaps he told the soldier to say it was the minister. (*Anxiously.*) Mrs. Anderson: do you think it can have been that?

ANDERSON.   Tell her the truth if it is so, Judith. She will learn it from the first neighbor she meets in the street. (JUDITH *turns away and covers her eyes with her hands.*)

ESSIE.   (*Wailing.*) But what will they do to him? Oh, what will they do to him? Will they hang him? (JUDITH *shudders convulsively, and throws herself into the chair in which Richard sat at the tea table.*)

ANDERSON.   (*Patting Essie's shoulder and trying to comfort her.*) I hope not. I hope not. Perhaps if you're very quiet and patient, we may be able to help him in some way.

ESSIE.   Yes—help him—yes, yes, yes. I'll be good.

ANDERSON.   I must go to him at once, Judith.

JUDITH.   (*Springing up.*) Oh no. You must go away—far away, to some place of safety.

ANDERSON.   Pooh!

JUDITH.   (*Passionately.*) Do you want to kill me? Do you think I can bear to live for days and days with every knock at the door—every footstep—giving me a spasm of terror? to lie awake for nights and nights in an agony of dread, listening for them to come and arrest you?

ANDERSON.   Do you think it would be better to know that I had run away from my post at the first sign of danger?

JUDITH.   (*Bitterly.*) Oh, you won't go. I know it. You'll stay; and I shall go mad.

ANDERSON.   My dear, your duty—

JUDITH.   (*Fiercely.*) What do I care about my duty?

ANDERSON.   (*Shocked.*) Judith!

JUDITH.   I am doing my duty. I am clinging to my duty. My duty is to get you away, to save you, to leave him to his fate. (ESSIE *utters a cry of distress and sinks on the chair at the fire, sobbing silently.*) My instinct is the same as hers—to save him above all things, though it would be so much better for him to die! so much greater! But I know you will take your own way as he took it. I have no power. (*She sits down sullenly on the railed seat.*) I'm only a woman: I can do nothing but sit here and suffer. Only, tell him I tried to save you—that I did my best to save you.

ANDERSON.   My dear, I am afraid he will be thinking more of his own danger than of mine.

JUDITH.   Stop; or I shall hate you.

ANDERSON.   (*Remonstrating.*) Come, come, come! How am I to leave you if you talk like this? You are quite out of your senses. (*He turns to* ESSIE.) Essie.

ESSIE.   (*Eagerly rising and drying her eyes.*) Yes?

ANDERSON.   Just wait outside a moment, like a good girl: Mrs. Anderson is not well. (ESSIE *looks doubtful.*) Never fear: I'll come to you presently; and I'll go to Dick.

ESSIE.   You are sure you will go to him? (*Whispering.*) You won't let her prevent you?

ANDERSON.   (*Smiling.*) No, no: it's all right. All right. (*She goes.*) That's a good girl. (*He closes the door, and returns to* JUDITH.)

JUDITH.   (*Seated—rigid.*) You are going to your death.

ANDERSON.   (*Quaintly.*) Then I shall go in my best coat, dear. (*He turns to the press, beginning to take off his coat.*) Where—? (*He stares at the empty nail for a moment; then looks quickly round to the fire; strides across to it; and lifts Richard's coat.*) Why, my dear, it seems that he has gone in my best coat.

JUDITH.   (*Still motionless.*) Yes.

ANDERSON.   Did the soldiers make a mistake?

JUDITH.   Yes: they made a mistake.

ANDERSON.   He might have told them. Poor fellow, he was too upset, I suppose.

JUDITH.   Yes: he might have told them. So might I.

ANDERSON.   Well, it's all very puzzling—almost funny. It's curious how these little things strike us even in the most— (*He breaks off and begins putting on Richard's coat.*) I'd better take him his own coat. I know what he'll say— (*Imitating Richard's sardonic manner.*) "Anxious about my soul, Pastor, and also about your best coat." Eh?

JUDITH.   Yes, that is just what he will say to you. (*Vacantly.*) It doesn't matter: I shall never see either of you again.

ANDERSON.   (*Rallying her.*) Oh pooh, pooh, pooh! (*He sits down *beside her.*) Is this how to keep your promise that I shan't be ashamed of my brave wife?

JUDITH.   No: this is how I break it. I cannot keep my promises to him: why should I keep my promises to you?

ANDERSON.   Don't speak so strangely, my love. It sounds insincere to me. (*She looks unutterable reproach at him.*) Yes, dear, nonsense is always insincere; and my dearest is talking nonsense. Just nonsense. (*Her face darkens into dumb obstinacy. She stares straight before her, and does not look at him again, absorbed in Richard's fate. He scans her face; sees that his rallying has produced no effect; and gives it up, making no further effort to conceal his anxiety.*) I wish I knew what has frightened you so. Was there a struggle? Did he fight?

JUDITH.   No. He smiled.

ANDERSON.   Did he realize his danger, do you think?

JUDITH.   He realized yours.

ANDERSON.   Mine!

JUDITH.   (*Monotonously.*) He said "See that you get him safely out of harm's way." I promised: I can't keep my promise. He said, "Don't for your life let him know of my danger." I've told you of it. He said that if you found it out, you could not save him—that they will hang him and not spare you.

ANDERSON.   (*Rising in generous indignation.*) And you think that I will let a man with that much good in him die like a dog, when a few words might make him die like a Christian. I'm ashamed of you, Judith.

JUDITH.   He will be steadfast in his religion as you are in yours; and you may depend on him to the death. He said so.

ANDERSON.   God forgive him! What else did he say?

JUDITH.   He said goodbye.

ANDERSON.   (*Fidgeting nervously to and fro in great concern.*) Poor fellow, poor fellow! You said goodbye to him in all kindness and charity, Judith, I hope.

JUDITH.   I kissed him.

ANDERSON.   What! Judith!

JUDITH.   Are you angry?

ANDERSON.   No, no. You were right: you were right. Poor fellow, poor fellow! (*Greatly distressed.*) To be hanged like that at his age! And then did they take him away?

JUDITH.   (*Wearily.*) Then you were here: that's the next thing I remember. I suppose I fainted. Now bid me goodbye, Tony. Perhaps I shall faint again. I wish I could die.

ANDERSON.   No, no, my dear: you must pull yourself together and be sensible. I am in no danger—not the least in the world.

JUDITH.   (*Solemnly.*) You are going to your death, Tony—your sure death, if God will let innocent men be murdered. They will not let you see him: they will arrest you the moment you give your name. It was for you the soldiers came.

ANDERSON. (*Thunderstruck.*) For me! ! ! (*His fists clench; his neck thickens; his face reddens; the fleshy purses under his eyes become injected with hot blood; the man of peace vanishes, transfigured into a choleric and formidable man of war. Still, she does not come out of her absorption to look at him: her eyes are steadfast with a mechanical reflection of Richard's steadfastness.*)

JUDITH. He took your place: he is dying to save you. That is why he went in your coat. That is why I kissed him.

ANDERSON. (*Exploding.*) Blood an' owns!° (*His voice is rough and dominant, his gesture full of brute energy.*) Here! Essie, Essie!

ESSIE. (*Running in.*) Yes.

ANDERSON. (*Impetuously.*) Off with you as hard as you can run, to the inn. Tell them to saddle the fastest and strongest horse they have. (JUDITH *rises breathless, and stares at him incredulously.*) —the chestnut mare, if she's fresh—without a moment's delay. Go into the stable yard and tell the black man there that I'll give him a silver dollar if the horse is waiting for me when I come, and that I am close on your heels. Away with you. (*His energy sends* ESSIE *flying from the room. He pounces on his riding boots; rushes with them to the chair at the fire; and begins pulling them on.*)

JUDITH. (*Unable to believe such a thing of him.*) You are not going to him!

ANDERSON. (*Busy with the boots.*) Going to him! What good would that do? (*Growling to himself as he gets the first boot on with a wrench.*) I'll go to them, so I will. (*To* JUDITH *peremptorily.*) Get me the pistols: I want them. And money, money: I want money— all the money in the house. (*He stoops over the other boot, grumbling.*) A great satisfaction it would be to him to have my company on the gallows. (*He pulls on the boot.*)

JUDITH. You are deserting him, then?

ANDERSON. Hold your tongue, woman; and get me the pistols. (*She goes to the press and takes from it a leather belt with two pistols, a powder horn, and a bag of bullets attached to it. She throws it on the table. Then she unlocks a drawer in the press and takes out a purse.* ANDERSON *grabs the belt and buckles it on, saying*) If they took him for me in my coat, perhaps they'll take me for him in his. (*Hitching the belt into its place.*) Do I look like him?

JUDITH. (*Turning with the purse in her hand.*) Horribly unlike him.

ANDERSON. (*Snatching the purse from her and emptying it on the table.*) Hm! We shall see.

JUDITH. (*Sitting down helplessly.*) Is it of any use to pray, do you think, Tony?

ANDERSON. (*Counting the money.*) Pray! Can we pray Swindon's rope off Richard's neck?

JUDITH. God may soften Major Swindon's heart.

ANDERSON. (*Contemptuously—pocketing a handful of money.*) Let him, then. I am not God; and I must go to work another way.

° **Blood an' owns:** blood and wounds (of Christ); a strong oath.

(JUDITH *gasps at the blasphemy. He throws the purse on the table.*) Keep that. I've taken 25 dollars.

JUDITH.   Have you forgotten even that you are a minister?

ANDERSON.   Minister be—faugh! My hat: where's my hat? (*He snatches up hat and cloak, and puts both on in hot haste.*) Now listen, you. If you can get a word with him by pretending you're his wife, tell him to hold his tongue until morning: that will give me all the start I need.

JUDITH.   (*Solemnly.*) You may depend on him to the death.

ANDERSON.   You're a fool, a fool, Judith. (*For a moment checking the torrent of his haste, and speaking with something of his old quiet and impressive conviction.*) You don't know the man you're married to. (ESSIE *returns. He swoops at her at once.*) Well: is the horse ready?

ESSIE.   (*Breathless.*) It will be ready when you come.

ANDERSON.   Good. (*He makes for the door.*)

JUDITH.   (*Rising and stretching out her arms after him involuntarily.*) Won't you say goodbye?

ANDERSON.   And waste another half minute! Psha! (*He rushes out like an avalanche.*)

ESSIE.   (*Hurrying to* JUDITH.) He has gone to save Richard, hasn't he?

JUDITH.   To save Richard! No: Richard has saved him. He has gone to save himself. Richard must die.

ESSIE *screams with terror and falls on her knees, hiding her face.* JUDITH, *without heeding her, looks rigidly straight in front of her, at the vision of Richard, dying.*

END OF ACT II

The Devil's Disciple, Act II: Discussion

The first of the four scenes in Act II opens with Judith anxiously awaiting Anderson's arrival and feverishly embracing him when he comes. This contrasts sharply with the opening of Act I, just as her deep concern for her husband's return and his safety contrasts with Mrs. Dudgeon's sound sleep and lack of curiosity as to why Christy instead of her husband shows up. The simple domestic action clearly indicates that the conflict will shift in Act II as different attitudes are engaged.

Scene one develops one side of the conflict in Act II, that between Judith and her husband. She is revealed as basically a little girl, a "good girl," the kind she kept telling Essie to be in Act I: "really respectable," "unspotted by contact with such men" as Dick Dudgeon, ready to say "Amen" to any kind of pious expression and to express shock at the slightest impropriety. Anderson treats her like a pampered child because he has to. He has to comfort her ("Why, you've been crying"); pat her verbally on the head ("That's right. Now you make me happy"); remind her what she should be doing ("And you're going to make the tea, aren't you?"); and be careful not to say upsetting things to her ("Well, well: never mind, pet. He's a bad man; and you hate him as he deserves"). Her responses are likewise those of a pampered child: tears come whether in anxiety for her husband's safety, in admiration of his bravery, or in dismay at his invitation to the Devil's Disciple. She is as self-centered as Mrs. Dudgeon: what shocks her is that Dick may cross her threshold, not that he may lose his life. Anderson can afford to cater to her silliness, even enjoy it, so long as it does not get in his way; but when the time comes for decisive action at the end of the act, he doesn't care how upset she gets, and he can't even be bothered with saying goodbye. In the first scene he calls her "dear" and "pet"; in the last he calls her "woman" and "you."

Scene two is essentially a confrontation between the minister and Dick, which sets Judith's sense of "duty" in the full light of what one's real sense of duty should be. Anderson's hospitality and his Christian charity are open to all: "You might have raised the latch and come in, Mr. Dudgeon. Nobody stands on much ceremony with us." "I think that a man's life is worth saving, whoever it belongs to." "On those terms, sir, I will accept your enmity or any man's." He throws his own wet cloak in a heap on the chair in front of the fire and hangs Dick's on the back to dry. His wife wants him to have some tea before he goes to Mrs. Dudgeon, but he declines gracefully with, "I shall enjoy it more when I come back, dear." In general, he counters Dick's cynicism and suspicion simply by being "a man," and Dick acknowledges by his behavior and his words that he has been well countered. Part of the purpose of the scene is to show that Anderson is more than simply a peacemaker or a right-minded minister who is "above . . . insults" and "whom everybody respects." His sense of duty has nothing of selfishness or priggishness in it. Hence we are well-prepared for his change at the end of the act (if a little surprised), when, symbolically wearing Dick's coat, he flies into the kind of action we would expect from the Devil's Disciple. Judith may not "know the man [she's] married to," but we do—and we guess what his instinctive sense of right action can lead him to.

The scene also shows what Dick is capable of. Anderson cushions his belligerency, and Dick takes it with good grace. He is no boor: he knocks before he enters (as Christy does not), and he "knows how to turn a compliment." The bluster we had from him in Act I is muted, and we are prepared, long before he puts on the minister's best coat, for the calm and gentlemanly skill with which he handles the British sergeant, much as Anderson would have done under similar circumstances.

Scene three, between Dick and Judith, sets her in conflict with the other half of the Dudgeon-Anderson "alliance." She is as much a ninny with Dick as she is with her husband: she cries, feels put upon, pointedly sits as far from him as possible, totally misunderstands his comment about a stranger taking them "for man and wife," and falls into a dead faint when she kisses him. Dick hardly knows how to handle her. He has accepted Anderson's hospitality and won't leave, but putting up with her is exasperating. He is drawn to the "beauty and peace of this home," but he knows that such peace at the price Anderson pays for it is not for him. Still, the temptation is real, and the fact that he sits drinking tea, even though "It's not in my nature . . . to be domesticated," leads to his being arrested.

The fourth scene, between Anderson and Judith after his return from Mrs. Dudgeon, dramatizes the clash of values between Judith and Dudgeon-Anderson from a different point of view. Her shallow comprehension of what Dick has done and Anderson will do—her feeble romantic belief in how and why men can be depended on "to the death"—is here pitted against the instinctive, selfless, practical responses of both men in their "hour of trial." Her concern is still largely for herself. After he wakes her, she flutters around like a wounded sparrow and never once makes any attempt to give a coherent account of what happened (all of which, of course, is melodramatically satisfying to the spectator). It takes Essie's sudden entrance to bring her "to her senses." Even after that she remains incoherent. She "turns away and covers her eyes with her hands," or implores Anderson to go "far away, to some place of safety," or bemoans the fact that "I'm only a woman; I can do nothing but sit here and suffer," or speaks riddles to him about the mistake that was made. She so misunderstands her husband's nature and clear-sighted sense of duty, and so foolishly worships what she sees as Dick's glorious sacrificial act that she literally immobilizes herself. The frenzy of her initial response, "What shall I do? Oh my God, what shall I do?" subsides into a kind of stupor, until she is reduced to uttering such nonsense as, "Is it of any use to pray, do you think, Tony?" or such romantic twaddle as, "To save Richard! No: Richard has saved him. He has gone to save himself. Richard must die."

The double function of character-on-stage is clearly underscored in the analysis we have made of the scene structuring in Act II: Dick and Anderson are strongly individualized, the one still mocking, flippant, clear-headed, unruffled, wary of human contacts; the other straightforward, forgiving, duty-bound, compassionate. Despite these differences, there is more similarity than difference between them: both are masters of any situation, both are detached yet intensely involved, both are instinctively charitable, both instinctively able to do the right thing at the right time. The symbolic representation of one man as two is clearly shown as Dick "becomes" Anderson by putting on the minister's coat, and Anderson "becomes" Dick by wearing Dudgeon's coat. Representationally, the coats are different; symbolically, they are the same reversible model.

As we have seen, Judith takes over Mrs. Dudgeon's role (the latter is conveniently dispatched) as the embodiment of misguided Puritanism, "good girl" variety. She is peevish, uncharitable when it really counts, weak-willed, politely unpleasant. She comes close to being simply a mouthpiece for romantic, self-centered nonsense whose reactions allow Dudgeon-Anderson to say and do the right things, but Shaw also gives her such a range of self-conscious poses that she is, at the same time, disarmingly real.

QUESTIONS

1. One of a playwright's problems is to keep the plot moving while, at the same time, filling in necessary background details and preparing for later events. At the beginning of Act II, what purposes are served by the following?

    (a) the reference to the town clock.

    (b) the reference to the British soldiers.

    (c) the fact that it is raining when the act opens and that the rain stops soon after.

    (d) the fact that Anderson believes Major Swindon intends to hang Dick—and that Anderson is anxious to warn him.

2. How has the confrontation between Judith and Dick been prepared for in Act I? What tells us in Act I that he is essentially as thoughtful a person as Anderson is? Is Judith attracted to him even before he makes his "noble gesture"? Explain.

3. What does Dick mean by his comment to Judith, "I see there is another side to domestic joy"? How does her comment, "How dare you belittle him by putting yourself in his place?" reveal her self-centeredness? (Has Dick put himself in Anderson's place?)

4. How does the Sergeant's opening remark immediately put him in the same category with Mrs. Dudgeon and Judith (and later General Burgoyne)?

5. How does Anderson misunderstand Judith's dismay? What does he think has happened? How does what she says and does support both his interpretation and the true interpretation? How have we been prepared to believe that he will react to her the way he does?

6. How does Judith's sharp reaction to Essie's arrival qualify her earlier and later actions in the scene? She keeps acting as if she is torn between her "duty" to save Anderson and her "instinct" to save Dick, but what shows that her chief concern remains for herself?

7. A good part of the melodramatic delight of Act II comes from the fact that it takes Anderson so long to understand what really happened in his absence, even when it seems clear at so many different points. For instance, when he asks point blank, "Did the soldiers make a mistake?" what does he mean?

8. How has Anderson's sudden switch been carefully prepared for? Nothing that has been said to him or that has happened to him before has ruffled him. Why does he react so vigorously now? How have even the pistols been prepared for?

9. Trace through the act Shaw's handling of the coats belonging to Dick and Anderson. How does he make it possible for the switch to take place, and how does he focus our attention all along on these essential props?

10. What kinds of irony are illustrated by the following:

   (a) *JUDITH.*   Do you think there is really any danger?
   ANDERSON.   Not the least in the world.

   (b) *JUDITH.*   O how brave you are, my dear!

   (c) *ANDERSON.*   It's a terrible thing to think of what death must mean to a man like that.

   (d) *ANDERSON.*   After all, my dear, if you watch people carefully, you'll be surprised to find how like hate is to love. . . . Come: depend on it, my dear, you are really fonder of Richard than you are of me, if you only knew it.

   (e) *ANDERSON.*   And even if I were in danger, I have duties here which I must not forsake. But you are a free man. Why should you run any risk? [There is a double irony here.]

   (f) *RICHARD.*   Did you ever arrest a man of my cloth, Sergeant?
   SERGEANT.   Well, no sir. At least only an army chaplain.

   (g) *SERGEANT.*   You're a game one. You ought to a bin a soldier, sir.

The world of a play:
Settings and conventions

(a) Plays are written to be staged, either in a theater or in the imagination.

Since plays are written to be staged, if only imaginatively, a reader must consider some problems of production, particularly setting and stage movement. In the scene from *Hamlet* the only necessaries are something on which the Queen can sit and a curtain behind which Polonius can hide. Should the room be her bedchamber and should Hamlet force her to sit on the bed? The play does not tell us. One critic has suggested that she sits as if "enthroned" on a chair when Hamlet enters, to emphasize to him her position. The thought is a happy one, not because of any regality she might suggest (Hamlet would certainly not look at her that way), but because the seated position—imperious posture and all: "enthroned"—gives an added visual irony to her rapid wilting. It also puts Hamlet physically in the dominant position, standing over her, which underscores his psychological dominance. When she tries to leave, it is probably more effective to have her rise and be forced back onto the chair than to have her standing initially and then suddenly be made to sit. The only reason to have her sit at all is to emphasize visually the power Hamlet has over her. It makes sense to convey that impression from the very beginning of the encounter, but a case can be made for the opposite. All Shakespeare's words actually tell us is that with, "Come, come, sit you down," he forces her to sit.

Polonius behind the arras is an even simpler matter. The only essentials are that the arras be not too far from the chair (if Hamlet has to cross half the stage to get to it, this will detract from the necessary swiftness of his response), and that enough movement should be shown, when Polonius calls out, to account for Hamlet's finding him with one thrust. Awareness of the lunge, thrust, and wild exaltation that accompanies "How now? a rat? Dead for a ducat, dead!" is essential, but the awareness need not be, for a reader, cluttered with quite all the details a director must deal with. In general, this is true of Elizabethan plays as a group. The stage they were written for was "unlocalized"—that is, a neutral acting area with little scenery and few props, which became for the spectator whatever the play's dialogue required.

It is a different matter with most modern plays. If we turn to the extensive stage directions that precede Acts I and II of *The*

Devil's Disciple, we can readily see that Shaw expects actor, director, and reader alike to pay close attention to the physical setting. Act I takes place in what he calls the "general dwelling room" of the Dudgeon farmhouse: the kitchen, living room, and dining room rolled into one. Its condition, as we have seen, defines the character of its chief occupant, Mrs. Dudgeon, and Shaw tells us so. The chairs are "uncushioned and unpainted"; the kitchen table is bare save for a candle in a tin holder; against one wall is a "shamelessly ugly black horsehair sofa"; a "locked" cupboard stands on top of a "dwarf dresser full of common crockery"; the shutters are closed against the "black night"; and the fire is only embers. The immediate impression given as the curtain rises is of bleakness, ugliness, and lifelessness.

In direct contrast stands the "general dwelling room" of Minister Anderson's house, in which Act II takes place. Shaw says that the Andersons are "no better off than the Dudgeons," and this room, too, serves as kitchen, dining room, and living room. But what a difference! The chairs, though not cushioned, are "stained and polished"; the kitchen table is covered with oilcloth; on it there is a tea service, consisting of "two thick cups and saucers of the plainest ware, with milk jug and bowl to match . . . on a black japanned tray"; next to the tea service is a "wooden trencher with a big loaf upon it, and a square half-pound of butter in a crock"; places are set; there is a rug on the floor and plaster on the ceiling between the beams; engravings hang on the walls and ornamental knickknacks stand on the mantelpiece; the front window (larger than the Dudgeons') has a red curtain; the shutters are open; and the room is bathed in "cozy firelight." There is nothing fancy or rich about the Andersons' room, but it clearly defines a cheerfulness and sociability totally missing in its counterpart.

Obviously, a director must pay close attention to suggestions made by the playwright, either explicitly and in detail, as with Shaw, or implicitly and rather loosely, as with Shakespeare. As readers, we do not *have* to imagine any setting very exactly, even Shaw's: he tells us more than as readers we absolutely need to bear in mind. But there is often great advantage in reading a play, especially the "revealing" parts of it, as if we were directors preparing it in our minds for staging. When details are given specifically, as with the two "general dwelling rooms," a concern for more than just a casual recognition that there is a difference between the two rooms will highlight the symbolic difference between the Dudgeon and Anderson households. More subtly, even the elements of setting about which a play is not specific and which we must therefore devise and thrust upon the text—e.g., that the Queen sits on a bed (with suggestions of Oedipus complexes, mother fixations, etc.)—can and do add up to an interpretation of the play.

Similarly, as readers we do not absolutely need to pay close attention to movement on the stage. Shakespeare says nothing about this; Shaw says a lot: in both cases, as readers we can (and do!) ignore many of the suggestions and specific indications. But, again, we are wise to put ourselves in the director's role, particularly in those places where the stage business conveys a considerable part of the meaning. We have already discussed in detail the movement suggested by the dialogue in the scene from *Hamlet*, and it is clear that a reader who recreates the movement in his mind's eye is getting more "meaning" out of *Hamlet* than one who does not.

In *The Devil's Disciple* Shaw provides a running commentary on what his characters are doing and thinking. Most of it indicates quite specifically what should be done in staging the text; some of it is simply Shaw writing "asides" to the reader, usually witty and relevant but hardly necessary to the play as a script. (In fact, none of the commentary is essential; if it were, *The Devil's Disciple* would be a bad play.) What the stage directions and the commentary provide is a kind of author's guide to the director, and it makes sense to pay attention to it.

If we look again at the opening stage directions for Act I, we can readily outline in our imaginations the following set:

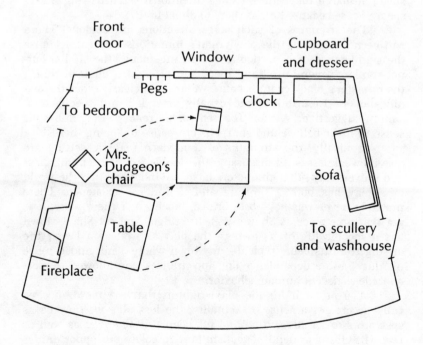

Shaw describes the fireplace in some detail, but there is no need for a reader's sketch of that. All that is essential is a clear idea of the working plan of the room for character movement. Also, it makes little sense for the reader to try to plot all the stage movement; but he must see the broad outlines, particularly when a number of characters are on stage at the same time.

For instance, in the sketch above, the dotted lines and arrows indicate that during the course of the act the table and the chairs around it are moved. When the play opens, Mrs. Dudgeon is sitting in the railed chair with her feet on the fender of the fireplace. Shaw calls the railed chair "comparatively a chair of state." When the Devil's Disciple makes his grand entrance into a room full of relatives waiting to hear the reading of the will, the kitchen table occupies the center of the room (and of the stage), and the railed chair stands next to the window. The relatives are spread around the periphery of the room; the lawyer and the minister are seated at either end of the table. Just before the will is read, Dick takes the railed chair and seats himself facing the audience at the center of the table, surrounded by all the other characters, who center their attention, and ours, on him. He thus assumes possession of his mother's chair—the "chair of state"—indicating that he will assume possession of her home once the will is read. (We have seen that the same sort of effect was obtained on the Elizabethan stage, although there are no stage directions to tell us—in Shakespeare's case because he was there to direct it all.)

The strengths of such stage directions are obvious. There can be no mistaking the playwright's intentions: we cannot miss the significance of a particular set arrangement (the similar-but-not-similar "general dwelling" rooms) or prop (the "chair of state"; the minister's black coat) because we are told clearly what the significance is. Descriptions are usually extended and specific, not simply suggestive. We are focused on a "reality" that dulls our sense of make-believe and sharpens our sense of "being there."

Ironically, the strengths of a modern realistic setting are also its weaknesses. In discussing the double function (uniqueness and universality) that characters have, we indicated that the world of a play has both a limiting and a limitless existence. There probably never was a Websterbridge, but even if there were, it is not the same place as Shaw's Websterbridge. And yet Shaw's town has a specific life of its own in the play as well as a larger life arising from its being typical—any town where a misguided sense of "duty" and a dependence on "appearances" are allowed to masquerade as decent human behavior.

The problem for the playwright is that the more successfully he creates a sense of actuality, the less able we may be as spectators to see his setting and his people as *symbolic* as well as *real*. His efforts at detailed realism may foreclose our opportunities to participate imaginatively. We sit enthralled, but perhaps with too many of the decisions and insights made *for* us, not *by* us. The recognition of the universal in the specific demands intellectual, or reflective, participation, not simply emotional identification. If we do not concern ourselves enough with the "reality" of Webster-bridge and General Burgoyne, and Mrs. Dudgeon's and Mrs. Anderson's "general dwelling" rooms, we may be deluded into dismissing the whole human experience of the play as a charade, as "a ballet of bloodless categories" (to use a phrase of A. C. Bradley's), as an intellectual game. On the other hand, if we concern ourselves too much with these perspectives of physical and literal reality, we shall lose the "meaning" of the play in a succession of momentary responses to its tugs of sympathy and pain. We are entertained but not enlightened.

(b) Theaters of different times and places have different conventions.

Almost all plays have been staged in some sort of theater, a public gathering place with specific areas for the actors and the audience. If that fact seems obvious enough, what may not be obvious is that until relatively recent times theaters were open-air structures and performances were daytime affairs. Even less obvious is that the theater most of us think of when we use the word is also a recent development, and that current "experimentation" in theater form and play production (such as the theater-in-the-round arrangement) is essentially a return to earlier dramatic conventions.

A *convention* is a particular man-made way of doing something: an accepted behavior pattern that one is not usually conscious of and considers "normal and natural." For instance, it is conventional for Americans to wear black when in mourning, not white; to wear rings on the fingers or on the ears, but not in the nose; to assume that marriage is a partnership of equals. Other societies have considered usages just the opposite to be "normal and natural."

Like any other form of behavior, the theater has conventions, some of which are universal, others of which are different for different places and times. The most obvious universal is the fact that the theater offers live people operating in the here and now. No matter how many times a given play is seen or read, it is always viewed in the present tense; real people are in the process of acting in the present and preparing the future. Whether or not we know the outcome of any speech or act is irrelevant to our intense absorption in the on-going experience; in fact, the involvement in any good play is enhanced by our knowledge of the consequences of what unfolds. The novel and short story are oriented toward "recall"; they are past tense forms in comparison to the play.

Universal also is the fact that the action of a play takes place in some kind of playing area. In most of the "theaters" of the world this playing area is a platform or stage, usually raised and set apart—or marked off—from those watching the performance; but plays have been presented in town squares, or in courtyards, or in open fields especially prepared for performances.

Whatever the physical arrangement, two other essential ingredients are present: an actor or actors who pretend to be persons they are not, and spectators. Almost universal is the fact that the actors speak, do not simply mime—although miming is still one of the dramatic genres. Moreover, in most instances the speeches are set down by an author (or playwright), although there may be partial improvisation, as in modern "happenings," or sixteenth century Italian Commedia dell' Arte, in which the actors had type-characters and a well-defined plot in mind and made up the dialogue as the plot progressed. Carefully structured spoken dialogue, however, remains almost essential to dramatic form; and consequently, another universal of the drama is that a play has a beginning and an end within the confines of a given "theater"—and takes place usually within the space of a few hours.

We have said that the essence of drama is confrontation, and as we have looked at the structuring of the scene from *Hamlet* and the first two acts from *The Devil's Disciple* we have concentrated on that fact. By extension and implication we have also referred to the spectator's (or reader's) active involvement in the stage business as a silent but by no means inert participant. We, too, are confronted; and it is this immediacy, this constant response to present action, that makes the drama, in Eric Bentley's words, "the closest link with the people . . . of all the arts."

If we look at the particulars of any given theater of the past, we soon recognize that apart from the universals of the drama that we have been discussing, a great variety of different conventions obtains. So accustomed are we to specific, detailed settings and costuming (in television dramas as well as in what is called "live theater") that we unthinkingly assume that the theater as we know it is certainly *the* theater, and that any deviation from it is simply interesting but offbeat experimentation. We can't discuss in detail the vast differences between the conventions of Greek and Elizabethan theater, say, and the modern realistic theater, but we will be able to study reactions against realism as revealed in other modern plays in this book. Since the modern realistic theater is the kind more familiar to us, we will deal with its conventions first, pointing out strengths and weaknesses.

The conventional commercial theater (or school auditorium used for staging plays) was fixed in form during the last century and has changed very little since. It is an enclosed structure and must, therefore, be artificially lighted whenever performances are given. The areas set aside for actors and spectators are separate, with the stage usually raised above the floor level where the audience sits. The separation of actors and spectators is physically apparent in the raised stage, in the orchestra pit, which often occurs immediately in front of the stage, and in the curtain which covers the proscenium arch (i.e., the large opening framing the stage) and is drawn back during performances. The sense of separation is further enhanced by the fact that during a performance the auditorium is in darkness, while bright lights of all kinds, on the stage and in the auditorium itself, bathe the stage in brilliance.

Another characteristic of the modern theater till quite recently is the attention given to stage setting, as in *The Devil's Disciple*. Elaborate and painstakingly designed sets endeavor to persuade the audience that this is a *real* "general dwelling room," or whatever. Historically "correct" costumes and makeup strive to take us back to the particular century, or, if modern, create visual impressions of people as lifelike as the girl in the next seat. Little is required of the imagination. When the curtain goes up, it is as if a wall had been removed so that the spectators can overhear and oversee what is going on in a real room. Since common sense says that confusion (and impossible cost) would result from too many walls being removed in the course of an evening, few modern plays have more than two or three sets and many of them only one.

Along with emphasis on realistic settings and realistic costumes naturally goes an expectation that the characters will behave like "real" people. Modern plays dispense with "asides" to the audience because people seldom utter asides of that nature. Soliloquies do not appear because in the real world people speak their private thoughts aloud for others to hear only if they are mentally disturbed. Speaking in verse, highly wrought "oratorical" passages, and language studded with imagery are normally taboo on the same grounds. "Natural" acting and speaking—with the word "natural" pointing to the attempt to approximate everyday reality as far as possible—are what most television, movie, and theater audiences look for today.

We have mentioned Shaw's extensive use of stage directions and his preoccupation with the physical arrangements of his stage. In both he was operating within the framework of modern theater practice. We have suggested that there are decided strengths in presenting as "real" a make-believe world as possible: if the sights and sounds are familiar or imaginatively acceptable, and if the characters "speak our language," it stands to reason that we are the more easily absorbed into the action.

However, as we also suggested earlier, we can pay a price for such faithfulness to the real world. For one, the experiences that can be explored are limited to the ones appropriate to a realistic physical environment. And with such an environment it is often difficult for the audience to see "real" people in the dual function we have spoken of as individual characters with universal significance.

Further, and more important, the technical virtuosity of the playwright, stage designer, costumer, director—and the total separation of stage and audience, one in the brightest light, the other in darkness—creates an atmosphere in which the spectator may be asked simply to respond from the guts, as it were. His imagination may never be sufficiently required to exercise itself, and neither may his critical faculty, the power that involves itself deeply in what goes on but keeps its distance at the same time, assessing, interpreting, acutely conscious that before it is a *play* deliberately acting itself out for spectators, not a slice of life that one intrudes himself into casually and secretly.

Now read Act III of *The Devil's Disciple*. At the end of it we make some observations on how it is put together. Following that come some questions for you to answer about Act III and about the play as a whole.

ACT III

Early next morning the SERGEANT, *at the British headquarters in the Town Hall, unlocks the door of a little empty panelled waiting room, and invites* JUDITH *to enter. She has had a bad night, probably a rather delirious one; for even in the reality of the raw morning, her fixed gaze comes back at moments when her attention is not strongly held.*

The SERGEANT *considers that her feelings do her credit, and is sympathetic in an encouraging military way. Being a fine figure of a man, vain of his uniform and of his rank, he feels specially qualified, in a respectful way, to console her.*

SERGEANT.   You can have a quiet word with him here, mum.

JUDITH.   Shall I have long to wait?

SERGEANT.   No, mum, not a minute. We kep him in the Bridewell° for the night; and he's just been brought over here for the court martial. Don't fret, mum: he slep like a child, and has made a rare good breakfast.

JUDITH.   (*Incredulously.*) He is in good spirits!

SERGEANT.   Tip top, mum. The chaplain looked in to see him last night; and he won seventeen shillings off him at spoil five.° He spent it among us like the gentleman he is. Duty's duty, mum, of course; but you're among friends here. (*The tramp of a couple of soldiers is heard approaching.*) There: I think he's coming. (RICHARD *comes in, without a sign of care or captivity in his bearing. The* SERGEANT *nods to the two soldiers, and shows them the key of the room in his hand. They withdraw.*) Your good lady, sir.

RICHARD.   (*Going to her.*) What! My wife. My adored one. (*He takes her hand and kisses it with a perverse, raffish gallantry.*) How long do you allow a brokenhearted husband for leave-taking, Sergeant?

SERGEANT.   As long as we can, sir. We shall not disturb you till the court sits.

RICHARD.   But it has struck the hour.

SERGEANT.   So it has, sir; but there's a delay. General Burgoyne's just arrived—Gentlemanly Johnny we call him, sir—and he won't have done finding fault with everything this side of half past. I know him, sir: I served with him in Portugal. You may count on twenty minutes, sir; and by your leave I won't waste any more of them. (*He goes out, locking the door.* RICHARD *immediately drops his raffish manner and turns to* JUDITH *with considerate sincerity.*)

RICHARD.   Mrs. Anderson: this visit is very kind of you. And how are you after last night? I had to leave you before you recovered; but

---

° **Bridewell:** prison; Bridewell is a London jail.
° **spoil five:** a card game.

I sent word to Essie to go and look after you. Did she understand the message?

JUDITH.   (*Breathless and urgent.*) Oh, don't think of me: I haven't come here to talk about myself. Are they going to—to— (*meaning* "*to hang you* ")?

RICHARD.   (*Whimsically.*) At noon, punctually. At least, that was when they disposed of Uncle Peter. (*She shudders.*) Is your husband safe? Is he on the wing?

JUDITH.   He is no longer my husband.

RICHARD.   (*Opening his eyes wide.*) Eh?

JUDITH.   I disobeyed you. I told him everything. I expected him to come here and save you. I wanted him to come here and save you. He ran away instead.

RICHARD.   Well, that's what I meant him to do. What good would his staying have done? They'd only have hanged us both.

JUDITH.   (*With reproachful earnestness.*) Richard Dudgeon: on your honor, what would you have done in his place?

RICHARD.   Exactly what he has done, of course.

JUDITH.   Oh, why will you not be simple with me—honest and straightforward? If you are so selfish as that, why did you let them take you last night?

RICHARD.   (*Gaily.*) Upon my life, Mrs. Anderson, I don't know. I've been asking myself that question ever since; and I can find no manner of reason for acting as I did.

JUDITH.   You know, you did it for his sake, believing he was a more worthy man than yourself.

RICHARD.   (*Laughing.*) Oho! No: that's a very pretty reason, I must say; but I'm not so modest as that. No: it wasn't for his sake.

JUDITH.   (*After a pause, during which she looks shamefacedly at him, blushing painfully.*) Was it for my sake?

RICHARD.   (*Gallantly.*) Well, you had a hand in it. It must have been a little for your sake. You let them take me, at all events.

JUDITH.   Oh, do you think I have not been telling myself that all night? Your death will be at my door. (*Impulsively, she gives him her hand, and adds, with intense earnestness*) If I could save you as you saved him, I would do it, no matter how cruel the death was.

RICHARD.   (*Holding her hand and smiling, but keeping her almost at arm's length.*) I am very sure I shouldn't let you.

JUDITH.   Don't you see that I can save you?

RICHARD.   How? by changing clothes with me, eh?

JUDITH.   (*Disengaging her hand to touch his lips with it.*) Don't (*meaning* "*Don't jest* ") No: by telling the Court who you really are.

RICHARD.   (*Frowning.*) No use: they wouldn't spare me; and it would spoil half his chance of escaping. They are determined to cow us by making an example of somebody on that gallows today. Well, let us cow them by showing that we can stand by one another to the death. That is the only force that can send Burgoyne back across the Atlantic and make America a nation.

JUDITH.   (*Impatiently.*) Oh, what does all that matter?

RICHARD.   (*Laughing.*) True: what does it matter? what does anything matter? You see, men have these strange notions, Mrs. Anderson; and women see the folly of them.

JUDITH.   Women have to lose those they love through them.

RICHARD.   They can easily get fresh lovers.

JUDITH.   (*Revolted.*) Oh! (*Vehemently.*) Do you realize that you are going to kill yourself?

RICHARD.   The only man I have any right to kill, Mrs. Anderson. Don't be concerned: no woman will lose her lover through my death. (*Smiling.*) Bless you, nobody cares for me. Have you heard that my mother is dead?

JUDITH.   Dead!

RICHARD.   Of heart disease—in the night. Her last word to me was her curse: I don't think I could have borne her blessing. My other relatives will not grieve much on my account. Essie will cry for a day or two; but I have provided for her: I made my own will last night.

JUDITH.   (*Stonily, after a moment's silence.*) And I!

RICHARD.   (*Surprised.*) You?

JUDITH.   Yes, I. Am I not to care at all?

RICHARD.   (*Gaily and bluntly.*) Not a scrap. Oh, you expressed your feelings towards me very frankly yesterday. What happened may have softened you for the moment; but believe me, Mrs. Anderson, you don't like a bone in my skin or a hair on my head. I shall be as good a riddance at 12 today as I should have been at 12 yesterday.

JUDITH.   (*Her voice trembling.*) What can I do to show you that you are mistaken?

RICHARD.   Don't trouble. I'll give you credit for liking me a little better than you did. All I say is that my death will not break your heart.

JUDITH.   (*Almost in a whisper.*) How do you know? (*She puts her hands on his shoulders and looks intently at him.*)

RICHARD.   (*Amazed—divining the truth.*) Mrs. Anderson! (*The bell of the town clock strikes the quarter. He collects himself, and removes her hands, saying rather coldly*) Excuse me: they will be here for me presently. It is too late.

JUDITH.   It is not too late. Call me as witness: they will never kill you when they know how heroically you have acted.

RICHARD.   (*With some scorn.*) Indeed! But if I don't go through with it, where will the heroism be? I shall simply have tricked them; and they'll hang me for that like a dog. Serve me right too!

JUDITH.   (*Wildly.*) Oh, I believe you want to die.

RICHARD.   (*Obstinately.*) No I don't.

JUDITH. Then why not try to save yourself? I implore you—listen. You said just now that you saved him for my sake—yes (*clutching him as he recoils with a gesture of denial*) a little for my sake. Well, save yourself for my sake. And I will go with you to the end of the world.

RICHARD. (*Taking her by the wrists and holding her a little way from him, looking steadily at her.*) Judith.

JUDITH. (*Breathless—delighted at the name.*) Yes.

RICHARD. If I said—to please you—that I did what I did ever so little for your sake, I lied as men always lie to women. You know how much I have lived with worthless men—aye, and worthless women too. Well, they could all rise to some sort of goodness and kindness when they were in love. (*The word love comes from him with true Puritan scorn.*) That has taught me to set very little store by the goodness that comes out red hot. What I did last night, I did in cold blood, caring not half so much for your husband, or (*ruthlessly*) for you (*she droops, stricken*) as I do for myself. I had no motive and no interest: all I can tell you is that when it came to the point whether I would take my neck out of the noose and put another man's into it, I could not do it. I don't know why not: I see myself as a fool for my pains; but I could not and I cannot. I have been brought up standing by the law of my own nature; and I may not go against it, gallows or no gallows. (*She has slowly raised her head and is now looking full at him.*) I should have done the same for any other man in the town, or any other man's wife. (*Releasing her.*) Do you understand that?

JUDITH. Yes: you mean that you do not love me.

RICHARD. (*Revolted—with fierce contempt.*) Is that all it means to you?

JUDITH. What more—what worse—can it mean to me? (*The SER-GEANT knocks. The blow on the door jars on her heart.*) Oh, one moment more. (*She throws herself on her knees.*) I pray to you—

RICHARD. Hush! (*Calling.*) Come in. (*The SERGEANT unlocks the door and opens it. The guard is with him.*)

SERGEANT. (*Coming in.*) Time's up, sir.

RICHARD. Quite ready, Sergeant. Now, my dear. (*He attempts to raise her.*)

JUDITH. (*Clinging to him.*) Only one thing more—I entreat, I implore you. Let me be present in the court. I have seen Major Swindon: he said I should be allowed if you asked it. You will ask it. It is my last request: I shall never ask you anything again. (*She clasps his knee.*) I beg and pray it of you.

RICHARD. If I do, will you be silent?

JUDITH. Yes.

RICHARD. You will keep faith?

JUDITH. I will keep— (*She breaks down, sobbing.*)

RICHARD. (*Taking her arm to lift her.*) Just—her other arm, Sergeant.

They go out, she sobbing convulsively, supported by the two men. Meanwhile, the Council Chamber is ready for the court martial. It is a large, lofty room, with a chair of state in the middle under a tall canopy with a gilt crown, and maroon curtains with the royal monogram G.R.° In front of the chair is a table, also draped in maroon, with a bell, a heavy inkstand, and writing materials on it. Several chairs are set at the table. The door is at the right hand of the occupant of the chair of state when it has an occupant: at present it is empty. MAJOR SWINDON, a pale, sandy haired, very conscientious looking man of about 45, sits at the end of the table with his back to the door, writing. He is alone until the SERGEANT announces the General in a subdued manner which suggests that Gentlemanly Johnny has been making his presence felt rather heavily.

SERGEANT.   The General, sir.

SWINDON *rises hastily. The* GENERAL *comes in: the* SERGEANT *goes out. General Burgoyne is 55, and very well preserved. He is a man of fashion, gallant enough to have made a distinguished marriage by an elopement, witty enough to write successful comedies, aristocratically-connected enough to have had opportunities of high military distinction. His eyes, large, brilliant, apprehensive, and intelligent, are his most remarkable feature: without them his fine nose and mouth would suggest rather more fastidiousness and less force than go to the making of a first rate general. Just now the eyes are angry and tragic, and the mouth and nostrils tense.*

BURGOYNE.   Major Swindon, I presume.

SWINDON.   Yes. General Burgoyne, if I mistake not. (*They bow to one another ceremoniously.*) I am glad to have the support of your presence this morning. It is not particularly lively business, hanging this poor devil of a minister.

BURGOYNE.   (*Throwing himself into Swindon's chair.*) No, sir, it is not. It is making too much of the fellow to execute him: what more could you have done if he had been a member of the Church of England?° Martyrdom, sir, is what these people like: it is the only way in which a man can become famous without ability. However, you have committed us to hanging him; and the sooner he is hanged the better.

SWINDON.   We have arranged it for 12 o'clock. Nothing remains to be done except to try him.

BURGOYNE.   (*Looking at him with suppressed anger.*) Nothing—except to save your own necks, perhaps. Have you heard the news from Springtown?

SWINDON.   Nothing special. The latest reports are satisfactory.

° **G.R.:** George Rex; George III was King of England at the time of the American Revolution.
° **Church of England:** Anderson is a Presbyterian; the Church of England is the established episcopal church in England.

BURGOYNE.   (*Rising in amazement.*) Satisfactory, sir! Satisfactory!!
(*He stares at him for a moment, and then adds, with grim intensity*) I am glad you take that view of them.

SWINDON.   (*Puzzled.*) Do I understand that in your opinion—

BURGOYNE.   I do not express my opinion. I never stoop to that habit
of profane language which unfortunately coarsens our profession.
If I did, sir, perhaps I should be able to express my opinion of the
news from Springtown—the news which you (*severely*) have
apparently not heard. How soon do you get news from your supports here?—in the course of a month, eh?

SWINDON.   (*Turning sulkily.*) I suppose the reports have been taken
to you, sir, instead of to me. Is there anything serious?

BURGOYNE.   (*Taking a report from his pocket and holding it up.*)
Springtown's in the hands of the rebels. (*He throws the report on
the table.*)

SWINDON.   (*Aghast.*) Since yesterday!

BURGOYNE.   Since two o'clock this morning. Perhaps we shall be in
their hands before two o'clock tomorrow morning. Have you
thought of that?

SWINDON.   (*Confidently.*) As to that, General, the British soldier will
give a good account of himself.

BURGOYNE.   (*Bitterly.*) And therefore, I suppose, sir, the British officer need not know his business: the British soldier will get him
out of all his blunders with the bayonet. In future, sir, I must ask
you to be a little less generous with the blood of your men, and a
little more generous with your own brains.

SWINDON.   I am sorry I cannot pretend to your intellectual eminence,
sir. I can only do my best, and rely on the devotion of my countrymen.

BURGOYNE.   (*Suddenly becoming suavely sarcastic.*) May I ask are
you writing a melodrama, Major Swindon?

SWINDON.   (*Flushing.*) No, sir.

BURGOYNE.   What a pity! What a pity! (*Dropping his sarcastic tone
and facing him suddenly and seriously.*) Do you at all realize, sir,
that we have nothing standing between us and destruction but our
own bluff and the sheepishness of these colonists? They are men
of the same English stock as ourselves: six to one of us (*repeating
it emphatically*) six to one, sir; and nearly half our troops are
Hessians, Brunswickers, German dragoons, and Indians with scalping knives. These are the countrymen on whose devotion you rely!
Suppose the colonists find a leader! Suppose the news from Springtown should turn out to mean that they have already found a
leader! What shall we do then? Eh?

SWINDON.   (*Sullenly.*) Our duty, sir, I presume.

BURGOYNE.   (*Again sarcastic—giving him up as a fool.*) Quite so,
quite so. Thank you, Major Swindon, thank you. Now you've settled the question, sir—thrown a flood of light on the situation.
What a comfort to me to feel that I have at my side so devoted

and able an officer to support me in this emergency! I think, sir, it will probably relieve both our feelings if we proceed to hang this dissenter without further delay (*he strikes the bell*) especially as I am debarred by my principles from the customary military vent for my feelings. (*The* SERGEANT *appears.*) Bring your man in.

SERGEANT.   Yes, sir.

BURGOYNE.   And mention to any officer you may meet that the court cannot wait any longer for him.

SWINDON.   (*Keeping his temper with difficulty.*) The staff is perfectly ready, sir. They have been waiting your convenience for fully half an hour. Perfectly ready, sir.

BURGOYNE.   (*Blandly.*) So am I. (*Several officers come in and take their seats. One of them sits at the end of the table furthest from the door, and acts throughout as clerk of the court, making notes of the proceedings. The uniforms are those of the 9th, 20th, 21st, 24th, 47th, 53rd, and 62nd British Infantry. One officer is a Major General of the Royal Artillery. There are also German officers of the Hessian Rifles, and of German dragoon and Brunswicker regiments.*) Oh, good morning, gentlemen. Sorry to disturb you, I am sure. Very good of you to spare us a few moments.

SWINDON.   Will you preside, sir?

BURGOYNE.   (*Becoming additionally polished, lofty, sarcastic, and urbane now that he is in public.*) No, sir: I feel my own deficiencies too keenly to presume so far. If you will kindly allow me, I will sit at the feet of Gamaliel.° (*He takes the chair at the end of the table next the door, and motions* SWINDON *to the chair of state, waiting for him to be seated before sitting down himself.*)

SWINDON.   (*Greatly annoyed.*) As you please, sir. I am only trying to do my duty under excessively trying circumstances. (*He takes his place in the chair of state.*)

BURGOYNE, *relaxing his studied demeanor for the moment, sits down and begins to read the report with knitted brows and careworn looks, reflecting on his desperate situation and Swindon's uselessness.* RICHARD *is brought in.* JUDITH *walks beside him. Two soldiers precede and two follow him, with the* SERGEANT *in command. They cross the room to the wall opposite the door; but when* RICHARD *has just passed before the chair of state the* SERGEANT *stops him with a touch on the arm, and posts himself behind him, at his elbow.* JUDITH *stands timidly at the wall. The four soldiers place themselves in a squad near her.*

BURGOYNE.   (*Looking up and seeing Judith.*) Who is that woman?

SERGEANT.   Prisoner's wife, sir.

SWINDON.   (*Nervously.*) She begged me to allow her to be present; and I thought—

° **Gamaliel:** teacher of St. Paul.

BURGOYNE.   (*Completing the sentence for him ironically.*) You thought it would be a pleasure for her. Quite so, quite so. (*Blandly.*) Give the lady a chair; and make her thoroughly comfortable.

The SERGEANT *fetches a chair and places it near Richard.*

JUDITH.   Thank you, sir. (*She sits down after an awestricken curtsy to* BURGOYNE, *which he acknowledges by a dignified bend of his head.*)

SWINDON.   (*To* RICHARD, *sharply.*) Your name, sir?

RICHARD.   (*Affable, but obstinate.*) Come: you don't mean to say that you've brought me here without knowing who I am?

SWINDON.   As a matter of form, sir, give your name.

RICHARD.   As a matter of form then, my name is Anthony Anderson, Presbyterian minister in this town.

BURGOYNE.   (*Interested.*) Indeed! Pray, Mr. Anderson, what do you gentlemen believe?

RICHARD.   I shall be happy to explain if time is allowed me. I cannot undertake to complete your conversion in less than a fortnight.

SWINDON.   (*Snubbing him.*) We are not here to discuss your views.

BURGOYNE.   (*With an elaborate bow to the unfortunate* SWINDON.) I stand rebuked.

SWINDON.   (*Embarrassed.*) Oh, not you, I as—

BURGOYNE.   Don't mention it. (*To* RICHARD, *very politely.*) Any political views, Mr. Anderson?

RICHARD.   I understand that that is just what we are here to find out.

SWINDON.   (*Severely.*) Do you mean to deny that you are a rebel?

RICHARD.   I am an American, sir.

SWINDON.   What do you expect me to think of that speech, Mr. Anderson?

RICHARD.   I never expect a soldier to think, sir.

BURGOYNE *is boundlessly delighted by this retort, which almost reconciles him to the loss of America.*

SWINDON.   (*Whitening with anger.*) I advise you not to be insolent, prisoner.

RICHARD.   You can't help yourself, General. When you make up your mind to hang a man, you put yourself at a disadvantage with him. Why should I be civil to you? I may as well be hanged for a sheep as a lamb.

SWINDON.   You have no right to assume that the court has made up its mind without a fair trial. And you will please not address me as General. I am Major Swindon.

RICHARD.   A thousand pardons. I thought I had the honor of addressing Gentlemanly Johnny.

Sensation among the officers. The SERGEANT *has a narrow escape from a guffaw.*

BURGOYNE.   (*With extreme suavity.*) I believe I am Gentlemanly Johnny, sir, at your service. My more intimate friends call me General Burgoyne. (RICHARD *bows with perfect politeness.*) You will understand, sir, I hope, since you seem to be a gentleman and a man of some spirit in spite of your calling, that if we should have the misfortune to hang you, we shall do so as a mere matter of political necessity and military duty, without any personal ill-feeling.

RICHARD.   Oh, quite so. That makes all the difference in the world, of course.

They all smile in spite of themselves; and some of the younger officers burst out laughing.

JUDITH.   (*Her dread and horror deepening at every one of these jests and compliments.*) How can you?

RICHARD.   You promised to be silent.

BURGOYNE.   (*To* JUDITH, *with studied courtesy.*) Believe me, Madam, your husband is placing us under the greatest obligation by taking this very disagreeable business so thoroughly in the spirit of a gentleman. Sergeant: give Mr. Anderson a chair. (*The* SERGEANT *does so.* RICHARD *sits down.*) Now, Major Swindon: we are waiting for you.

SWINDON.   You are aware, I presume, Mr. Anderson, of your obligations as a subject of His Majesty King George the Third.

RICHARD.   I am aware, sir, that His Majesty King George the Third is about to hang me because I object to Lord North's robbing me.

SWINDON.   That is a treasonable speech, sir.

RICHARD.   (*Briefly.*) Yes. I meant it to be.

BURGOYNE.   (*Strongly deprecating this line of defense, but still polite.*) Don't you think, Mr. Anderson, that this is rather—if you will excuse the word—a vulgar line to take? Why should you cry out robbery because of a stamp duty and a tea duty and so forth? After all, it is the essence of your position as a gentleman that you pay with a good grace.

RICHARD.   It is not the money, General. But to be swindled by a pig-headed lunatic like King George—

SWINDON.   (*Scandalized.*) Chut, sir—silence!

SERGEANT.   (*In stentorian tones, greatly shocked.*) Silence!

BURGOYNE.   (*Unruffled.*) Ah, that is another point of view. My position does not allow of my going into that, except in private. But (*shrugging his shoulders*) of course, Mr. Anderson, if you are determined to be hanged (JUDITH *flinches*) there's nothing more to be said. An unusual taste! however (*With a final shrug.*)—!

SWINDON.   (*To* BURGOYNE.) Shall we call witnesses?

RICHARD.   What need is there of witnesses? If the townspeople here had listened to me, you would have found the streets barricaded, the houses loopholed, and the people in arms to hold the town against you to the last man. But you arrived, unfortunately, before we had got out of the talking stage; and then it was too late.

SWINDON.   (*Severely.*) Well, sir, we shall teach you and your townspeople a lesson they will not forget. Have you anything more to say?

RICHARD.   I think you might have the decency to treat me as a prisoner of war, and shoot me like a man instead of hanging me like a dog.

BURGOYNE.   (*Sympathetically.*) Now there, Mr. Anderson, you talk like a civilian, if you will excuse my saying so. Have you any idea of the average marksmanship of the army of His Majesty King George the Third? If we make you up a firing party, what will happen? Half of them will miss you: the rest will make a mess of the business and leave you to the provo-marshal's pistol. Whereas we can hang you in a perfectly workmanlike and agreeable way. (*Kindly.*) Let me persuade you to be hanged, Mr. Anderson?

JUDITH.   (*Sick with horror.*) My God!

RICHARD.   (*To* JUDITH.) Your promise! (*To* BURGOYNE.) Thank you, General: that view of the case did not occur to me before. To oblige you, I withdraw my objection to the rope. Hang me, by all means.

BURGOYNE.   (*Smoothly.*) Will 12 o'clock suit you, Mr. Anderson?

RICHARD.   I shall be at your disposal then, General.

BURGOYNE.   (*Rising.*) Nothing more to be said, gentlemen. (*They all rise.*)

JUDITH.   (*Rushing to the table.*) Oh, you are not going to murder a man like that, without a proper trial—without thinking of what you are doing—without—(*She cannot find words.*)

RICHARD.   Is this how you keep your promise?

JUDITH.   If I am not to speak, you must. Defend yourself: save yourself: tell them the truth.

RICHARD.   (*Worriedly.*) I have told them truth enough to hang me ten times over. If you say another word you will risk other lives; but you will not save mine.

BURGOYNE.   My good lady, our only desire is to save unpleasantness. What satisfaction would it give me to have a solemn fuss made, with my friend Swindon in a black cap and so forth? I am sure we are greatly indebted to the admirable tact and gentlemanly feeling shown by your husband.

JUDITH.   (*Throwing the words in his face.*) Oh, you are mad. Is it nothing to you what wicked thing you do if only you do it like a gentleman? Is it nothing to you whether you are a murderer or not, if only you murder in a red coat? (*Desperately.*) You shall not hang him: that man is not my husband.

The officers look at one another, and whisper: some of the Germans asking their neighbors to explain what the woman has said. BURGOYNE, *who has been visibly shaken by Judith's reproach, recovers himself promptly at this new development.* RICHARD *meanwhile raises his voice above the buzz.*

RICHARD.   I appeal to you, gentlemen, to put an end to this. She will not believe that she cannot save me. Break up the court.

BURGOYNE.   (*In a voice so quiet and firm that it restores silence at once.*) One moment, Mr. Anderson. One moment, gentlemen. (*He*

resumes his seat. SWINDON *and the officers follow his example.*)
Let me understand you clearly, madam. Do you mean that this
gentleman is not your husband, or merely—I wish to put this with
all delicacy—that you are not his wife?

JUDITH.   I don't know what you mean. I say that he is not my husband
—that my husband has escaped. This man took his place to save
him. Ask anyone in the town—send out into the street for the
first person you find there, and bring him in as a witness. He will
tell you that the prisoner is not Anthony Anderson.

BURGOYNE.   (*Quietly, as before.*) Sergeant.

SERGEANT.   Yes, sir.

BURGOYNE.   Go out into the street and bring in the first townsman you
see there.

SERGEANT.   (*Making for the door.*) Yes, sir.

BURGOYNE.   (*As the* SERGEANT *passes.*) The first clean, sober townsman you see.

SERGEANT.   Yes, sir. (*He goes out.*)

BURGOYNE.   Sit down, Mr. Anderson—if I may call you so for the
present. (RICHARD *sits down.*) Sit down, madam, whilst we wait.
Give the lady a newspaper.

RICHARD.   (*Indignantly.*) Shame!

BURGOYNE.   (*Keenly, with a half smile.*) If you are not her husband,
sir, the case is not a serious one—for her. (RICHARD *bites his lip,
silenced.*)

JUDITH.   (*To* RICHARD, *as she returns to her seat.*) I couldn't help
it. (*He shakes his head. She sits down.*)

BURGOYNE.   You will understand, of course, Mr. Anderson, that you
must not build on this little incident. We are bound to make an
example of somebody.

RICHARD.   I quite understand. I suppose there's no use in my explaining.

BURGOYNE.   I think we should prefer independent testimony, if you
don't mind.

The SERGEANT, *with a packet of papers in his hand, returns con-
ducting* CHRISTY, *who is much scared.*

SERGEANT.   (*Giving Burgoyne the packet.*) Dispatches, sir. Delivered by a corporal of the 33rd. Dead beat with hard riding, sir.

BURGOYNE *opens the dispatches, and presently becomes absorbed
in them. They are so serious as to take his attention completely
from the court martial.*

THE SERGEANT.   (*To* CHRISTY.) Now then. Attention; and take
your hat off. (*He posts himself in charge of Christy, who stands
on Burgoyne's side of the court.*)

RICHARD.   (*In his usual bullying tone to* CHRISTY.) Don't be frightened, you fool: you're only wanted as a witness. They're not going
to hang you.

SWINDON.   What's your name?

CHRISTY.   Christy.

RICHARD.   (*Impatiently.*) Christopher Dudgeon, you blatant idiot. Give your full name.

SWINDON.   Be silent, prisoner. You must not prompt the witness.

RICHARD.   Very well. But I warn you you'll get nothing out of him unless you shake it out of him. He has been too well brought up by a pious mother to have any sense or manhood left in him.

BURGOYNE.   (*Springing up and speaking to the* SERGEANT *in a startling voice.*) Where is the man who brought these?

SERGEANT.   In the guard-room, sir.

BURGOYNE *goes out with a haste that sets the officers exchanging looks.*

SWINDON.   (*To* CHRISTY.) Do you know Anthony Anderson, the Presbyterian minister?

CHRISTY.   Of course I do (*implying that Swindon must be an ass not to know it*).

SWINDON.   Is he here?

CHRISTY.   (*Staring round.*) I don't know.

SWINDON.   Do you see him?

CHRISTY.   No.

SWINDON.   You seem to know the prisoner?

CHRISTY.   Do you mean Dick?

SWINDON.   Which is Dick?

CHRISTY.   (*Pointing to* RICHARD.) Him.

SWINDON.   What is his name?

CHRISTY.   Dick.

RICHARD.   Answer properly, you jumping jackass. What do they know about Dick?

CHRISTY.   Well, you are Dick, ain't you? What am I to say?

SWINDON.   Address me, sir; and do you, prisoner, be silent. Tell us who the prisoner is.

CHRISTY.   He's my brother Dick—Richard—Richard Dudgeon.

SWINDON.   Your brother!

CHRISTY.   Yes.

SWINDON.   You are sure he is not Anderson.

CHRISTY.   Who?

RICHARD.   (*Exasperatedly.*) Me, me, me, you—

SWINDON.   Silence, sir.

SERGEANT.   (*Shouting.*) Silence.

RICHARD.   (*Impatiently.*) Yah! (*To* CHRISTY.) He wants to know am I Minister Anderson. Tell him, and stop grinning like a zany.

CHRISTY.   (*Grinning more than ever.*) You Pastor Anderson! (*To* SWINDON.) Why, Mr. Anderson's a minister—a very good man; and Dick's a bad character: the respectable people won't speak to him. He's the bad brother: I'm the good one. (*The officers laugh outright. The soldiers grin.*)

SWINDON.   Who arrested this man?

SERGEANT. I did, sir. I found him in the minister's house, sitting at tea with the lady with his coat off, quite at home. If he isn't married to her, he ought to be.

SWINDON. Did he answer to the minister's name?

SERGEANT. Yes, sir, but not to a minister's nature. You ask the chaplain, sir.

SWINDON. (*To* RICHARD, *threateningly.*) So, sir, you have attempted to cheat us. And your name is Richard Dudgeon?

RICHARD. You've found it out at last, have you?

SWINDON. Dudgeon is a name well known to us, eh?

RICHARD. Yes: Peter Dudgeon, whom you murdered, was my uncle.

SWINDON. Hm! (*He compresses his lips, and looks at* RICHARD *with vindictive gravity.*)

CHRISTY. Are they going to hang you, Dick?

RICHARD. Yes. Get out: they've done with you.

CHRISTY. And I may keep the china peacocks?

RICHARD. (*Jumping up.*) Get out. Get out, you blithering baboon, you. (CHRISTY *flies, panic-stricken.*)

SWINDON. (*Rising—all rise.*) Since you have taken the minister's place, Richard Dudgeon, you shall go through with it. The execution will take place at 12 o'clock as arranged; and unless Anderson surrenders before then, you shall take his place on the gallows. Sergeant: take your man out.

JUDITH. (*Distracted.*) No, no—

SWINDON. (*Fiercely dreading a renewal of her entreaties.*) Take that woman away.

RICHARD. (*Springing across the table with a tiger-like bound, and seizing* SWINDON *by the throat.*) You infernal scoundrel—

The SERGEANT *rushes to the rescue from one side, the soldiers from the other. They seize* RICHARD *and drag him back to his place.* SWINDON, *who has been thrown supine on the table, rises, arranging his stock.° He is about to speak, when he is anticipated by* BURGOYNE, *who has just appeared at the door with two papers in his hand: a white letter and a blue dispatch.*

BURGOYNE. (*Advancing to the table, elaborately cool.*) What is it? What's happening? Mr. Anderson: I'm astonished at you.

RICHARD. I am sorry I disturbed you, General. I merely wanted to strangle your understrapper there. (*Breaking out violently at* SWINDON.) Why do you raise the devil in me by bullying the woman like that? You oatmeal faced dog, I'd twist your cursed head off with the greatest satisfaction. (*He puts out his hands to the* SERGEANT.) Here: handcuff me, will you; or I'll not undertake to keep my fingers off him.

The SERGEANT *takes out a pair of handcuffs and looks to* BURGOYNE *for instructions.*

° **stock:** neck scarf.

BURGOYNE.   Have you addressed profane language to the lady, Major
     Swindon.
SWINDON.   (*Very angry.*) No, sir, certainly not. That question should
     not have been put to me. I ordered the woman to be removed, as
     she was disorderly; and the fellow sprang at me. Put away those
     handcuffs. I am perfectly able to take care of myself.
RICHARD.   Now you talk like a man, I have no quarrel with you.
BURGOYNE.   Mr. Anderson—
SWINDON.   His name is Dudgeon, sir, Richard Dudgeon. He is an
     impostor.
BURGOYNE.   (*Brusquely.*) Nonsense, sir: you hanged Dudgeon at
     Springtown.
RICHARD.   It was my uncle, General.
BURGOYNE.   Oh, your uncle. (*To* SWINDON, *handsomely.*) I beg your
     pardon, Major Swindon. (SWINDON *acknowledges the apology
     stiffly.* BURGOYNE *turns to* RICHARD.) We are somewhat unfor-
     tunate in our relations with your family. Well, Mr. Dudgeon, what
     I wanted to ask you is this. Who is (*reading the name from the
     letter*) William Maindeck Parshotter?
RICHARD.   He is the Mayor of Springtown.
BURGOYNE.   Is William—Maindeck and so on—a man of his word?
RICHARD.   Is he selling you anything?
BURGOYNE.   No.
RICHARD.   Then you may depend upon him.
BURGOYNE.   Thank you, Mr.—'m Dudgeon. By the way, since you are
     not Mr. Anderson, do we still—eh, Major Swindon? (*Meaning "do
     we still hang him?"*)
RICHARD.   The arrangements are unaltered, General.
BURGOYNE.   Ah, indeed. I am sorry. Good morning, Mr. Dudgeon.
     Good morning, madam.
RICHARD.   (*Interrupting Judith almost fiercely as she is about to
     make some wild appeal, and taking her arm resolutely.*) Not one
     word more. Come.

*She looks imploringly at him, but is overborne by his determina-
tion. They are marched out by the four soldiers: the* SERGEANT,
very sulky, walking between SWINDON *and* RICHARD, *whom he
watches as if he were a dangerous animal.*

BURGOYNE.   Gentlemen: we need not detain you. Major Swindon: a
     word with you. (*The officers go out.* BURGOYNE *waits with un-
     ruffled serenity until the last of them disappears. Then he becomes
     very grave, and addresses Swindon for the first time without his
     title.*) Swindon: do you know what this is (*showing him the
     letter*)?
SWINDON.   What?
BURGOYNE.   A demand for a safe-conduct for an officer of their militia
     to come here and arrange terms with us.
SWINDON.   Oh, they are giving in.

BURGOYNE. They add that they are sending the man who raised Springtown last night and drove us out; so that we may know that we are dealing with an officer of importance.

SWINDON. Pooh!

BURGOYNE. He will be fully empowered to arrange the terms of—guess what.

SWINDON. Their surrender, I hope.

BURGOYNE. No: our evacuation of the town. They offer us just six hours to clear out.

SWINDON. What monstrous impudence!

BURGOYNE. What shall we do, eh?

SWINDON. March on Springtown and strike a decisive blow at once.

BURGOYNE. (*Quietly.*) Hm! (*Turning to the door.*) Come to the adjutant's office.

SWINDON. What for?

BURGOYNE. To write out that safe-conduct. (*He puts his hand on the door knob to open it.*)

SWINDON. (*Who has not budged.*) General Burgoyne.

BURGOYNE. (*Returning.*) Sir?

SWINDON. It is my duty to tell you, sir, that I do not consider the threats of a mob of rebellious tradesmen a sufficient reason for our giving way.

BURGOYNE. (*Imperturbable.*) Suppose I resign my command to you, what will you do?

SWINDON. I will undertake to do what we have marched south from Quebec to do, and what General Howe has marched north from New York to do: effect a junction at Albany and wipe out the rebel army with our united forces.

BURGOYNE. (*Enigmatically.*) And will you wipe out our enemies in London, too?

SWINDON. In London! What enemies?

BURGOYNE. (*Forcibly.*) Jobbery and snobbery, incompetence and Red Tape. (*He holds up the dispatch and adds, with despair in his face and voice*) I have just learnt, sir, that General Howe is still in New York.

SWINDON. (*Thunderstruck.*) Good God! He has disobeyed orders!

BURGOYNE. (*With sardonic calm.*) He has received no orders, sir. Some gentleman in London forgot to dispatch them: he was leaving town for his holiday, I believe. To avoid upsetting his arrangements, England will lose her American colonies; and in a few days you and I will be at Saratoga with 5,000 men to face 18,000 rebels in an impregnable position.

SWINDON. (*Appalled.*) Impossible!

BURGOYNE. (*Coldly.*) I beg your pardon?

SWINDON. I can't believe it! What will History say?

BURGOYNE. History, sir, will tell lies, as usual. Come: we must send the safe-conduct. (*He goes out.*)

SWINDON.   (*Following distractedly.*) My God, my God! We shall be wiped out.

As noon approaches there is excitement in the market place. The gallows which hangs there permanently for the terror of evildoers, with such minor advertizers and examples of crime as the pillory, the whipping post, and the stocks, has a new rope attached, with the noose hitched up to one of the uprights, out of reach of the boys. Its ladder, too, has been brought out and placed in position by the town beadle,° who stands by to guard it from unauthorized climbing. The Websterbridge townsfolk are present in force, and in high spirits; for the news has spread that it is the devil's disciple and not the minister that the Continentals (so they call Burgoyne's forces) are about to hang: consequently the execution can be enjoyed without any misgivings as to its righteousness, or to the cowardice of allowing it to take place without a struggle. There is even some fear of a disappointment as midday approaches and the arrival of the beadle with the ladder remains the only sign of preparation. But at last reassuring shouts of Here they come: Here they are, are heard; and a company of soldiers with fixed bayonets, half British infantry, half Hessians, tramp quickly into the middle of the market place, driving the crowd to the sides.

THE SERGEANT.   Halt. Front. Dress. (*The soldiers change their column into a square enclosing the gallows, their petty officers, energetically led by the* SERGEANT, *hustling the persons who find themselves inside the square out at the corners.*) Now then! Out of it with you: out of it. Some o' you'll get strung up yourselves presently. Form that square there, will you, you damned Hoosians. No use talkin' German to them: talk to their toes with the butt end of your muskets: they'll understand that. Get out of it, will you. (*He comes upon* JUDITH, *standing near the gallows.*) Now then: you've no call here.

JUDITH.   May I not stay? What harm am I doing?

SERGEANT.   I want none of your argufying. You ought to be ashamed of yourself, running to see a man hanged that's not your husband. And he's no better than yourself. I told my major he was a gentleman; and then he goes and tries to strangle him, and calls his blessed Majesty a lunatic. So out of it with you, double quick.

JUDITH.   Will you take these two silver dollars and let me stay?

The SERGEANT, *without an instant's hesitation, looks quickly and furtively round as he shoots the money dexterously into his pocket. Then he raises his voice in virtuous indignation.*

THE SERGEANT.   Me take money in the execution of my duty! Certainly not. Now I'll tell you what I'll do, to teach you to corrupt the King's officer. I'll put you under arrest until the execution's over. You just stand there; and don't let me see you as much as move

---

° **beadle:** a minor parish official.

from that spot until you're let. (*With a swift wink at her he points to the corner of the square behind the gallows on his right, and turns noisily away, shouting*) Now then, dress up and keep 'em back, will you.

Cries of Hush and Silence are heard among the townsfolk; and the sound of a military band, playing the Dead March from Saul,° is heard. The crowd becomes quiet at once; and the Sergeant and petty officers, hurrying to the back of the square, with a few whispered orders and some stealthy hustling cause it to open and admit the funeral procession, which is protected from the crowd by a double file of soldiers. First come Burgoyne and Swindon, who, on entering the square, glance with distaste at the gallows, and avoid passing under it by wheeling a little to the right and stationing themselves on that side. Then Mr. Brudenell, the chaplain, in his surplice, with his prayer book open in his hand, walking beside Richard, who is moody and disorderly. He walks doggedly through the gallows framework, and posts himself a little in front of it. Behind him comes the executioner, a stalwart soldier in his shirtsleeves. Following him, two soldiers haul a light military wagon. Finally comes the band, which posts itself at the back of the square, and finishes the Dead March. Judith, watching Richard painfully, steals down to the gallows, and stands leaning against its right post. During the conversation which follows, the two soldiers place the cart under the gallows, and stand by the shafts, which point backwards. The executioner takes a set of steps from the cart and places it ready for the prisoner to mount. Then he climbs the tall ladder which stands against the gallows, and cuts the string by which the rope is hitched up; so that the noose drops dangling over the cart, into which he steps as he descends.

RICHARD. (*With suppressed impatience, to* BRUDENELL.) Look here, sir: this is no place for a man of your profession. Hadn't you better go away?

SWINDON. I appeal to you, prisoner, if you have any sense of decency left, to listen to the ministrations of the chaplain, and pay due heed to the solemnity of the occasion.

THE CHAPLAIN. (*Gently reproving Richard.*) Try to control yourself, and submit to the divine will. (*He lifts his book to proceed with the service.*)

RICHARD. Answer for your own will, sir, and those of your accomplices here. (*Indicating* BURGOYNE *and* SWINDON.) I see little divinity about them or you. You talk to me of Christianity when you are in the act of hanging your enemies. Was there ever such blasphemous nonsense! (*To* SWINDON, *more rudely.*) You've got up the solemnity of the occasion, as you call it, to impress the people with your own dignity—Handel's music and a clergyman to

---

° **Saul**: oratorio by George Frederick Handel.

make murder look like piety! Do you suppose *I* am going to help you? You've asked me to choose the rope because you don't know your own trade well enough to shoot me properly. Well, hang away and have done with it.

SWINDON.   (*To the* CHAPLAIN.) Can you do nothing with him, Mr. Brudenell?

CHAPLAIN.   I will try, sir. (*Beginning to read.*) Man that is born of woman hath—

RICHARD.   (*Fixing his eyes on him.*) "Thou shalt not kill."

The book drops in Brudenell's hands.

CHAPLAIN.   (*Confessing his embarrassment.*) What am I to say, Mr. Dudgeon?

RICHARD.   Let me alone, man, can't you!

BURGOYNE.   (*With extreme urbanity.*) I think, Mr. Brudenell, that as the usual professional observations seem to strike Mr. Dudgeon as incongruous under the circumstances, you had better omit them until—er—until Mr. Dudgeon can no longer be inconvenienced by them. (BRUDENELL, *with a shrug, shuts his book and retires behind the gallows.*) You seem in a hurry, Mr. Dudgeon.

RICHARD.   (*With the horror of death upon him.*) Do you think this is a pleasant sort of thing to be kept waiting for? You've made up your mind to commit murder: well, do it and have done with it.

BURGOYNE.   Mr. Dudgeon: we are only doing this—

RICHARD.   Because you're paid to do it.

SWINDON.   You insolent— (*He swallows his rage.*)

BURGOYNE.   (*With much charm of manner.*) Ah, I am really sorry that you should think that, Mr. Dudgeon. If you knew what my commission cost me, and what my pay is, you would think better of me. I should be glad to part from you on friendly terms.

RICHARD.   Hark ye, General Burgoyne. If you think that I like being hanged, you're mistaken. I don't like it; and I don't mean to pretend that I do. And if you think I'm obliged to you for hanging me in a gentlemanly way, you're wrong there too. I take the whole business in devilish bad part; and the only satisfaction I have in it is that you'll feel a good deal meaner than I'll look when it's over. (*He turns away, and is striding to the cart when* JUDITH *advances and interposes with her arms stretched out to him.* RICHARD, *feeling that a very little will upset his self-possession, shrinks from her, crying*) What are you doing here? This is no place for you. (*She makes a gesture as if to touch him. He recoils impatiently.*) No: go away, go away: you'll unnerve me. Take her away, will you.

JUDITH.   Won't you bid me goodbye?

RICHARD.   (*Allowing her to take his hand.*) Oh goodbye, goodbye. Now go—go—quickly. (*She clings to his hand—will not be put off with so cold a last farewell—at last, as he tries to disengage himself, throws herself on his breast in agony.*)

SWINDON. (*Angrily to the sergeant, who, alarmed at Judith's movement, has come from the back of the square to pull her back, and stopped irresolutely on finding that he is too late.*) How is this? Why is she inside the lines?

SERGEANT. (*Guiltily.*) I dunno, sir. She's that artful—can't keep her away.

BURGOYNE. You were bribed.

SERGEANT. (*Protesting.*) No, sir—

SWINDON. (*Severely.*) Fall back. (*He obeys.*)

RICHARD. (*Imploringly to those around him, and finally to BURGOYNE, as the least stolid of them.*) Take her away. Do you think I want a woman near me now?

BURGOYNE. (*Going to JUDITH and taking her hand.*) Here, madam: you had better keep inside the lines; but stand here behind us; and don't look.

RICHARD, *with a great sobbing sigh of relief as she releases him and turns to BURGOYNE, flies for refuge to the cart and mounts into it. The executioner takes off his coat and pinions him.*

JUDITH. (*Resisting Burgoyne quietly and drawing her hand away.*) No: I must stay. I won't look. (*She goes to the right of the gallows. She tries to look at Richard, but turns away with a frightful shudder, and falls on her knees in prayer. BRUDENELL comes towards her from the back of the square.*)

BURGOYNE. (*Nodding approvingly as she kneels.*) Ah, quite so. Do not disturb her, Mr. Brudenell: that will do very nicely. (*BRUDENELL nods also, and withdraws a little, watching her sympathetically. BURGOYNE resumes his former position, and takes out a handsome gold chronometer.*) Now then, are those preparations made? We must not detain Mr. Dudgeon.

By this time Richard's hands are bound behind him; and the noose is round his neck. The two soldiers take the shafts of the wagon, ready to pull it away. The executioner, standing in the cart behind Richard, makes a sign to the sergeant.

SERGEANT. (*To BURGOYNE.*) Ready, sir.

BURGOYNE. Have you anything more to say, Mr. Dudgeon? It wants two minutes of twelve still.

RICHARD. (*In the strong voice of a man who has conquered the bitterness of death.*) Your watch is two minutes slow by the town clock, which I can see from here, General. (*The town clock strikes the first stroke of twelve. Involuntarily the people flinch at the sound, and a subdued groan breaks from them.*) Amen! my life for the world's future!

ANDERSON. (*Shouting as he rushes into the market place.*) Amen; and stop the execution. (*He bursts through the line of soldiers opposite Burgoyne, and rushes, panting, to the gallows.*) I am Anthony Anderson, the man you want.

The crowd, intensely excited, listens with all its ears. JUDITH, *half rising, stares at him; then lifts her hands like one whose dearest prayer has been granted.*

SWINDON.   Indeed. Then you are just in time to take your place on the gallows. Arrest him.

At a sign from the sergeant, two soldiers come forward to seize ANDERSON.

ANDERSON.   (*Thrusting a paper under Swindon's nose.*) There's my safe-conduct, sir.

SWINDON.   (*Taken aback.*) Safe-conduct! Are you—!

ANDERSON.   (*Emphatically.*) I am. (*The two soldiers take him by the elbows.*) Tell these men to take their hands off me.

SWINDON.   (*To the men.*) Let him go.

SERGEANT.   Fall back.

The two men return to their places. The townsfolk raise a cheer; and begin to exchange exultant looks, with a presentiment of triumph as they see their Pastor speaking with their enemies in the gate.

ANDERSON.   (*Exhaling a deep breath of relief, and dabbing his perspiring brow with his handkerchief.*) Thank God, I was in time!

BURGOYNE.   (*Calm as ever, and still watch in hand.*) Ample time, sir. Plenty of time. I should never dream of hanging any gentleman by an American clock. (*He puts up his watch.*)

ANDERSON.   Yes: we are some minutes ahead of you already, General. Now tell them to take the rope from the neck of that American citizen.

BURGOYNE.   (*To the executioner in the cart—very politely.*) Kindly undo Mr. Dudgeon.

The executioner takes the rope from Richard's neck, unties his hands, and helps him on with his coat.

JUDITH.   (*Stealing timidly to Anderson.*) Tony.

ANDERSON.   (*Putting his arm round her shoulders and bantering her affectionately.*) Well, what do you think of your husband now, eh? —eh? ?—eh? ? ?

JUDITH.   I am ashamed— (*She hides her face against his breast.*)

BURGOYNE.   (*To* SWINDON.) You look disappointed, Major Swindon.

SWINDON.   You look defeated, General Burgoyne.

BURGOYNE.   I am, sir; and I am humane enough to be glad of it. (RICHARD *jumps down from the cart,* BRUDENELL *offering his hand to help him, and runs to* ANDERSON, *whose left hand he shakes heartily, the right being occupied by* JUDITH.) By the way, Mr. Anderson, I do not quite understand. The safe-conduct was for a commander of the militia. I understand you are a—(*He looks as pointedly as his good manners permit at the riding boots, the pistols, and Richard's coat, and adds*)—a clergyman.

ANDERSON.   (*Between* JUDITH *and* RICHARD.) Sir: it is in the hour of trial that a man finds his true profession. This foolish young man (*Placing his hand on Richard's shoulder.*) boasted himself the Devil's Disciple; but when the hour of trial came to him, he found that it was his destiny to suffer and be faithful to the death. I thought myself a decent minister of the gospel of peace; but when the hour of trial came to me, I found that it was my destiny to be a man of action, and that my place was amid the thunder of the captains and the shouting. So I am starting life at fifty as Captain Anthony Anderson of the Springtown militia; and the Devil's Disciple here will start presently as the Reverend Richard Dudgeon, and wag his pow in my old pulpit, and give good advice to this silly sentimental little wife of mine. (*Putting his other hand on her shoulder. She steals a glance at Richard to see how the prospect pleases him.*) Your mother told me, Richard, that I should never have chosen Judith if I'd been born for the ministry. I am afraid she was right; so, by your leave, you may keep my coat and I'll keep yours.

RICHARD.   Minister—I should say Captain. I have behaved like a fool.

JUDITH.   Like a hero.

RICHARD.   Much the same thing, perhaps. (*With some bitterness towards himself.*) But no: if I had been any good, I should have done for you what you did for me, instead of making a vain sacrifice.

ANDERSON.   Not vain, my boy. It takes all sorts to make a world— saints as well as soldiers. (*Turning to* BURGOYNE.) And now, General, time presses; and America is in a hurry. Have you realized that though you may occupy towns and win battles, you cannot conquer a nation?

BURGOYNE.   My good sir, without a Conquest you cannot have an aristocracy. Come and settle the matter at my quarters.

ANDERSON.   At your service, sir. (*To* RICHARD.) See Judith home for me, will you, my boy. (*He hands her over to him.*) Now, General. (*He goes busily up the market place towards the Town Hall, leaving* JUDITH *and* RICHARD *together.* BURGOYNE *follows him a step or two; then checks himself and turns to* RICHARD.)

BURGOYNE.   Oh, by the way, Mr. Dudgeon, I shall be glad to see you at lunch at half-past one. (*He pauses a moment, and adds, with politely veiled slyness*) Bring Mrs. Anderson, if she will be so good. (*To* SWINDON, *who is fuming.*) Take it quietly, Major Swindon: your friend the British soldier can stand up to anything except the British War Office. (*He follows Anderson.*)

SERGEANT.   (*To* SWINDON.) What orders, sir?

SWINDON.   (*Savagely.*) Orders! What use are orders now! There's no army. Back to quarters, and be d— (*He turns on his heel and goes.*)

SERGEANT.   (*Pugnacious and patriotic, repudiating the idea of defeat.*) 'Tention. Now then: cock up your chins, and show 'em you don't care a damn for 'em. Slope arms! Fours! Wheel! Quick march!

The drum marks time with a tremendous bang; the band strikes up British Grenadiers; and the SERGEANT, BRUDENELL, *and the English troops march off defiantly to their quarters. The townsfolk press in behind, and follow them up the market, jeering at them; and the town band, a very primitive affair, brings up the rear, playing Yankee Doodle.* ESSIE, *who comes in with them, runs to* RICHARD.

ESSIE.   Oh, Dick!

RICHARD.   (*Good-humoredly, but wilfully.*) Now, now: come, come! I don't mind being hanged: but I will not be cried over.

ESSIE.   No, I promise. I'll be good. (*She tries to restrain her tears, but cannot.*) I—I want to see where the soldiers are going to. (*She goes a little way up the market, pretending to look after the crowd.*)

JUDITH.   Promise me you will never tell him.

RICHARD.   Don't be afraid.

They shake hands on it.

ESSIE.   (*Calling to them.*) They're coming back. They want you.

Jubilation in the market. The townsfolk surge back again in wild enthusiasm with their band, and hoist RICHARD *on their shoulders, cheering him.*

CURTAIN

The Devil's Disciple, Act III: Discussion

In Act III Dick's antagonists are first Judith and then General Burgoyne. The opening confrontation between Judith and the Sergeant serves to set the time and Dick's frame of mind, and to reaffirm Judith's intense involvement in his fate and in him. It also gives Shaw a chance to suggest what will be the center of the conflict in the act: the concern for "appearances" that infests the British military mind. Gentlemanly Johnny Burgoyne will be Dick's chief adversary, but here the Sergeant, with his brainless delight in Dick's behaving "like the gentleman he is," sets the tone.

The second confrontation, in which Judith tries to convince Dick to save himself, builds on the conflict of values dramatized in Act II. The experiences of the previous evening have done little to change her superficial understanding of courage and self-sacrifice. She ignores the fact that correcting the mistake will not help Dick at all, and her "instinct" to save him is as self-centered as was her "duty" to save her husband. She says at the outset, "Oh, don't think of me: I haven't come here to talk about myself"; but in reality her principal concern is whether "for [her] sake" he will try to save himself. She even goes so far as to say, "I will go with you to the end of the world," as if that had any reference to his situation. She has shown that her instincts are as wrong as her sense of duty; and we are shown by his response to the mistaken arrest and to her open profession of love that his instincts and sense of duty—as romantically oriented, in a sense, as hers—are one and the same and that they lead to right action. The difference between their romanticism is that she sees his behavior as chivalrously motivated; he sees it as a simple, inexplicable necessity— and a decidedly disagreeable one. She gradually comes to her senses as the act proceeds, but in this scene she is still very much the spoiled child, however appealing.

The remainder of the play pits Dick (and, to a lesser extent, Anderson) against General Burgoyne and the British military mind. Gentlemanly Johnny may have wit and polish; he may express sympathetic feelings; he may have the grace to accept defeat without rancor or complaint. But he is perfectly content with a senseless hanging and is concerned only about a "solemn fuss" being made: he says to Judith, ". . . our only desire is to save unpleasantness." Swindon, the Sergeant, and Brudenell have none of his suavity or his civilized indifference, but they play the same game. They are all in various ways concerned with appearances, with the forms of things, not the spirit; with duty and discipline and good order at any cost. The Sergeant says politely to Judith,

"Duty's duty, mum, of course; but you're among friends here." Of course. Burgoyne thinks the hanging is politically unwise, but says to Swindon, ". . . you have committed us to hanging him, and the sooner he is hanged the better." Swindon tells Burgoyne that the hanging is scheduled for twelve o'clock and that "Nothing remains to be done except to try him." Later he says to Dick, "You have no right to assume that the court has made up its mind without a fair trial." The General comments on neither statement; both are in good form. The Chaplain tries to impress on Dick the "solemnity of the occasion"; Dick mocks the "blasphemous nonsense" by intoning "Thou shalt not kill." Judith's retort to Burgoyne defines the frame of the British military mind: "Oh you are mad. Is it nothing to you what wicked thing you do if only you do it like a gentleman?"

The three acts together form a three-pronged attack on three varieties of "blasphemous nonsense": hypocritical and self-serving piety; overblown and self-serving romanticism; complacent and self-serving gentility. The double-headed hero, Dudgeon-Anderson —the Devil's Disciple and the minister of the Gospel—puts self-serving in the proper light. They change coats and functions, but essentially they are the same man, each true to the "law of [his] own nature," each unconsciously motivated to serving others, not self, each a different side of the same flippable coin. (Anderson's action in going to the relief of Springtown rather than to replace Dick may seem to suggest a difference in makeup, but remember that Dick has tried unsuccessfully to raise Websterbridge.) Anderson was no misfit as a pastor, nor was Dick as the community gadfly. And neither is a misfit in his new role.

QUESTIONS

1. How has the Sergeant's behavior in Act II prepared for the switch in the focus of the central conflict in Act III, just as Judith's behavior in Act I prepared for the switch in Act II?

2. At the end of Act II, Anderson says to his wife, "You're a fool, a fool, Judith. You don't know the man you're married to." Show how her behavior proves that she also doesn't know the man she has fallen for? Consider, among other details, her shock at his "good spirits," her silly "Was it for my sake?" and her incredible answer, after he had explained himself bluntly and then asked, "Do you understand that?"—"Yes, you mean that you do not love me." How does his self-control, common sense, and lightheartedness make her behavior more inane than it might be otherwise? (After all, she is trying to save his neck.)

3. What is the purpose of the first confrontation between Burgoyne and Swindon? What do we find out that we need to know? Since this information could have been reported by a courier, what other purposes are served by having it come out in the dialogue between the two men? What kind of man is each shown to be?

4. The trial scene is a mockery of justice, but it proceeds in such a lighthearted vein that we might take it all as a joke, except that we know Peter Dudgeon has already been hanged after just such a "trial" and that the British fully intend to hang Dick. What is Shaw's purpose in making the scene a compound of "jests and compliments"?

5. Why is Brudenell introduced as part of the "solemnity of the occasion"? How does his presence and Dick's rejection of him recall the conflict in Act I?

6. How relevant are comments like, "History, sir, will tell lies, as usual," and "making America a nation," and "America is in a hurry"?

7. Why is it significant that the townspeople carry Dick off on their shoulders at the end of the play? What had been his attitude toward them and their attitude toward him?

8. What indications are there in the language Judith uses as well as in what she says in Act III, scenes two and three, that she has grown up?

9. Select at least three quotations that show how Burgoyne's use of language characterizes him. Do the same for Swindon.

10. What is the effect of Burgoyne's maintaining his civilized gentility to the very end? Why is it significant that he refers to himself as "humane enough to be glad" when Anderson saves Dick, even though there are several places where he could have easily called the hanging off? What makes him an engaging fellow despite the fact that Dick dead or alive is equally acceptable to him?

11. Essie is in tears again at the end of Act III. She has ended each act in this condition. What is Shaw's purpose in making her behave thus?

ESSAY QUESTIONS

1. Show to what extent the three kinds of "blasphemous nonsense" referred to (hypocritical and self-serving piety, overblown and self-serving romanticism, complacent and self-serving gentility) are manifestations of essentially the same thing. Show to what extent they are distinct.

2. Melodrama—the word Shaw himself applied to his play—allows us to look on at the good-guys vs. bad-guys struggle without testing anything we believe. We know that no matter how dark things seem, everything will turn out for the best in the end, so our only involvement is a kind of curiosity about how clever the plot may be and a smug self-assurance that we saw through it all along. Show that *The Devil's Disciple* is more than a "threadbare popular melodrama," that Shaw uses the form to comment seriously

on religion, romantic attitudes, and gentlemanly behavior. Consider that both Dick and the minister are religious, romantic, and gentlemanly.

3. If we look down our noses at Judith's shallow hero-worshiping, devil-damning, how do we look at our own? Nothing could be more "romantic" than Dick's willingness to die for Anderson and the latter's last-minute rescue of Dick; no devil ever got his due more summarily than Mrs. Dudgeon. If we find such developments highly satisfying (and we do), how is our reaction different from Judith's? Can it be said that Shaw is mocking our behavior as well as hers? Discuss.

Botticelli

Terrence McNally is one of a group of young American playwrights whose works have been performed in a number of experimental and established theaters on both coasts of the United States, and way stations in between, during the 1960s and into the 1970s. *Botticelli* is a one-scene extended confrontation, a dual game, one verbal and civilized that frames the second unspoken one—a brutal, inhuman action. Juxtaposed, the two "games" reveal, as one observer has put it, the "banality of violence."

This short play shows the power of direct dramatic speech to reveal the appalling gulf that separates, in all of us, what we talk about from what we do, that shows in a handful of breaths what the difference is between knowing the facts and knowing ⁺he spirit.

Botticelli

TERRENCE McNALLY

(1939–   )

CAST

WAYNE
STU
MAN

SCENE: *Jungle foliage. Afternoon sun and shadows. Insect noises.*
Two soldiers, WAYNE *and* STU, *crouching with rifles.*

WAYNE.   No, I'm not Marcel Proust.
STU.   Proust was a stylist.
WAYNE.   And he died *after* World War I.
STU.   You sure?
WAYNE.   1922.
STU.   Yeah?
WAYNE.   November 4, 19—
STU.   All right! (*Then.*) What's up?
WAYNE.   (*Stiffening.*) I thought I heard something. (*Relaxes.*)
STU.   Are you a . . . let's see . . . are you a Polish concert pianist who
      donated a large part of the proceeds from his concerts to the
      cause of Polish nationalism?
WAYNE.   Oh, that's a real brain crusher, that one is!
STU.   Well, are you?
WAYNE.   No, I'm not Paderewski.
STU.   Are you sure you're dead?
WAYNE.   Oh, brother!
STU.   A dead European male in the arts beginning with *P*?
WAYNE.   Why don't you write it down?
STU.   Got it! You're a controversial Russian poet, novelist, dramatist
      and short-story writer.
WAYNE.   Sorry. I'm not Pushkin.
STU.   Pushkin wasn't considered controversial.
WAYNE.   Who says?
STU.   I do.

WAYNE.   He was part Negro.

STU.   What's controversial about that?

WAYNE.   Dumas *père*?

STU.   Don't change the subject. Controversial Russian writer. Come on. I've got you stumped, hunh? Look at you. Drew a blank. Hunh? Hunh?

WAYNE.   I hope it's not Boris Pasternak you're crowing about.

STU.   Drop dead, will you?

WAYNE.   Then give up, hunh? (*Tenses.*) Sshh! (*Relaxes.*) Not yet.

STU.   You'd think he'd starve in there by now.

WAYNE.   Maybe he has. Why don't you go see?

STU.   And get a grenade in the face. That tunnel could be half a mile long for all we know. He's buried in there like a groundhog. No, sir, I'm holding tight, staying right where I am, sergeant's orders. I got all the time in the world to wait for that bugger to stick his head out. (WAYNE *starts making a cigarette.*) Are you a . . . ? I'm running dry. P's the hardest letter in the alphabet.

WAYNE.   Wanna turn on?

STU.   How much we got left?

WAYNE.   If he's not out of there by tonight we're in trouble.

STU.   Do you keep a diary?

WAYNE.   Sure. Every night.

STU.   No, who you are! Does he keep a diary?

WAYNE.   I'm not Samuel Pepys.

STU.   Smart ass! (*They smoke.*) Would you say this is the best part of the whole war?

WAYNE.   What is?

STU.   This. Pot.

WAYNE.   No. I'd say Raquel Welch was.

STU.   Yeah.

WAYNE.   What'd you think of her?

STU.   I didn't.

WAYNE.   Those goddamn white leather boots up to here . . . and that yellow miniskirt. . . .

STU.   Hey, are you the outstanding English baroque composer?

WAYNE.   I'm not Henry Purcell. I thought Raquel Welch looked like a sexy . . . ostrich.

STU.   Do the words "Rape of the Lock" mean anything to you?

WAYNE.   No, and they don't mean anything to Alexander Pope either.

STU.   Nuts!

WAYNE.   Look, let me tell you who I am, hunh?

STU.   No, I said.

WAYNE.   Brother, you're stubborn.

STU.   And *you're* a Victorian playwright!

WAYNE.   I'm not Arthur Wing Pinero.

STU.   Sir.

WAYNE.   Hunh?

STU.   Sir Arthur Wing Pinero.

WAYNE.   I know!

STU.   You didn't say it.

WAYNE.   I'd rather talk about Raquel Welch.

STU.   Sure you would. You're getting stoned.

WAYNE.   I'm not getting laid.

STU.   You still worrying about that letter from Susan?

WAYNE.   Not since Raquel Welch I'm not.

STU.   I bet.

WAYNE.   Let her get a divorce. I don't care. Hell, the only mistake I made was thinking I had to marry her. I should've sent her to Puerto Rico. She could've had a vacation on me, too.

STU.   Only you had scruples.

WAYNE.   Leave me alone.

STU.   Jesuit high school, Dominican college scruples.

WAYNE.   God, you're insensitive. Wait'll *you* get married.

STU.   Maybe I never will.

WAYNE.   Yeah!

STU.   I might not.

WAYNE.   You'd marry the first girl who looked twice at you. Yours is one wedding I wouldn't wanna miss. There's always Marlene Schroll.

STU.   *As You Desire Me!*

WAYNE.   What the—?

STU.   You wrote *As You Desire Me.*

WAYNE.   I'm not Luigi Pirandello!

STU.   Okay, but simmer down, hunh?

WAYNE.   It's a dumb game.

STU.   Your idea.

WAYNE.   I was trying to kill time.

STU.   Well, if we had something intelligent to discuss. . . .

WAYNE.   What's wrong with Raquel Welch?

STU.   Nothing. She's the quintessence of intelligence.

WAYNE.   I'm gonna bust you in the mouth. (*Pause.*) I should have burned my draft card.

STU.   Are you a Russian composer?

WAYNE.   I'm not Prokofiev.

STU.   An Italian composer?

WAYNE.   I'm not Puccini.

STU.   An Italian composer?

WAYNE.   I'm not Ponchielli.

STU.   An Italian composer?

WAYNE.   What are you, a record?

STU.   An Italian composer?

WAYNE.   All right, who?

STU.   Pizzarella.

WAYNE.   Go to hell.

STU.   What's wrong with Pizzarella?

WAYNE.   There's no Italian composer called Pizzarella.

STU.   How do you know?

WAYNE.   I know!

STU.   Well, maybe there is.

WAYNE.   Yeah, and you just made him up. Pizzarella. Look, if you're gonna play, play fair. Boy, you haven't changed since college. Even in charades you'd try to put something over.

STU.   Like when?

WAYNE.   Like when you did *The Brothers Karamazov*. Only you did it in Russian. How could anybody guess *The Brothers Karamazov* in a game of charades when *you* were doing it in Russian?

STU.   It would've been too easy in English.

WAYNE.   No wonder you never made the chess and bridge teams. Those are precise games. You don't muck with the rules in *them*. (*Pause.*) Typical. Sulk now.

STU.   I'm thinking.

WAYNE.   (*Rolls over on his back, looks up at the sky.*) You know what I can't get over?

STU.   Mmmmmm.

WAYNE.   Poor Father Reilly.

STU.   Yeah.

WAYNE.   I mean just dropping dead like that. God, we were lucky having him for a teacher. And of all places to drop dead. He loved Rome the same way some men love women. I think he lived for his summer vacations. As much as he gave his students, his heart was always in Rome on the Spanish Steps or the Pincio. And I guess it was all those steps and hills that finally killed him. A great man.

STU.   Wayne?

WAYNE.   Yeah?

STU.   An Italian composer?

WAYNE.   (*Holding up his hand, fingers together and pointing.*) You know what this is? (STU *shakes his head no.*) It's one week's supply of *this!* (*He gestures with his middle finger.*)

STU.   I just thought of two more.

WAYNE.   Real ones?

STU.   Give up. You'll see.

WAYNE.   If they're not, buddy! . . .

STU.   (*Looking at his watch.*) You've got fifteen seconds.

WAYNE.   Unh . . . unh . . . unh . . . quit making me nervous . . . unh. . . .

STU.   Ten!

WAYNE.   Palestrina!

STU.   Who else?

WAYNE.   Palestrina and . . . unh. . . .

STU.   Pizzarella?

WAYNE.   Can it! Palestrina and. . . .

STU.   Five seconds.

WAYNE.   Pergolesi. Giovanni Pergolesi! (*A burst of machine gun fire is heard; they both flatten out.*) That dirty little. . . . (*Aims, ready to fire.*)

STU.   (*In a terse whisper.*) Homosexual Greek philosopher.

WAYNE.   Brother, are you warped. I mean that's disgusting.

STU.   Come on.

WAYNE.   Plato wasn't homosexual.

STU.   You were right there, climbing the Acropolis.

WAYNE.   Your mind is really sick. A remark like that turns my stomach.

STU.   Who made any remarks?

WAYNE.   It's not even funny. (*Firing stops.*) Where the hell is he?

STU.   Come on, buster, stick your neck out.

WAYNE.   He's shooting to see if anybody's out here. We'll just have to sit tight.

STU.   Apropos the Parthenon, did you by any chance supervise the rebuilding of it?

WAYNE.   I'm not Phidias. What are we on now? Your Greek kick?

STU.   You're a fine one to talk about *that*.

WAYNE.   There's something crawling on you.

STU.   Hey! What the hell is it? This country. Bugs in your shoes, bugs in your hair, bugs in your food. Look at him go. Eight legs . . . no, ten! . . . I guess those are wings . . . nice antennae. . . . I used to be scared of bugs.

WAYNE.   Do you have to have a conversation with it?

STU.   Bonsoir, bug. (*Crushes bug.*)

WAYNE.   I could never do that.

STU.   Bugs have souls now, too?

WAYNE.   Shut up about all that, will you?

STU.   I don't suppose you're an Italian poet?

WAYNE.   I'm not Petrarch, Einstein.

STU.   It was just a wild guess.

WAYNE.   You're never going to get me.

STU.   I'm not going to give up either.

WAYNE.   Stubborn, stubborn, stubborn!

STU.   I'd lose all self-respect if I weren't.

WAYNE.   Sshh.

STU.   I mean the only reason to begin a game is to win it.

WAYNE.   I said shut up! (MAN *has come out of the tunnel. He's young, emaciated. He pauses at the entrance, quivering like a frightened rabbit. The lights focus on his face during the following.*) Look at the little bugger.

STU.   Not so little through these sights.

WAYNE.   Not yet! He has to come this way. Wait'll he's closer.

STU.   You're not a French painter? A great master of the classical school?

WAYNE. I'm not Poussin.

STU. I've got another one. Impressionist.

WAYNE. French.

STU. Yeah.

WAYNE. I'm not Pissarro.

STU. I can't think of anymore *P*s.

WAYNE. All right, you gave up. I'm—

STU. No! (MAN *has begun to move cautiously away from tunnel opening.*)

WAYNE. Here he comes. Quiet now.

STU. Were you an Italian sculptor working with Giotto on the campanile in Florence?

WAYNE. I'm not Pisano. Get ready.

STU. Okay, and this is it, Wayne. Did you write a famous *Lives*?

WAYNE. I'm not Plutarch, Let's go!

(MAN'S *face contorts with pain as he is cut down by a seemingly endless volley of gunfire. He falls, twitches, finally lies still.* WAYNE *and* STU *appear.*)

STU. Is he dead? I just asked!

WAYNE. Let's get back to camp.

STU. Okay, I give up. Who are you?

WAYNE. Pollaiuolo.

STU. Who?

WAYNE. Pollaiuolo. Antonio del Pollaiuolo.

STU. That's like Pizzarella.

(*They start moving off. Lights stay on* MAN'S *face.*)

WAYNE. The famous Italian painter, sculptor and goldsmith, 1432 to 1498.

STU. Well, I never heard of him.

WAYNE. He's famous for his landscapes and the movement he put into the human body.

STU. Never heard of him.

WAYNE. He influenced Dürer, Signorelli and Verrocchio.

STU. *Them* I've heard of.

WAYNE. Portrait of a Man? The Labors of Hercules? David? The Martyrdom of St. Sebastian? Tobias and the Angel?

STU. Never heard of him.

WAYNE. The tomb of Sixtus IV?

STU. Never heard of him.

WAYNE. Good God, he was a contemporary of Botticelli!

STU. Never heard of him.

WAYNE. Christ, you're dumb.

STU. I NEVER HEARD OF HIM.

(*Lights stay on* MAN'S *face. Slow fade*)

CURTAIN

QUESTIONS

1. The setting is simply stated as "Jungle foliage. Afternoon sun and shadows. Insect noises." Why that particular setting, besides the fact that the play was written and first presented when American involvement in the Viet Nam War was at its height? What difference would there be, if any, if the setting were: "Outskirts of a flattened Normandy village. Afternoon sun and shadows. Truck noises in the distance"?

2. What nationality are Wayne and Stu? How do you know? Why are they sitting by this tunnel opening? What game are they playing? Why are they playing it?

3. Characterize the two soldiers. Are they essentially two-of-a-kind or do you see distinct differences between them? Would your characterization be different if the opening confrontation went something like the following (and continued on in the same vein)?

    WAYNE.   No, I'm not Arnold Palmer.
    STU.   Palmer is a belter.
    WAYNE.   And he won his first Open *after* the '50s?
    STU.   You sure?
    WAYNE.   1960.
    STU.   Yeah?
    WAYNE.   June, 19—

    Would your reaction to what they finally do be any different if their game had been based on famous American athletes or movie stars rather than on European writers and artists? Why or why not? If you think your reaction would be different, what kind of influence are you attributing to an education in history, literature, and the arts? To a probable lack of such an education?

4. What's the connection between the identification game and the assignment the two soldiers have?

5. Why is the third character simply called "Man"? Why not "Enemy Soldier"? Who thinks of him as nothing more, and nothing less, than simply "Man"?

6. What do you take to be the purpose of the following:
    (a) Stu's reference to the letter from Susan.
    (b) Stu's reference to "Jesuit high school. Dominican college scruples."
    (c) "Poor Father Reilly."
    (d) The argument about Plato.
    (e) *STU.*   Bonsoir, bug (*Crushes bug*).
        WAYNE.   I could never do that.
    (f) *WAYNE.*   "[Pollaiuolo's] famous for his landscapes and the movement he put into the human body."

7. What commentary do Stu's repeated words—"Never heard of him" finally make on the *action* that has taken place? What is revealed by their being finally shouted? How is what they imply the same

as or different from the comment the speaker makes in the following Thomas Hardy poem, also based on an enemy vs. enemy confrontation?

The Man He Killed

Had he and I but met
By some old ancient inn
We should have sat us down to wet
Right many a nipperkin!°

But ranged as infantry,
And staring face to face,
I shot at him as he at me,
And killed him in his place.

I shot him dead because—
Because he was my foe,
Just so: my foe of course he was;
That's clear enough; although

He thought he'd 'list,° perhaps
Off-hand like—just as I—
Was out of work—had sold his traps°—
No other reason why.

Yes; quaint and curious war is!
You shoot a fellow down
You'd treat if met where any bar is,
Or help to half-a-crown.

8. We commented in the headnote that one observer has said that *Botticelli* reveals the "banality of violence." What do you think the phrase means and how accurate do you think it is as a commentary on the play? In the light of your answer, if you were directing the play or taking one of the speaking parts, what attitudes and gestures would you think it most important to emphasize as you spoke the lines?

° **nipperkin:** half-pint mug.
° **list:** enlist.
° **traps:** belongings; "tools of his trade."

Day of Absence

For almost two decades Douglas Turner Ward has been deeply involved in the theater: acting, directing, writing, and managing. In the late 1960s he helped launch the Negro Ensemble Company in New York City and at present is the Company's Artistic Director. As *Day of Absence* will demonstrate, he has the satirist's ability to keep his thumbs on the jugular without succumbing to the urge to apply final pressure. Satire is a form of humor, but not the kind that produces belly-laughs; rather it's the kind that aims to bring a purging smile of recognition—the recognition that we are none of us innocent bystanders when it comes to vice and folly.

Unlike *The Devil's Disciple* and most plays of the last hundred years or so, which proceed in a carefully ordered, tightly knit storyline fashion—usually a series of scenes that build logically one out of the other—*Day of Absence* is a loosely connected series of episodes, each of which reveals a different aspect of the near chaos that results from a strange disruption of the "normal" life of a small Southern town.

Day of Absence

DOUGLAS TURNER WARD

(1933–   )

The time is now.

Play opens in unnamed Southern town of medium population on a somnolent cracker morning—meaning no matter the early temperature, it's gonna get hot. The hamlet is just beginning to rouse itself from the sleepy lassitude of night.

NOTES ON PRODUCTION

No scenery is necessary—only actors shifting in and out on an almost bare stage and freezing into immobility as focuses change or blackouts occur.

Play is conceived for performance by a Negro cast, a reverse minstrel show done in white face. Logically, it might also be performed by whites—at their own risk. If any producer is faced with choosing between opposite hues, author strongly suggests: "Go 'long wit the blacks—besides all else, they need the work more."

If acted by the latter, race members are urged to go for broke, yet cautioned not to ham it up too broadly. In fact—it just might be more effective if they aspire to serious tragedy. Only qualification needed for Caucasian casting is that the company fit a uniform pattern—insipid white.

Before any horrifying discrimination doubts arise, I hasten to add that a bona fide white actor should be cast as the AN-NOUNCER in all productions, likewise a Negro thespian in pure native black as RASTUS. This will truly subvert any charge that the production is unintegrated.

All props, except essential items (chairs, brooms, rags, mop, debris) should be imaginary (phones, switchboard, mikes, eating utensils, food, etc.). Actors should indicate their presence through mime.

The cast of characters develops as the play progresses. In the interest of economical casting, actors should double or triple in roles wherever possible.

Production concept
This is a red-white-and-blue play—meaning that the entire production should be designed around the basic color scheme of our

patriotic trinity. Lighting should illustrate, highlight, and detail time, action, and mood—opening scenes stage-lit with white rays of morning, transforming to panic reds of afternoon, flowing into ominous blues of evening. Costuming should be orchestrated around the same color scheme. In addition, subsidiary usage of grays, khakis, yellow, pinks, and patterns of stars and bars should be employed. All actors (ANNOUNCER and RASTUS excepted, of course) should wear white shoes or sneakers, and all women characters clothed in knee-length frocks should wear white stockings. Blond wigs, both for males and females, can be used in selected instances. Makeup should have uniform consistency, with individual touches thrown in to enhance personal identity.

Sample models of makeup and costuming

MARY: *Kewpie-doll face, ruby-red lips painted to valentine pursing, moon-shaped rough circles implanted on each cheek, blond wig of fat flowing ringlets, dazzling ankle-length snow-white nightie.*

MAYOR: *Seersucker white ensemble, ten-gallon hat, red string tie, and blue belt.*

CLEM: *Khaki pants, bareheaded, and blond.*

LUKE: *Blue work jeans, strawhatted.*

CLUB WOMAN: *Yellow dress patterned with symbols of Dixie, gray hat.*

CLAN: *A vertible,° riotous advertisement of red-white-and-blue combinations with stars and bars tossed in.*

PIOUS: *White ministerial garb with black cleric's collar topping his snow-white shirt.*

OPERATORS: *All in red with different color wigs.*

All other characters should be carefully defined through costuming which typifies their identity.

SCENE: *Street.*

TIME: *Early morning.*

CLEM.   (*Sitting under a sign suspended by invisible wires and bold-printed with the lettering:* "Store".) Morning, Luke . . .

LUKE.   (*Sitting a few paces away under an identical sign.*) Morning, Clem . . .

CLEM.   Gon be a hot day.

LUKE.   Looks that way . . .

CLEM.   Might rain though . . .

LUKE.   Might.

CLEM.   Hope it does . . .

LUKE.   Me too . . .

° **vertible:** changeable.

CLEM.   Farmers could use a little wet spell for a change . . . How's the Missis?

LUKE.   Same.

CLEM.   'N the kids?

LUKE.   Them too . . . How's yourns?

CLEM.   Fine, thank you . . . (*They both lapse into drowsy silence, waving lethargically from time to time at imaginary passersby.*) Hi, Joe . . .

LUKE.   Joe . . .

CLEM.   How'd it go yesterday, Luke?

LUKE.   Fair.

CLEM.   Same wit me . . . Business don't seem to git no better or no worse. Guess we in a rut, Luke, don't it 'pear that way to you?— Morning, Ma'm.

LUKE.   Morning . . .

CLEM.   Tried display, sales, advertisement, stamps—everything—yet merchandising stumbles 'round in the same old groove. . . . But— that's better than plunging downwards, I reckon.

LUKE.   Guess it is.

CLEM.   Morning, Bret. How's the family? . . . That's good.

LUKE.   Bret—

CLEM.   Morning, Sue.

LUKE.   How do, Sue.

CLEM.   (*Staring after her.*) Fine hunk of woman.

LUKE.   Sure is.

CLEM.   Wonder if it's any good?

LUKE.   Bet it is.

CLEM.   Sure like to find out!

LUKE.   So would I.

CLEM.   You ever try?

LUKE.   Never did . . .

CLEM.   Morning, Gus . . .

LUKE.   Howdy, Gus.

CLEM.   Fine, thank you. (*They lapse into silence again. CLEM rouses himself slowly, begins to look around quizzically.*) Luke . . . ?

LUKE.   Huh?

CLEM.   Do you . . . er, er—feel anything—funny . . . ?

LUKE.   Like what?

CLEM.   Like . . . er—something—strange?

LUKE.   I dunno . . . haven't thought about it.

CLEM.   I mean . . . like something's wrong—outta place, unusual?

LUKE.   I don't know . . . What you got in mind?

CLEM.   Nothing . . . just that—just that—like somp'um's outta kilter. I got a funny feeling somp'um's not up to snuff. Can't figger out what it is . . .

LUKE.   Maybe it's in your haid . . .

CLEM.   No, not like that . . . Like somp'um's happened—or happening —gone haywire, loony.

LUKE.   Well, don't worry 'bout it, it'll pass.

CLEM.   Guess you right (*attempts return to somnolence but doesn't succeed*). I'm sorry, Luke, but you sure you don't feel nothing peculiar . . . ?

LUKE.   (*Slightly irked.*) Toss it out your mind. Clem! We got a long day ahead of us. If something's wrong, you'll know 'bout it in due time. No use worrying about it 'till it comes and if it's coming, it will. Now, relax!

CLEM.   All right, you right . . . Hi, Margie . . .

LUKE.   Marge.

CLEM.   (*Unable to control himself.*) Luke, I don't give a damn what you say. Somp'um's topsy-turvy, I just know it!

LUKE.   (*Increasingly irritated.*) Now look here, Clem—it's a bright day, it looks like it's gon git hotter. You say the wife and kids are fine and the business is no better or no worse? Well, what else could be wrong? . . . If somp'um's gon happen, it's gon happen anyway and there ain't a damn fool thing you kin do to stop it! So you ain't helping me, yourself or nobody else by thinking 'bout it. It's not gon be no better or no worse when it gits here. It'll come to you when it gits ready to come and it's gon be the same whether you worry about it or not. So stop letting it upset you! (LUKE *settles back in his chair*. CLEM *does likewise*. LUKE *shuts his eyes. After a few moments, they reopen. He forces them shut again. They reopen in greater curiosity. Finally, he rises slowly to an upright position in the chair, looks around frowningly. Turns slowly to* CLEM.) Clem? . . . You know something? . . . Somp'um is peculiar . . .

CLEM.   (*Vindicated.*) I knew it, Luke! I jist knew it! Ever since we been sitting here, I been having that feeling!

(*Scene is blacked out abruptly. Lights rise on another section of the stage where a young couple lie in bed under an invisible wire-suspension sign lettered "*HOME*." Loud, insistent sounds of baby yells are heard.* JOHN, *the husband, turns over trying to ignore the cries;* MARY, *the wife, is undisturbed.* JOHN'S *efforts are futile; the cries continue until they cannot be denied. He bolts upright, jumps out of bed, and disappears offstage. Returns quickly and tries to rouse* MARY.)

JOHN.   Mary . . . (*Nudges her, pushes her, yells into her ear, but she fails to respond.*) Mary, get up . . . Get up!

MARY.   Ummm . . . (*Shrugs away, still sleeping.*)

JOHN.   GET UP!

MARY.   Ummmmmmmmm!

JOHN.   Don't you hear the baby's bawling? . . . NOW GET UP!

MARY.   (*Mumbling drowsily.*) What baby . . . whose baby . . . ?

JOHN.   Yours!

MARY.   Mine? That's ridiculous . . . what'd you say . . . ? Somebody's baby bawling? . . . How could that be so? (*Hearing screams.*)

Who's crying? Somebody's crying! . . . What's crying? . . . *Where's Lula?*

JOHN.   I don't know. You better get up.

MARY.   That's outrageous! . . . What time is it?

JOHN.   Late 'nuff! Now rise up!

MARY.   You must be joking . . . I'm sure I still have four or five hours' sleep in store—even more after that head-splittin' blowout last night . . . (*Tumbles back under covers.*)

JOHN.   Nobody told you to gulp those last six bourbons—

MARY.   Don't tell me how many bourbons to swallow, not after you guzzled the whole stinking bar! . . . Get up? . . . You must be cracked . . . Where's Lula? She must be here, she always is . . .

JOHN.   Well, she ain't here yet, so get up and muzzle that brat before she does drive me cuckoo!

MARY.   (*Springing upright, finally realizing gravity of situation.*) Whaddaya mean Lula's not here? She's always here, she must be here . . . Where else kin she be? She supposed to be . . . She just can't *not* be here—call her!

(*Blackout as* JOHN *rushes offstage. Scene shifts to a trio of* TELEPHONE OPERATORS *perched on stools before imaginary switchboards. Chaos and bedlam are taking place to the sound of buzzes. Effect of following dialogue should simulate rising pandemonium.*)

FIRST OPERATOR.   The line is busy—
SECOND OPERATOR.   Line is busy—
THIRD OPERATOR.   Is busy—
FIRST OPERATOR.   Doing best we can—
SECOND OPERATOR.   Having difficulty—
THIRD OPERATOR.   Soon as possible—
FIRST OPERATOR.   Just one moment—
SECOND OPERATOR.   Would you hold on—
THIRD OPERATOR.   Awful sorry, madam—
FIRST OPERATOR.   Would you hold on, please—
SECOND OPERATOR.   Just a second, please—
THIRD OPERATOR.   Please hold on, please—
FIRST OPERATOR.   The line is busy.
SECOND OPERATOR.   The line is busy—
THIRD OPERATOR.   The line is busy—
FIRST OPERATOR.   Doing best we can—
SECOND OPERATOR.   Hold on, please—
THIRD OPERATOR.   Can't make connections—
FIRST OPERATOR.   Unable to put it in—
SECOND OPERATOR.   Won't plug through—
THIRD OPERATOR.   Sorry, madam—
FIRST OPERATOR.   If you'd wait a moment—
SECOND OPERATOR.   Doing best we can—
THIRD OPERATOR.   Sorry—

FIRST OPERATOR.   One moment—
SECOND OPERATOR.   Just a second—
THIRD OPERATOR.   Hold on—
FIRST OPERATOR.   Yes—
SECOND OPERATOR.   *Stop it!*—
THIRD OPERATOR.   *How do I know*—
FIRST OPERATOR.   You another one!
SECOND OPERATOR.   *Hold on, dammit!*
THIRD OPERATOR.   *Up yours, too!*
FIRST OPERATOR.   The line is busy—
SECOND OPERATOR.   *The line is busy*—
THIRD OPERATOR.   *The line is busy*—

>   (*The switchboard clamors a cacophony of buzzes as* OPERATORS *plug connections with the frenzy of a Chaplin movie. Their replies degenerate into a babble of gibberish. At the height of frenzy, the* SUPERVISOR *appears.*)

SUPERVISOR.   What's the snarl-up?
FIRST OPERATOR.   Everybody calling at the same time, Ma'am!
SECOND OPERATOR.   Board can't handle it!
THIRD OPERATOR.   Like everybody in big New York City is trying to squeeze a call through to lil ole us!
SUPERVISOR.   God! . . . Somp'um terrible musta happened! . . . Buzz the emergency frequency hookup to the Mayor's office and find out what the hell's going on!

>   (*Scene blacks out quickly to* CLEM *and* LUKE.)

CLEM.   (*Something slowly dawning on him.*) Luke . . . ?
LUKE.   Yes, Clem?
CLEM.   (*Eyes roving around in puzzlement.*) Luke . . . ?
LUKE.   (*Irked.*) I said what, Clem!
CLEM.   Luke . . . ? Where—where is—the—the—?
LUKE.   The *what?*
CLEM.   Nigras . . . ?
LUKE.   What . . . ?
CLEM.   Nigras . . . Where is the Nigras, where is they, Luke . . . ? *All the Nigras!* . . . I don't see no Nigras . . . !
LUKE.   Whatcha mean . . . ?
CLEM.   (*Agitatedly.*) Luke there ain't a darkey in sight. . . . And if you remember, we ain't seen a nappy hair all morning . . . The Nigras, Luke! We ain't laid eyes on nary a coon this whole morning!
LUKE.   You must be crazy or something, Clem!
CLEM.   Think about it, Luke, we been sitting here for an hour or more—try and recollect if you remember seeing just *one* go by!
LUKE.   (*Confused.*) I don't recall . . . But . . . but there musta been some . . . The heat musta got you, Clem! How in hell could that be so?
CLEM.   (*Triumphantly.*) Just think, Luke! . . . Look around ya . . .

Now, every morning mosta people walkin 'long this street is colored. They's strolling by going to work, they's waiting for the buses, they's sweeping sidewalks, cleaning stores, starting to shine shoes and wetting the mops—Right? . . . Well, look around you, Luke—Where is they? (LUKE *paces up and down, checking.*) I told you, Luke, they ain't nowhere to be seen.

LUKE.   This . . . this . . . some kind of holiday for 'em—or something?

CLEM.   I don't know, Luke . . . but . . . but what I do know is they ain't here'n we haven't seen a solitary one . . . It's scarifying, Luke . . . !

LUKE.   Well . . . Maybe they's jist standing 'n walking and shining on other streets—Let's go look!

(*Scene blacks out to* JOHN *and* MARY. *Baby cries are as insistent as ever.*)

MARY.   (*At end of patience.*) Smother it!

JOHN.   (*Beyond his.*) That's a hell of a thing to say 'bout your own child! You should know what to do to hush her up!

MARY.   Why don't you try?

JOHN.   You had her!

MARY.   You shared in borning her!

JOHN.   Possibly not!

MARY.   Why, you lousy—!

JOHN.   What good is a mother who can't shut up her own daughter?

MARY.   I told you she yells louder every time I try to lay hands on her—Where's Lula? Didn't you call her?

JOHN.   I told you I can't get the call through!

MARY.   Try again—

JOHN.   It's no use! I tried numerous times and can't even git through to the switchboard. You've got to quiet her down yourself. (*Firmly.*) Now, go in there and clam her up 'fore I lose my patience! (MARY *exits. Soon, we hear the yells increase. She rushes back in.*)

MARY.   She won't let me touch her, just screams louder!

JOHN.   Probably wet 'n soppy!

MARY.   Yes! Stinks something awful! Phooooey! I can't stand that filth and odor!

JOHN.   That's why she's screaming! Needs her didee changed—go change it!

MARY.   How you 'spect me to when I don't know how? Suppose I faint?

JOHN.   Well let her blast away. I'm getting outta here.

MARY.   You can't leave me here like this!

JOHN.   Just watch me! . . . See this nice split-level cottage, peachy furniture, multicolored T.V., hi-fi set n' the rest? . . . Well, how you think I scraped 'em together while you curled up on your fat lil fanny? . . . By gitting outta here—not only *on time* . . . but *earlier!*—Beating a frantic crew of nice young executives to the punch—gitting there fustest with the mostest brown-nosing you ever saw! Now if I goof one day—just ONE DAY!—you reckon I'd stay ahead? NO! . . . There'd be a wolf pack trampling over my prostrate body, racing to replace my smiling face against the boss's left rump! . . . *No, mam!* I'm zooming outta here on time, just as I always have, and what's more—you gon fix me some breakfast. *I'm hungry!*

MARY. But—

JOHN. No buts about it! (*Flash blackout as he gags on a mouthful of coffee.*) What you trying to do, STRANGLE ME? (*Jumps up and starts putting on jacket.*)

MARY. (*Sarcastically.*) What did you expect?

JOHN. (*In biting fury.*) That you could possibly boil a pot of water, toast a few slices of bread and fry a coupler eggs! . . . It was a mistaken assumption!

MARY. So they aren't as good as Lula's!

JOHN. That is an overstatement. Your efforts don't result in anything that could possibly be digested by man, mammal, or insect! . . . When I married you, I thought I was fairly acquainted with your faults and weaknesses—I chalked 'em up to human imperfection . . . But now I know I was being extremely generous, overoptimistic and phenomenally deluded!—You have no idea how useless you really are!

MARY. Then why'd you marry me?

JOHN. Decoration!

MARY. You shoulda married Lula!

JOHN. I might've if it wasn't 'gainst the segregation law! . . . But for the sake of my home, my child and my sanity, I will even take a chance on sacrificing my slippery grip on the status pole and drive by her shanty to find out whether she or someone like her kin come over here and prevent some ultimate disaster. (*Storms toward door, stopping abruptly at exit.*) Are you sure you kin make it to the bathroom wit'out Lula backing you up?

(*Blackout. Scene shifts to MAYOR'S office where a cluttered desk stands center stage amid paper debris.*)

MAYOR. (*Striding determinedly toward desk; stopping midway, bellowing.*) Woodfence! . . . Woodfence! . . . Woodfence! (*Receiving no reply, completes distance to desk.*) Jack-son! . . . Jackson!

JACKSON. (*Entering worriedly.*) Yes, sir . . . ?

MAYOR. Where's Vice-Mayor Woodfence, that no-good brother-in-law of mine?

JACKSON. Hasn't come in yet, sir.

MAYOR. *Hasn't come in?* . . . Damn bastard! Knows we have a crucial conference. Soon as he staggers through that door, tell him to shoot in here! (*Angrily focusing on his disorderly desk and littered surroundings.*) And git Mandy here to straighten up this mess—Rufus too! You know he shoulda been waiting to knock dust off my shoes soon as I step in. Get 'em in here! . . . What's the matter wit them lazy Nigras? . . . Already had to dress myself because of J. C., fix my own coffee without May-Belle, drive myself to work 'counta Bubber, feel my old bag's tits after Sapphi—*Never Mind!*—Git 'em in here—*Quick!*

JACKSON.   (*Meekly.*) They aren't . . . they aren't here, sir . . .

MAYOR.   Whaddaya mean they aren't here? Find out where they at. We got important business, man! You can't run a town wit laxity like this. Can't allow things to git snafued jist because a bunch of lazy Nigras been out gitting drunk and living it up all night! Discipline, man, discipline!

JACKSON.   That's what I'm trying to tell you, sir . . . they didn't come in, can't be found . . . none of 'em.

MAYOR.   Ridiculous, boy! Scare 'em up and tell 'em scoot here in a hurry befo' I git mad and fire the whole goddamn lot of 'em!

JACKSON.   But we can't find 'em, sir.

MAYOR.   Hogwash! Can't nobody in this office do anything right? Do I hafta handle every piddling little matter myself? Git me their numbers, I'll have 'em here befo' you kin shout to—

(THREE MEN *burst into room.*)

ONE.   Henry—they vanished.

TWO.   Disappeared into thin air!

THREE.   Gone wit'out a trace!

TWO.   Not a one on the street!

THREE.   In the house!

ONE.   On the job!

MAYOR.   Wait a minute! . . . Hold your water! Calm down—!

ONE.   But they've gone, Henry—GONE! All of 'em!

MAYOR.   What the hell you talking 'bout? Gone? Who's gone—?

ONE.   The Nigras, Henry! They gone!

MAYOR.   Gone? . . . Gone where?

TWO.   That's what we trying to tell ya—they just disappeared! The Nigras have disappeared, swallowed up, vanished! All of 'em! Every last one!

MAYOR.   Has everybody 'round here gone batty? . . . That's impossible, how could the Nigras vanish?

THREE.   Beats me, but it's happened!

MAYOR.   You mean a whole town of Nigras just evaporated like that —poof!—overnight?

ONE.   Right!

MAYOR.   Y'all must be drunk! Why, half this town is colored. How could they just sneak out?

TWO.   Don't ask me, but there ain't one in sight!

MAYOR.   Simmer down 'n put it to me easy-like.

ONE.   Well . . . I first suspected somp'um smelly when Sarah Jo didn't show up this morning and I couldn't reach her—

TWO.   Dorothy Jane didn't 'rive at my house—

THREE.   Georgia Mae wasn't at mine neither—and SHE sleeps in!

ONE. When I reached the office, I realized I hadn't seen nary one Nigra all morning! Nobody else had either—Wait a minute—Henry, have you?

MAYOR. Now that you mention it . . . no, I haven't . . .

ONE. They gone, Henry . . . Not a one on the street, not a one in our homes, not a single, last living one to be found nowheres in town. What we gon' do?

MAYOR. (*Thinking.*) Keep heads on your shoulders 'n put clothes on your back . . . They can't be far . . . Must be 'round somewheres . . . Probably playing hide 'n seek, that's it! . . . *Jackson!*

JACKSON. Yessir?

MAYOR. Immediately mobilize our Citizens Emergency Distress Committee!—order a fleet of sound trucks to patrol streets urging the population to remain calm—situation's not as bad as it looks—everything's under control! Then, have another squadron of squawk buggies drive slowly through all Nigra alleys, ordering them to come out wherever they are. If that don't git 'em, organize a vigilante search squad to flush 'em outta hiding! But most important of all, track down that lazy goldbricker Woodfence and tell him to git on top of the situation! By God, we'll find 'em even if we hafta dig 'em outta the ground!

(*Blackout. Scene shifts back to* JOHN *and* MARY *a few hours later. A funeral solemnity pervades their mood.*)

JOHN. Walked up to the shack, knocked on door, didn't git no answer. Hollered: "Lula? Lula . . . ?—not a thing. Went 'round the side, peeped in window—nobody stirred. Next door—nobody there. Crossed other side of street and banged on five or six other doors—not a colored person could be found! Not a man, neither woman or child—not even a black dog could be seen, smelt or heard for blocks around . . . They've gone, Mary.

MARY. What does it all mean, John?

JOHN. I don't know, Mary . . .

MARY. I always had Lula, John. Never missed a day at my side . . . That's why I couldn't accept your wedding proposal until I was sure you'd welcome me and her together as a package. How am I gonna git through the day? Baby don't know *me*, I ain't acquainted wit *it*. I've never lifted cover off pot, swung a mop or broom, dunked a dish or even pushed a dust rag. I'm lost wit'out Lula, I need her, John, I need her. (*Begins to weep softly.* JOHN *pats her consolingly.*)

JOHN. Courage, honey . . . Everybody in town is facing the same dilemma. We mustn't crack up . . .

(*Blackout. Scene shifts back to* MAYOR'S *office later in day. Atmosphere and tone resembles a wartime headquarters at the front.* MAYOR *is perched on ladder checking over huge map.*)

INDUSTRIALIST. Half the day is gone already, Henry. On behalf of the factory owners of this town, you've got to bail us out! Seventy-five percent of all production is paralyzed. With the Nigra absent, men are waiting for machines to be cleaned, floors to be swept, crates lifted, equipment delivered and bathrooms deodorized. Why, restrooms and toilets are so filthy until they not only cannot be sat in, but it's virtually impossible to get within hailing distance because of the stench!

MAYOR.   Keep your shirt on, Jeb—

BUSINESSMAN.   Business is even in worse condition, Henry. The volume of goods moving 'cross counters has slowed down to a trickle—almost negligible. Customers are not only not purchasing —but the absence of handymen, porters, sweepers, stockmovers, deliverers and miscellaneous dirty-work doers is disrupting the smooth harmony of marketing!

CLUBWOMAN.   Food poisoning, severe indigestitis, chronic diarrhea, advanced diaper chafings and a plethora of unsanitary household disasters dangerous to life, limb and property! . . . As a representative of the Federation of Ladies' Clubs, I must sadly report that unless the trend is reversed, a complete breakdown in family unity is imminent . . . Just as homosexuality and debauchery signaled the fall of Greece and Rome, the downgrading of Southern Bellesdom might very well prophesy the collapse of our indigenous institutions. . . . Remember—it has always been pure, delicate, lily-white images of Dixie femininity which provided backbone, inspiration and ideology for our male warriors in their defense against the onrushing black horde. If our gallant men are drained of this worship and idolatry—God knows! The cause won't be worth a Confederate nickel!

MAYOR.   (*Jumping off ladder.*) Stop this panicky defeatism, y'all hear me! All machinery at my disposal is being utilized. I assure you wit great confidence the damage will soon repair itself—Cheerful progress reports are expected any moment now—Wait! See here's Jackson . . . Well, Jackson?

JACKSON.   As of now, sir, all efforts are fruitless. Neither hide nor hair of them has been located. We have not unearthed a single one in our shack-to-shack search. Not a single one has heeded our appeal. Scoured every creek and cranny inside their hovels, turning furniture upside down and inside out, breaking down walls and tearing through ceilings. We made determined efforts to discover where'bouts of our faithful Uncle Toms and informers—but even they have vanished without a trace . . . Searching squads are on the verge of panic and hysteria, sir, wit hotheads among 'em campaigning for scorched earth policies. Nigras on a whole lack cellars, but there's rising sentiment favoring burning to find out whether they're underground—dug in!

MAYOR.   Absolutely counter such foolhardy suggestions! Suppose they are tombed in? We'd only accelerate the gravity of the situation using incendiary tactics! Besides, when they're rounded

up where will we put 'em if we've already burned up their shacks
—*in our own bedrooms?*

JACKSON. I agree, sir, but the mood of the crowd is becoming ir-
rational. In anger and frustration, they's forgetting their original
purpose was to *find* the Nigras!

MAYOR. At all costs! Stamp out all burning proposals! Must prevent
extremist notions from gaining ascendancy. Git wit it . . . Wait—'n
for Jehovah's sake, find out where the hell is that trifling slacker,
Woodfence!

COURIER. (*Rushing in.*) Mr. Mayor! . . . We've found some! We've
found some!

MAYOR. (*Excitedly.*) Where?

COURIER. In the—in the—(*Can't catch breath.*)

MAYOR. (*Impatiently.*) Where, man? Where?

COURIER. In the colored wing of the city hospital!

MAYOR. The hos—? The hospital! I shoulda known! How could those
helpless, crippled, cut and shot Nigras disappear from a hospital?
Should thought of that! . . . Tell me more, man!

COURIER. I—I didn't wait, sir . . . I—I ran in to report soon as I
heard—

MAYOR. Well git back on the phone, you idiot! Don't you know what
this means?

COURIER. Yes, sir. (*Races out.*)

MAYOR. Now we gitting somewhere! . . . Gentlemen, if one sole
Nigra is among us, we're well on the road to rehabilitation! Those
Nigras in the hospital must know somp'um 'bout the others
where'bouts . . . Scat back to your colleagues, boost up their morale
and inform 'em that things will zip back to normal in a jiffy!
(*They start to file out, then pause to observe the* COURIER *re-
entering dazedly.*) Well . . . ? Well, man . . . ? What's the matter
wit you, ninny? Tell me what else was said!

COURIER. They all . . . they all . . . they all in a—a coma, sir . . .

MAYOR. They all in a what . . . ?

COURIER. In a coma, sir . . .

MAYOR. Talk sense, man! . . . Whaddaya mean, they all in a coma?

COURIER. Doctor says every last one of the Nigras are jist laying in
bed . . . *still* . . . not moving . . . neither live or dead . . . laying
up there in a coma . . . every last one of 'em . . .

MAYOR. (*Sputters, then grabs phone.*) Get me Confederate Memorial
. . . Put me through to the Staff Chief . . . YES, this is the Mayor
. . . Sam? . . . What's this I hear? . . . But how could they be in
a coma, Sam? . . . You don't know! Well, what the hell you think
the city's paying you for! You've got 'nuff damn hacks and quacks
there to find out! . . . How could it be somp'um unknown? You
mean Nigras know somp'um 'bout drugs your damn butchers
don't? . . . Well, what the crap good are they? . . . All right, all
right, I'll be calm. . . . Now, tell me . . . Uh huh, uh huh . . .

Well, can't you give 'em some injections or somp'um . . . ?—You did . . . uh huh . . . *Did you try a lil rough treatment?*—that too, huh . . . All right, Sam, keep trying . . . (*Puts phone down deliberately, continuing absently.*) Can't wake 'em up. Just lay there. Them that's sick won't git no sicker, them that's half-well won't git no better, babies that's due won't be born and them that's come won't show no life. Nigras wit cuts won't bleed and them which need blood won't be transfused . . . He say dying Nigras is even refusing to pass away! (*Is silently perplexed for a moment, then suddenly breaks into action.*) Jackson? . . . Call up the police—*the jail!* Find out what's going on there! Them Nigras are captives! If there's one place we got darkies under control, it's there! Them sonsabitches too onery to act right either for colored or white! (*JACKSON exits.*) Keep your fingers crossed, citizens, them Nigras in jail are the most important Nigras we got!

(*All hands are raised conspicuously aloft, fingers prominently crossed. Seconds tick by. Soon JACKSON returns crestfallen.*)

JACKSON.   Sheriff Bull says they don't know whether they still on premises or not. When they went to rouse Nigra jailbirds this morning, cell block doors refused to swing open. Tried everything—even exploded dynamite charges—but it just wouldn't budge . . . Then they hoisted guards up to peep through barred windows, but couldn't see good 'nuff to tell whether Nigras was inside or not. Finally, gitting desperate, they power-hosed the cells wit water but had to cease 'cause Sheriff Bull said he didn't wanta jeopardize drowning the Nigras since it might spoil his chance of shipping a record load of cotton pickers to the State Penitentiary for cotton-snatching jubilee . . . Anyway—they ain't heard a Nigra-squeak all day.

MAYOR.   That so . . . ? *What 'bout trains 'n busses passing through?* There must be some dinges riding through?

JACKSON.   We checked . . . not a one on board.

MAYOR.   Did you hear whether any other towns lost their Nigras?

JACKSON.   Things are status quo everywhere else.

MAYOR.   (*Angrily.*) Then what they picking on us for?

COURIER.   (*Rushing in.*) Mr. Mayor! Your sister jist called—*hysterical!* She says Vice-Mayor Woodfence went to bed wit her last night, but when she woke up this morning he was gone! Been missing all day!

MAYOR.   Could Nigras be holding him hostage?

COURIER.   No, sir. Besides him—investigations reveal that dozens or more prominent citizens—two City Council members, the chairman of the Junior Chamber of Commerce, our City College All-Southern halfback, the chairlady of the Daughters of the Confederate Rebellion, Miss Cotton Sack Festival of the Year and numerous other miscellaneous nobodies—are absent wit'out leave. Dangerous evidence points to the conclusion that they been infiltrating!

MAYOR.   Infiltrating?
COURIER.   Passing all along!
MAYOR.   What?
COURIER.   Secret Nigras all the while!
MAYOR.   Naw!

(CLUBWOMAN *keels over in faint.* JACKSON, BUSINESSMAN *and* INDUSTRIALIST *begin to eye each other suspiciously.*)

COURIER.   Yessir!
MAYOR.   Passing?
COURIER.   Yessir!
MAYOR.   Secret Nig—?
COURIER.   Yessir!
MAYOR.   (*Momentarily stunned to silence.*) The dirty mongrelizers!
   . . . Gentlemen, this is a grave predicament indeed . . . It pains me
   to surrender priority of our states rights credo, but it is my solemn
   task and frightening duty to inform you that we have no other
   recourse but to seek outside help for deliverance.

   (*Blackout. Lights rise again on Huntley-Brinkley-Murrow-Severeid-
   Cronkite-Reasoner-type* ANNOUNCER *grasping a hand-held micro-
   phone [imaginary] a few hours later. He is vigorously, excitedly
   mouthing his commentary, but no sound escapes his lips. During
   this dumb, wordless section of his broadcast, a bedraggled assort-
   ment of figures marching with picket signs occupies his attention.
   On their picket signs are inscribed various appeals and slogans.*
   "CINDY LOU UNFAIR TO BABY JOE" . . . "CAP'N SAM MISS BIG BOY"
   . . . "RETURN LIL BLUE TO MARS JIM" . . . "INFORMATION RE-
   QUESTED BOUT MAMMY GAIL" . . . "BOSS NATHAN PROTEST TO FAST
   LEROY." *Trailing behind the* MARCHERS, *forcibly isolated, is a*
   WOMAN *dressed in widow black holding a placard which reads:*
   "WHY DIDN'T YOU TELL US—YOUR DEFILED WIFE AND 11 ABSENT
   MONGRELS.")

ANNOUNCER.   (*Who has been silently mouthing his delivery during
   the picketing procession, is suddenly heard as if caught in the
   midst of commentary.*) Factories standing idle from the loss of
   nonessential workers. Stores remaining shuttered from the ab-
   sconding of uncrucial personnel. Fruit, vegetables and other edible
   foodstuffs rotting in warehouses, with uncollected garbage threatening pestilence and pollution . . . Also, each second somewheres
   in this former utopia below the Mason and Dixon, dozens of de-
   crepit old men and women usually tended by faithful nurses and
   servants are popping off like flies—abandoned by sons, daughters
   and grandchildren whose refusal to provide these doddering souls
   with bedpans and other soothing necessities results in their hasty,
   nasty, messy departures . . .

   An equally wretched fate lurks in wait for juveniles of the town
   as hundreds of new born infants HUNGER for the comforting
   embraces of devoted nannies while being forced to endure the
   presence of strange parents . . .

But most critically affected of all by this complete drought of Afro-American resources are policemen and other public safety guardians denied their daily quota of Negro arrests. One officer known affectionately as "Two-a-Day-Pete" because of his un-blemished record of TWO Negro headwhippings per day has al-ready been carted off to the County Insane Asylum—strait jack-eted, screaming and biting, unable to withstand the shock of having his spotless slate sullied by interruption . . . It is feared that similar attacks are soon expected among municipal judges prevented for the first time in years of distinguished bench-sitting from sentencing one single Negro to corrective institutions . . .

Ladies and gentlemen, as you trudge in from the joys and head-aches of workday chores and dusk begins to descend on this sleepy Southern hamlet, we *repeat*—today—before early morning dew had dried upon magnolia blossoms, your comrade citizens of this lovely Dixie village awoke to the realization that some— pardon me! not some but *all*—of their Negroes were missing . . . Absent, vamoosed, departed, at bay, fugitive, away, gone and so far unretrieved . . .

In order to dispel your incredulity, gauge the temper of your suffering compatriots and just possibly prepare you for the likeli-hood of an equally nightmarish eventuality, we have gathered a cross section of this city's most distinguished leaders for exclusive interviews . . . First, Mr. Council Clan, grand dragoon of this area's most active civic organizations and staunch bellwether of the political opposition . . . Mr. Clan, how do you *account* for this incredible disappearance?

CLAN.   A *plot*, plain and simple, that's what it is, as plain as the corns on your feet!

ANNOUNCER.   Whom would you consider responsible?

CLAN.   I could go on all night.

ANNOUNCER.   Cite a few.

CLAN.   Too numerous.

ANNOUNCER.   Just one?

CLAN.   Name names when time comes.

ANNOUNCER.   Could you be referring to native Negroes?

CLAN.   Ever try quarantining lepers from their spots?

ANNOUNCER.   Their organizations?

CLAN.   Could you slice a nose off a mouth and still keep a face?

ANNOUNCER.   Commies?

CLAN.   Would you lop off a titty from a chest and still have a breast?

ANNOUNCER.   Your city government?

CLAN.   Now you talkin'!

ANNOUNCER.   State administration?

CLAN.   Warming up!

ANNOUNCER.   Federal?

CLAN.   Kin a blind man see?

ANNOUNCER.   The Court?

CLAN. Is a pig clean?

ANNOUNCER. Clergy?

CLAN. Do a polecat stink?!

ANNOUNCER. Well, Mr. Clan, with this massive complicity, how do you think the plot could've been prevented from succeeding?

CLAN. If I'da been in office, it never woulda happened.

ANNOUNCER. Then you're laying the major blame at the doorstep of the present administration?

CLAN. Damn tooting!

ANNOUNCER. But from your oft-expressed views, Mr. Clan, shouldn't you and your followers be delighted at the turn of events? After all—isn't it one of the main policies of your society to *drive* the Negroes away? *Drive* 'em back where they came from?

CLAN. Drivvve, boy! Driiiivvve! That's right! . . . When we say so and not befo'. Ain't supposed to do nothing 'til we tell 'em. Got to stay put until we exercise our God-given right to tell 'em when to git!

ANNOUNCER. But why argue if they've merely jumped the gun? Why not rejoice at this premature purging of undesirables?

CLAN. The time ain't ripe yet, boy . . . The time ain't ripe yet.

ANNOUNCER. Thank you for being so informative, Mr. Clan—Mrs. Aide? Mrs. Aide? Over here, Mrs. Aide . . . Ladies and gentlemen, this city's Social Welfare Commissioner, Mrs. Handy Anna Aide . . . Mrs. Aide, with all your freeloading Negroes seemingly AWOL, haven't developments alleviated the staggering demands made upon your Welfare Department? Reduction of relief requests, elimination of case loads, removal of chronic welfare dependents, et cetera?

AIDE. Quite the contrary. Disruption of our pilot projects among Nigras saddles our white community with extreme hardship . . . You see, historically, our agencies have always been foremost contributors to the Nigra Git-A-Job movement. We pioneered in enforcing social welfare theories which oppose coddling the fakers. We strenuously believe in helping Nigras help themselves by participating in meaningful labor. "Relief is Out, Work is In," is our motto. We place them as maids, cooks, butlers, and breast-feeders, cesspool-diggers, wash-basin maintainers, shoeshine boys, and so on—mostly on a volunteer self-work basis.

ANNOUNCER. Hired at prevailing salaried rates, of course?

AIDE. God forbid! Money is unimportant. Would only make 'em worse. Our main goal is to improve their ethical behavior. "Rehabilitation Through Positive Participation" is another motto of ours. All unwed mothers, loose-living malingering fathers, bastard children and shiftless grandparents are kept occupied through constructive muscle therapy. This provides 'em with less opportunity to indulge their pleasure-loving amoral inclinations.

ANNOUNCER. They volunteer to participate in these pilot projects?

AIDE. Heavens no! They're notorious shirkers. When I said the program is voluntary, I meant white citizens in overwhelming majorities do the volunteering. Placing their homes, offices, appliances and persons at our disposal for use in "Operation Uplift" . . . We would never dare place such a decision in the hands of the Nigra. It would never get off the ground! No, they have no choice in the matter. "Work or Starve" is the slogan we use to stimulate their awareness of what's good for survival.

ANNOUNCER.   And a good one it is. Thank you, Mrs. Aide, and good luck . . . Rev? . . . Rev? . . . Ladies and gentlemen, this city's foremost spiritual guidance counselor, Reverend Reb Pious . . . How does it look to you, Reb Pious?

PIOUS.   (*Continuing to gaze skyward.*) It's in *His* hands, son, it's in *His* hands.

ANNOUNCER.   How would you assess the disappearance, from a moral standpoint?

PIOUS.   An immoral act, son, morally wrong and ethically indefensible. A perversion of Christian principles to be condemned from every pulpit of this nation.

ANNOUNCER.   Can you account for its occurrence after the many decades of the Church's missionary activity among them?

PIOUS.   It's basically a reversion of the Nigra to his deep-rooted primitivism . . . Now, at last, you can understand the difficulties of the Church in attempting to anchor God's kingdom among ungratefuls. It's a constant, unrelenting, no-holds-barred struggle against Satan to wrestle away souls locked in his possession for countless centuries! Despite all our aid, guidance, solace and protection, Old Beezlebub still retains tenacious grips upon the Nigras' childish loyalty—comparable to the lure of bright flames to an infant.

ANNOUNCER.   But actual physical departure, Reb Pious? How do you explain that?

PIOUS.   Voodoo, my son, voodoo . . . With Satan's assist, they have probably employed some heathen magic which we cultivated, sophisticated Christians know absolutely nothing about. However, before long we are confident about counteracting this evil witchdoctory and triumphing in our Holy Savior's name. At this perilous juncture, true believers of all denominations are participating in joint, 'round-the-clock observances, offering prayers for our Master's swiftiest intercession. I'm optimistic about the outcome of His intervention . . . Which prompts me—if I may, sir—to offer these words of counsel to our delinquent Nigras . . . I say to you without rancor or vengeance, quoting a phrase of one of your greatest prophets, Booker T. Washington: "Return your buckets to where they lay and all will be forgiven."

ANNOUNCER.   A very inspirational appeal, Reb Pious. I'm certain they will find the tug of its magnet sincerity irresistible. Thank you, Reb Pious . . . All in all—as you have witnessed, ladies and gentlemen—this town symbolizes the face of disaster, suffering as severe a prostration as any city wrecked, ravaged and devastated by the holocaust of war. A vital, lively, throbbing organism brought to a screeching halt by the strange enigma of the missing Negroes . . .

　　We take you now to offices of the one man into whose hands has been thrust the final responsibility of rescuing this shuddering metropolis from the precipice of destruction . . . We give you the honorable Mayor, Henry R. E. Lee . . . Hello, Mayor Lee.

MAYOR. (*Jovially.*) Hello, Jack.

ANNOUNCER. Mayor Lee, we have just concluded interviews with some of your city's leading spokesmen. If I may say so, sir, they don't sound too encouraging about the situation.

MAYOR. Nonsense, Jack! The situation's as well in hand as it could be under the circumstances. Couldn't be better in hand. Underneath every dark cloud, Jack, there's always a ray of sunlight, ha, ha, ha.

ANNOUNCER. Have you discovered one, sir?

MAYOR. Well, Jack, I'll tell you . . . Of course we've been faced wit a little crisis, but look at it like this—we've faced 'em befo': Sherman marched through Georgia—*once!* Lincoln freed the slaves—*momentarily!* Carpetbaggers even put Nigras in the Governor's mansion, state legislature, Congress and the Senate of the United States. But what happened? Ole Dixie bounced right on back up . . . At this moment the Supreme Court's trying to put Nigras in our schools and the Nigra has got it in his haid to put hisself everywhere . . . But what you spect gon happen? Ole Dixie will kangaroo back even higher. Southern courage, fortitude, chivalry and superiority always wins out. . . . SHUCKS! We'll have us some Nigras befo' daylight is gone!

ANNOUNCER. Mr. Mayor, I hate to introduce this note, but in an earlier interview one of your chief opponents, Mr. Clan, hinted at your own complicity in the affair—

MAYOR. *A lot of poppycock!* Clan is politicking! I've beaten him four times outta four and I'll beat him four more times outta four! This is no time for partisan politics! What we need now is level-headedness and across-the-board unity. This typical, rash, mealy-mouth, shooting-off-at-the-lip of Clan and his ilk proves their insincerity, and voters will remember that in the next election! Won't you, voters? (*Has risen to the height of campaign oratory.*)

ANNOUNCER. Mr. Mayor! . . . Mr. Mayor! . . . Please—

MAYOR. I tell you, I promise you—

ANNOUNCER. *Please, Mr. Mayor!*

MAYOR. Huh? . . . Oh—yes, carry on.

ANNOUNCER. Mr. Mayor, your cheerfulness and infectious good spirits lead me to conclude that startling new developments warrant fresh-bound optimism. What concrete, declassified information do you have to support your claim that Negroes will reappear before nightfall?

MAYOR.   Because we are presently awaiting the pay-off of a masterful five-point supra-recovery program which can't help but reap us a bonanza of Nigras 'fore sundown! . . . First: Exhaustive efforts to pinpoint the where'bouts of our own missing darkies continue to zero in on the bull's-eye . . . Second: The President of the United States, following an emergency cabinet meeting, has designated us the prime disaster area of the century—National Guard is already on the way . . . Third: In an unusual, but bold, maneuver we have appealed to the NAACP 'n all other Nigra conspirators to help us git to the bottom of the vanishing act . . . Fourth: We have exercised our non-reciprocal option and requested that all fraternal Southern states express their solidarity by lending us some of their Nigras temporarily on credit . . . Fifth and foremost: We have already gotten consent of the Governor to round up all stray, excess and incorrigible Nigras to be shipped to us under escort of the state militia . . . That's why we've stifled pessimism and are brimming wit confidence that this full-scale concerted mobilization will ring down a jackpot of jigaboos 'fore light vanishes from sky!

ANNOUNCER.   Congratulations! What happens if it fails?

MAYOR.   Don't even think *that!* Absolutely no reason to suspect it will . . . (*Peers over shoulder, then whispers confidentially while placing hand over mouth by* ANNOUNCER'S *imaginary mike.*) But speculating on the dark side of your question—if we don't turn up some by nightfall, it may be all over. The harm has already been done. You see the South has always been glued together by the uninterrupted presence of its darkies. No telling how unstuck we might git if things keep on like they have—Wait a minute, it musta paid off already! Mission accomplished 'cause here's Jackson 'head a time wit the word . . . Well, Jackson, what's new?

JACKSON.   Situation on the home front remains static, sir—can't uncover scent or shadow. The NAACP and all other Nigra front groups 'n plotters deny any knowledge or connection wit the missing Nigras. Maintained this even after appearing befo' a Senate Emergency Investigating Committee which subpoenaed 'em to Washington posthaste and threw 'em in jail for contempt. A handful of Nigras who agreed to make spectacular appeals for ours to come back to us have themselves mysteriously disappeared. But, worst news of all, sir, is our sister cities and counties, inside and outside the state, have changed their minds, fallen back on their promises and refused to lend us any Nigras, claiming they don't have 'nuff for themselves.

MAYOR.   What 'bout Nigras promised by the Governor?

JACKSON.   Jailbirds and vagrants escorted here from chain gangs and other reservations either revolted and escaped en route or else vanished mysteriously on approaching our city limits . . . Deterioration rapidly escalates, sir. Estimates predict we kin hold out only one more hour before being overtaken by anarchistic turmoil . . . Some citizens seeking haven elsewheres have already fled, but on last report were being forcibly turned back by armed sentinels in other cities who wanted no parts of 'em—claiming they carried a jinx.

MAYOR.   That bad, huh?

JACKSON.   Worse, sir . . . we've received at least five reports of plots on your life.

MAYOR.   What?—We've gotta act quickly then!

JACKSON.   Run out of ideas, sir.

MAYOR.   Think harder, boy!

JACKSON.   Don't have much time, sir. One measly hour, then all hell gon break loose.

MAYOR.   Gotta think of something drastic, Jackson!

JACKSON.   I'm dry, sir.

MAYOR.   Jackson! Is there any planes outta here in the next hour?

JACKSON.   All transportation's been knocked out, sir.

MAYOR.   I thought so!

JACKSON.   What were you contemplating, sir?

MAYOR.   Don't ask me what I was contemplating! I'm still boss 'round here! Don't forgit it!

JACKSON.   Sorry, sir.

MAYOR.   Hold the wire! . . . Wait a minute . . . ! Waaaaait a minute —*goddammit!* All this time crapping 'round, diddling and fotsing wit puny lil solutions—all the while neglecting our ace in the hole, our trump card! Most potent weapon for digging Nigras outta the woodpile? All the while right befo' our eyes! . . . Ass! Why didn't you remind me?

JACKSON.   What is it, sir?

MAYOR.   *Me— That's what! Me!* a personal appeal from ME! *Directly to them!* . . . Although we wouldn't let 'em march to the polls and express their affection for me through the ballot box, we've always known I'm held highest in their esteem. A direct address from their beloved Mayor! . . . If they's anywheres close within the sound of my voice, they'll shape up! Or let us know by a sign they's ready to.

JACKSON.   You sure *that'll* turn the trick, sir?

MAYOR.   As sure as my ancestors befo' me who knew that when they puckered their lips to whistle, ole Sambo was gonna come a-lickety-splitting to answer the call! . . . That same chips-down blood courses through these Confederate gray veins of Henry R. E. Lee ! ! !

ANNOUNCER.   I'm delighted to offer our network's facilities for such a crucial public interest address, sir. We'll arrange immediately for your appearance on an international hookup, placing you in widest proximity to contact them wherever they may be.

MAYOR.   Thank you, I'm very grateful . . . Jackson, regrease the machinery and set wheels in motion. Inform townspeople what's being done. Tell 'em we're all in this together. The next hour is countdown. I demand absolute cooperation, citywide silence and inactivity. I don't want the Nigras frightened if they's nearby. This is the most important hour in the town's history. Tell 'em if one single Nigra shows up during the hour of decision, victory is within sight. I'm gonna git 'em that one—maybe all! Hurry and crack to it!

(ANNOUNCER *rushes out, followed by* JACKSON.)

(*Blackout. Scene reopens, with* MAYOR *seated, eyes front, spotlight illuminating him in semidarkness. Shadowy figures stand in the background, prepared to answer phones or aid in any other manner.* MAYOR *waits patiently until "Go" signal is given.*)

MAYOR.   (*Voice combining elements of confidence, tremolo and gravity.*) Good evening . . . Despite the fact that millions of you wonderful people throughout the nation are viewing and listening to this momentous broadcast—and I thank you for your concern and sympathy in this hour of our peril—I primarily want to concentrate my attention and address these remarks solely for the benefit of our departed Nigra friends who may be listening somewheres in our far-flung land to the sound of my voice . . . If you are—it is with heart-felt emotion and fond memories of our happy association that I ask—"Where are you . . . ?"

Your absence has left a void in the bosom of every single man, woman and child of our great city. I tell you—you don't know what it means for us to wake up in the morning and discover that your cheerful, grinning, happy-go-lucky faces are missing! . . . From the depths of my heart, I can meekly, humbly suggest what it means to me personally . . . You see—the one face I will never be able to erase from my memory is the face—not of my Ma, not of Pa, neither wife or child—but the image of the first woman I came to love so well when just a wee lad—the vision of the first human I laid clear sight on at childbirth—the profile—better yet the full face of my dear old . . . Jemimah—God rest her soul . . . Yes! My dear ole mammy, wit her round black moonbeam gleaming down upon me in the crib, teeth shining, blood-red bandana standing starched, peaked and proud, gazing down on me affectionately as she crooned me a Southern lullaby . . . Oh! It's a memorable picture I will eternally cherish in permanent treasure chambers of my heart, now and forever always . . .

Well, if this radiant image can remain so infinitely vivid to me all these many years after her unfortunate demise in the po' folks' home—*think* of the misery the rest of us must be suffering after being *freshly* denied your soothing presence!

We need ya. If you kin hear me, just contact this station 'n I will welcome you back personally. Let me just tell you that since you eloped, nothing has been the same. How could it? You're part of us, you belong to us. Just give us a sign and we'll be contented that all is well . . .

Now if you've skipped away on a little fun fest, we understand, ha, ha. We know you like a good time and we don't begrudge it to ya. Hell—er, er, we like a good time ourselves—who doesn't . . . In fact, think of all the good times we've had together, huh? We've had some real fun, you and us, yesiree! . . . Nobody knows better than you and I what fun we've had together. You singing us those old Southern coon songs and dancing those Nigra jigs and us clapping, prodding 'n spurring you on! Lots of fun, huh? . . . *Oh boy!* The times we've had together . . . If you've snucked away for a bit of fun by yourself, we'll go 'long wit ya—long as you let us know where you at so we won't be worried about you . . .

We'll go 'long wit you long as you don't take the joke too far. I'll admit a joke is a joke and you've played a *lulu!* . . . I'm warning you, we can't stand much more horsing 'round from you! Business is business 'n fun is fun! You've had your fun so now let's get down to business! Come on back, *you hear me!*

If you been hoodwinked by agents of some foreign government, I've been authorized by the President of these United States to inform you that this liberty-loving Republic is prepared to rescue you from their clutches. Don't pay no 'tention to their sireen songs and atheistic promises! You better off under our control and you know it! . . . If you been bamboozled by rabble-rousing nonsense of your own so-called leaders, we prepared to offer some protection. Just call us up! Just give us a sign! . . . Come on, give us a sign . . . give us a sign—even a teeny weeny one . . . ? (*Glances around checking, on possible communications. A bevy of head-shakes indicate no success.* MAYOR *returns to address with desperate fervor.*)

Now look—you don't know what you doing! If you persist in this disobedience, you know all too well the consequences! We'll track you to the end of the earth, beyond the galaxy, across the stars! We'll capture you and chastise you with all the vengeance we command! 'N you know only too well how stern we kin be when double-crossed! The city, the state and the entire nation will crucify you for this unpardonable defiance! (*Checks again.*) No call . . . ? No sign . . . ? Time is running out! Deadline slipping past! They gotta respond! They gotta! (*Resuming.*) Listen to me! I'm begging y'all, you've gotta come back . . . ! *Look, George!* (*Waves dirty rag aloft*) I brought the rag you wax the car wit . . . Remember, George . . . ? Don't this bring back memories, George, of all the days you spent shining that automobile to shimmering perfection . . . ? And you, Rufus! . . . Here's the polish and the brush! . . . 'Member, Rufus? . . . Remember the happy mornings you spent popping this rag and whisking this brush so furiously 'till it created music that was sympho-nee to the ear . . . ? And you—*Mandy?* . . . Here's the wastebasket you didn't dump this morning. I saved it just for you! . . . *Look,* all y'all out there . . . (*Signals and a three-person procession parades one after the other before the imaginary camera.*)

DOLL WOMAN.   (*Brandishing a crying baby [doll] as she strolls past and exits.*) She's been crying ever since you left, Caldonia . . .
MOP MAN.   (*Flashing mop.*) It's been waiting in the same corner, Buster . . .
BRUSH MAN.   (*Flagging toilet brush.*) It's been dry ever since you left, Washington . . .
MAYOR.   (*Jumping in on the heels of the last exit.*) Don't these things mean anything to y'all? By God! Are your memories so short? Is there nothing sacred to ya . . . Please come back, for my sake, please! All of you—even you questionable ones! I promise no harm will be done to you! Revenge is disallowed! We'll forgive everything! Just come on back and I'll git down on my knees —(*Immediately drops to knees.*) I'll be kneeling in the middle of Dixie Avenue to kiss the first shoe of the first one to show up . . . I'll smooch any other spot you request . . . Erase this nightmare 'n we'll concede any demand you make, just come on back—please? . . . Pleeeeeeeze!
VOICE.   (*Shouting.*) Time!
MAYOR.   (*Remaining on knees, frozen in a pose of supplication. After a brief, deadly silence, he whispers almost inaudibly.*) They wouldn't answer . . . they wouldn't answer . . .

(*Blackout as bedlam erupts offstage. Total blackness holds during a sufficient interval where offstage sound effects create the illusion of complete pandemonium, followed by a diminution which trails off into an expressionistic simulation of a city coming to a stricken standstill: industrial machinery clanks to halt, traffic blares to silence, etc. . . . . The stage remains dark and silent for a long moment, then lights rise again on the ANNOUNCER.*)

ANNOUNCER.   A pitiful sight, ladies and gentlemen. Soon after his unsuccessful appeal, Mayor Lee suffered a vicious pummeling from the mob and barely escaped with his life. National guardsmen and state militia were impotent in quelling the fury of a town venting its frustration in an orgy of destruction—a frenzy of rioting, looting and all other aberrations of a town gone berserk . . . Then—suddenly—as if a magic wand had been waved, madness evaporated and something more frightening replaced it: submission . . .
Even whimpering ceased. The city: exhausted, benumbed— Slowly its occupants slinked off into shadows, and by midnight the town was occupied exclusively by zombies. The fight and life had been drained out . . . Pooped . . . Hope ebbed away as completely as the beloved, absent Negroes . . . As our crew packed gear and crept away silently, we treaded softly—as if we were stealing away from a mausoleum . . . The face of a defeated city.

(*Blackout.*)

(*Lights rise slowly at the sound of rooster crowing, signaling the approach of a new day, the next morning. Scene is same as opening of play. CLEM and LUKE are huddled over dazedly,*

*trancelike. They remain so for a long count. Finally, a figure drifts
on stage, shuffling slowly.*)

LUKE. (*Gazing in silent fascination at the approaching figure.*) Clem
. . . ? Do you see what I see or am I dreaming . . . ?

CLEM. It's a . . . a Nigra, ain't it, Luke . . . ?

LUKE. Sure looks like one, Clem—but we better make sure—eyes
could be playing tricks on us . . . Does he still look like one to you,
Clem?

CLEM. He still does, Luke—but I'm scared to believe—

LUKE. Why . . . ? It looks like Rastus, Clem!

CLEM. Sure does, Luke . . . but we better not jump to no hasty
conclusion . . .

LUKE. (*In timid softness.*) That you, Rastus . . . ?

RASTUS. (*Stepin Fetchit, Willie Best, Nicodemus, Butterfly McQueen
and all the rest rolled into one.*) Why . . . howdy . . . Mr. Luke . . .
Mr. Clem . . .

CLEM. It is him, Luke! It is him!

LUKE. Rastus?

RASTUS. Yas . . . sah?

LUKE. Where was you yesterday?

RASTUS. (*Very, very puzzled.*) Yes . . . ter . . . day? . . . Yester
. . . day . . . ? Why . . . right . . . here . . . Mr. Luke . . .

LUKE. No you warn't, Rastus, don't lie to me! Where was you
yestiddy?

RASTUS. Why . . . I'm sure I was . . . Mr. Luke . . . Remember
. . . I made . . . that . . . delivery for you . . .

LUKE. That was *Monday*, Rastus, yestiddy was *Tuesday.*

RASTUS. Tues . . . day . . . ? You don't say . . . Well . . . well . . .
well . . .

LUKE. Where was you 'n all the other Nigras yesterday, Rastus?

RASTUS. I . . . thought . . . yestiddy . . . was . . . Monday, Mr. Luke
—I coulda swore it . . . ! . . . See how . . . things . . . kin git all
mixed up? . . . I coulda swore it . . .

LUKE. *Today* is *Wednesday*, Rastus. Where was you *Tuesday*?

RASTUS. Tuesday . . . huh? That's somp'um . . . I . . . don't remember . . . missing . . . a day . . . Mr. Luke . . . but I guess you
right . . .

LUKE. Then where was you?

RASTUS. Don't rightly know, Mr. Luke. I didn't know I had skipped
a day—But that jist goes to show you how time kin fly, don't it,
Mr. Luke . . . Uuh, uuh, uuh . . . (*He starts shuffling off, scratch-
ing head, a flicker of a smile playing across his lips. CLEM and
LUKE gaze dumbfoundedly as he disappears.*)

LUKE. (*Eyes sweeping around in all directions.*) Well . . . There's the
others, Clem . . . Back jist like they useta be . . . Everything's same
as always . . .

CLEM. Is it . . . Luke . . . ?

CURTAIN

QUESTIONS

1. To what aspect of the play do you take the author to be referring in his designation of it (in the subtitle) as a fantasy? When he insists in addition that the fantasy is satirical, he implies that its aim is to expose and deride one or more of the vices and follies of whch human beings are guilty. What vices or follies appear here in the whites apart from "racism"? The traditional Seven Deadly Sins are covetousness, lust, anger, gluttony, envy, sloth, and pride. Of which of these would you say that racism is a subdivision?

2. Satirical literature, like political cartooning, often uses caricature to obtain its effects. Would you say that the Whites in this play are accurately portrayed? Caricatured? Or both at once? Explain. If you feel that the author does caricature the Whites, would you call this simply reverse racism on his part? Or would you say it is the appropriate means for making Whites realize the caricature images they have always tended to apply to Blacks? What evidence for the former conclusion might you see in the playwright's instructions about the kind of White company needed to perform his play—"insipid white"? What evidence for the latter might you see in his observation that the play is conceived as "a reverse minstrel show." What was a minstrel show when *un*reversed? What caricature image of the Black man as the White has often seen him appears in the final episode of the play?

3. In what ways is White treatment of other Whites no better than White treatment of Blacks in the play? Point out examples. Why do you suppose the playwright chose to depict White–White relationships the way he does?

4. Why does it take Clem and Luke so long to put their fingers on what is "wrong—outta place, unusual"? How is this same inability to recognize the obvious repeated throughout the play in various other ways?

5. How would you describe the confrontation or conflict that is set in motion in the opening episode and developed in the ones that follow? How is it resolved, both in obvious ways and in not-so-obvious ways?

6. Ward's play calls for a great deal of miming, since, as he points out in his preliminary directions, all but the most essential props are to remain imaginary: "phones, switchboards, mikes, eating utensils, etc." Try for yourself the kind of miming that is called for by (a) the telephone switchboard speeches, using if possible a tall stool; and (b) the "Huntley-Brinkley-Murrow-Severeid-Cronkite-Reasoner type Announcer" episode, recording with your face and hands the Announcer's emotion as he sketches the dimensions of the disaster that has hit the town and then reads out loud the pleading placards of the marchers.

7. Taking your cues from the playwright's opening "Notes on Production," and in terms of the racial make-up of your class, put on

readings, or even "productions," of various episodes for the benefit of the rest of the class or of a group of classes. No scenery is necessary, but costuming is certainly possible and easily handled. You will find that the satire will come across more powerfully in preparation and production than it does in silent reading.

8. In their eagerness to make their point, satirists sometimes allow their characters to break away from the attitudes that are suited to them as characters in order to express more plainly the author's own attitudes. Ward does this with his Courier when he allows him to add to the list of White notables who have vanished along with the Blacks a disparaging allusion to "numerous other miscellaneous nobodies." As a White courier, holding the view that all Whites in the play hold, the Courier obviously would not speak in this way himself: the author's voice here pokes through behind him. How many other instances of this kind of "rupture" in the satire can you find? Does it make any difference to the effectiveness of the play? Why or why not?

9. "Show me your group's caricatures of other groups," someone once said, "and I will show you your own shortcomings." Choose one of the following pairs and describe briefly, or sketch in a drawing, the caricature images that you think either member of the pair usually holds of the other: (1) White teenager and Black teenager; (2) Black and Chicano; (3) Jew and Wasp; (4) Irishman and Italian; (5) Republican and Democrat; (6) rich man and poor man; (7) New Yorker and Londoner; (8) American and Russian; (9) movie cowboy and movie Indian. In the pair you have chosen what shortcomings, fears, or rivalries do you see obliquely reflected in the caricature images that the one group cherishes of the other? Why in your opinion do people tend to cling to these images? How do you think they might go about getting rid of them? Do you detect any such caricature images in your own thinking or that of your family?

The Glass Menagerie

The Glass Menagerie has been one of the staples of the modern American theater since its first highly successful Broadway run in 1945. It is a favorite with school, semiprofessional and professional theater groups, and it has been made into a movie (several times) and produced on television. Its popularity is easy to understand. It has enough pathos to satisfy any soap-opera addict, and yet it is an honest and compelling piece of stagecraft, with four superb parts that any actor would find challenging and satisfying.

Since World War II Tennessee Williams has been one of America's most successful and productive playwrights. A Southerner by birth and inclination (he adopted the name Tennessee, having grown up with the more prosaic Tom—Thomas Lanier Williams in full), he deals in most of his plays and short stories with a South of faded gentility, dissipated power, and fruitless hopes, with people unable or unwilling to make it in an openly acquisitive, hard-nosed, unfeeling world. In *The Glass Menagerie,* if not in some of his other works, Williams suggests the possibility that the people who *do* make it in the "world of reality" may be the real losers, rather than the gentle souls who, while seeming to be losers, keep alive a certain decency and dignity.

Williams has experimented in a variety of ways with departures from the conventions of the realistic theater, conventions which we discussed at some length in connection with *The Devil's Disciple* (see pages 67–70). His comments in the Production Notes for *The Glass Menagerie* are revealing not only for an actual production for this particular play or a staging of it in the theater of the mind, but also as a general statement on the value of any nonrealistic approach to drama.

The Glass Menagerie

TENNESSEE WILLIAMS

(1914–   )

Nobody, not even the rain, has such small hands.

E E CUMMINGS

CHARACTERS

AMANDA WINGFIELD (*the mother*)
>*A little woman of great but confused vitality clinging frantically to another time and place. Her characterization must be carefully created, not copied from type. She is not paranoiac, but her life is paranoia. There is much to admire in Amanda, and as much to love and pity as there is to laugh at. Certainly she has endurance and a kind of heroism, and though her foolishness makes her unwittingly cruel at times, there is tenderness in her slight person.*

LAURA WINGFIELD (*her daughter*)
>*Amanda, having failed to establish contact with reality, continues to live vitally in her illusions, but Laura's situation is even graver. A childhood illness has left her crippled, one leg slightly shorter than the other, and held in a brace. This defect need not be more than suggested on the stage. Stemming from this, Laura's separation increases till she is like a piece of her own glass collection, too exquisitely fragile to move from the shelf.*

TOM WINGFIELD (*her son*)
>*And the narrator of the play. A poet with a job in a warehouse. His nature is not remorseless, but to escape from a trap he has to act without pity.*

JIM O'CONNOR (*the gentleman caller*)
>*A nice, ordinary, young man.*

SCENE

An Alley in St. Louis
    part i. *Preparation for a Gentleman Caller*
    part ii. *The Gentleman calls*
Time: Now and the Past

PRODUCTION NOTES

Being a "*memory play*," The Glass Menagerie *can be presented with unusual freedom of convention. Because of its considerably delicate or tenuous material, atmospheric touches and subtleties of direction play a particularly important part. Expressionism and all other unconventional techniques in drama have only one valid aim, and that is a closer approach to truth. When a play employs unconventional techniques, it is not, or certainly shouldn't be, trying to escape its responsibility of dealing with reality, or interpreting experience, but is actually or should be attempting to find a closer approach, a more penetrating and vivid expression of things as they are. The straight realistic play with its genuine frigidaire and authentic ice-cubes, its characters that speak exactly as its audience speaks, corresponds to the academic landscape and has the same virtue of a photographic likeness. Everyone should know nowadays the unimportance of the photographic in art: that truth, life, or reality is an organic thing which the poetic imagination can represent or suggest, in essence, only through transformation, through changing into other forms than those which were merely present in appearance.*

    These remarks are not meant as a preface only to this particular play. They have to do with a conception of a new, plastic theatre which must take the place of the exhausted theatre of realistic conventions if the theatre is to resume vitality as a part of our culture.

the music

Another extra-literary accent in this play is provided by the use of music. A single recurring tune, "The Glass Menagerie," is used to give emotional emphasis to suitable passages. This tune is like circus music, not when you are on the grounds or in the immediate vicinity of the parade, but when you are at some distance and very likely thinking of something else. It seems under those circumstances to continue almost interminably and it weaves in and out of your preoccupied consciousness; then it is the lightest, most delicate music in the world and perhaps the saddest. It expresses the surface vivacity of life with the underlying strain of immutable and inexpressible sorrow. When you look at a piece of deli-

cately spun glass you think of two things: how beautiful it is and how easily it can be broken. Both of those ideas should be woven into the recurring tune, which dips in and out of the play as if it were carried on a wind that changes. It serves as a thread of connection and allusion between the narrator with his separate point in time and space and the subject of his story. Between each episode it returns as reference to the emotion, nostalgia, which is the first condition of the play. It is primarily Laura's music and therefore comes out most clearly when the play focuses upon her and the lovely fragility of glass which is her image.

the lighting

The lighting in the play is not realistic. In keeping with the atmosphere of memory, the stage is dim. Shafts of light are focused on selected areas or actors, sometimes in contradistinction to what is the apparent center. For instance, in the quarrel scene between Tom and Amanda, in which Laura has no active part, the clearest pool of light is on her figure. This is also true of the supper scene, when her silent figure on the sofa should remain the visual center. The light upon Laura should be distinct from the others, having a peculiar pristine clarity such as light used in early religious portraits of female saints or madonnas. A certain correspondence to light in religious paintings, such as El Greco's, where the figures are radiant in atmosphere that is relatively dusky, could be effectively used throughout the play. . . . A free, imaginative use of light can be of enormous value in giving a mobile, plastic quality to plays of a more or less static nature.

T. W.

SCENE 1

The Wingfield apartment is in the rear of the building, one of those vast hive-like conglomerations of cellular living-units that flower as warty growths in overcrowded urban centers of lower middle-class population and are symptomatic of the impulse of this largest and fundamentally enslaved section of American society to avoid fluidity and differentiation and to exist and function as one interfused mass of automatism.

The apartment faces an alley and is entered by a fire-escape, a structure whose name is a touch of accidential poetic truth, for all of these huge buildings are always burning with the slow and implacable fires of human desperation. The fire-escape is included in the set—that is, the landing of it and steps descending from it.

The scene is memory and is therefore nonrealistic. Memory takes a lot of poetic license. It omits some details; others are exaggerated, according to the emotional value of the articles it touches, for memory is seated predominantly in the heart. The interior is therefore rather dim and poetic.

At the rise of the curtain, the audience is faced with the dark, grim rear wall of the Wingfield tenement. This building, which runs parallel to the footlights, is flanked on both sides by dark, narrow alleys which run into murky canyons of tangled clotheslines, garbage cans and the sinister latticework of neighboring fire-escapes. It is up and down these side alleys that exterior entrances and exits are made, during the play. At the end of TOM'S opening commentary, the dark tenement wall slowly reveals (by means of a transparency) the interior of the ground floor Wingfield apart-ment.

Downstage is the living room, which also serves as a sleeping room for LAURA, the sofa unfolding to make her bed. Upstage, center, and divided by a wide arch or second proscenium with transparent faded portieres (or second curtain), is the dining room. In an old-fashioned what-not in the living room are seen scores of transparent glass animals. A blown-up photograph of the father hangs on the wall of the living room, facing the audience, to the left of the archway. It is the face of a very handsome young man in a doughboy's First World War cap. He is gallantly smiling, in-eluctably smiling, as if to say, "I will be smiling forever."

The audience hears and sees the opening scene in the dining room through both the transparent fourth wall of the building and the transparent gauze portieres of the dining-room arch. It is during this revealing scene that the fourth wall slowly ascends, out of sight. This transparent exterior wall is not brought down again until the very end of the play, during TOM'S final speech.

The narrator is an undisguised convention of the play. He takes whatever license with dramatic convention as is convenient to his purposes.

TOM enters dressed as a merchant sailor from alley, stage left, and strolls across the front of the stage to the fire-escape. There he stops and lights a cigarette. He addresses the audience.

TOM. Yes, I have tricks in my pocket, I have things up my sleeve. But I am the opposite of a stage magician. He gives you illusion that has the appearance of truth. I give you truth in the pleasant disguise of illusion.

To begin with, I turn back time. I reverse it to that quaint period, the thirties, when the huge middle class of America was matriculating in a school for the blind. Their eyes had failed them, or they had failed their eyes, and so they were having their fingers pressed forcibly down on the fiery Braille alphabet of a dissolving economy.

In Spain there was revolution. Here there was only shouting and confusion.

In Spain there was Guernica. Here there were disturbances of labor, sometimes pretty violent, in otherwise peaceful cities such as Chicago, Cleveland, Saint Louis . . .

This is the social background of the play.

(*Music*)

The play is memory.

Being a memory play, it is dimly lighted, it is sentimental, it is not realistic.

In memory everything seems to happen to music. That explains the fiddle in the wings.

I am the narrator of the play, and also a character in it.

The other characters are my mother, Amanda, my sister, Laura, and a gentleman caller who appears in the final scenes.

He is the most realistic character in the play, being an emissary from a world of reality that we were somehow set apart from.

But since I have a poet's weakness for symbols, I am using this character also as a symbol; he is the long delayed but always expected something that we live for.

There is a fifth character in the play who doesn't appear except in this larger-than-life-size photograph over the mantel.

This is our father who left us a long time ago.

He was a telephone man who fell in love with long distances; he gave up his job with the telephone company and skipped the light fantastic out of town . . .

The last we heard of him was a picture post-card from Mazatlan, on the Pacific coast of Mexico, containing a message of two words—

"Hello— Good-bye!" and no address.

I think the rest of the play will explain itself. . . .

(AMANDA'S *voice becomes audible through the portieres.*)

(*He divides the portieres and enters the upstage area.*)

(AMANDA *and* LAURA *are seated at a drop-leaf table. Eating is indicated by gestures without food or utensils.* AMANDA *faces the audience.* TOM *and* LAURA *are seated in profile.*)

(*The interior has lit up softly and through the scrim we see* AMANDA *and* LAURA *seated at the table in the upstage area.*)

AMANDA.   (*Calling.*) Tom?

TOM.   Yes, Mother.

AMANDA.   We can't say grace until you come to the table!

TOM.   Coming, Mother. (*He bows slightly and withdraws, reappearing a few moments later in his place at the table.*)

AMANDA.   (*To her son.*) Honey, don't *push* with your *fingers.* If you have to push with something, the thing to push with is a crust of bread. And chew—chew! Animals have sections in their stomachs which enable them to digest food without mastication, but human beings are supposed to chew their food before they swallow it down. Eat food leisurely, son, and really enjoy it. A well-cooked meal has lots of delicate flavors that have to be held in the mouth for appreciation. So chew your food and give your salivary glands a chance to function!

(TOM *deliberately lays his imaginary fork down and pushes his chair back from the table.*)

TOM.   I haven't enjoyed one bite of this dinner because of your constant directions on how to eat it. It's you that make me rush through meals with your hawk-like attention to every bite I take. Sickening—spoils my appetite—all this discussion of—animal's secretion—salivary glands—mastication!

AMANDA.   (*Lightly.*) Temperament like a Metropolitan star! (*He rises and crosses downstage.*) You're not excused from the table.

TOM.   I'm getting a cigarette.

AMANDA.   You smoke too much.

(LAURA *rises.*)

LAURA.   I'll bring in the blanc mange.

(*He remains standing with his cigarette by the portieres during the following.*)

AMANDA.   (*Rising.*) No, sister, no, sister—you be the lady this time and I'll be the darky.

LAURA.   I'm already up.

AMANDA.   Resume your seat, little sister—I want you to stay fresh and pretty—for gentlemen callers!

LAURA.   I'm not expecting any gentlemen callers.

AMANDA.   (*Crossing out to kitchenette. Airily.*) Sometimes they come when they are least expected! Why, I remember one Sunday afternoon in Blue Mountain— (*Enters kitchenette.*)

TOM.   I know what's coming!

LAURA.   Yes. But let her tell it.

TOM.   Again?

LAURA.   She loves to tell it.

(AMANDA *returns with bowl of dessert.*)

AMANDA.   One Sunday afternoon in Blue Mountain—your mother received—*seventeen!*—gentlemen callers! Why, sometimes there weren't chairs enough to accommodate them all. We had to send the nigger over to bring in folding chairs from the parish house.

TOM.   (*Remaining at portieres.*) How did you entertain those gentlemen callers?

AMANDA.   I understood the art of conversation!

TOM.   I bet you could talk.

AMANDA.   Girls in those days *knew* how to talk, I can tell you.

TOM.   Yes?

AMANDA.   They knew how to entertain their gentlemen callers. It wasn't enough for a girl to be possessed of a pretty face and a graceful figure—although I wasn't slighted in either respect. She also needed to have a nimble wit and a tongue to meet all occasions.

TOM.   What did you talk about?

AMANDA.   Things of importance going on in the world! Never anything coarse or common or vulgar. (*She addresses* TOM *as though he were seated in the vacant chair at the table though he remains by portieres. He plays this scene as though he held the book.*) My callers were gentlemen—all! Among my callers were some of the most prominent young planters of the Mississippi Delta—planters and sons of planters!

(TOM *motions for music and a spot of light on AMANDA.*)

(*Her eyes lift, her face glows, her voice becomes rich and elegiac.*)

There was young Champ Laughlin who later became vice-president of the Delta Planters Bank.

Hadley Stevenson who was drowned in Moon Lake and left his widow one hundred and fifty thousand in Government bonds.

There were the Cutrere brothers, Wesley and Bates. Bates was one of my bright particular beaux! He got in a quarrel with that wild Wainwright boy. They shot it out on the floor of Moon Lake Casino. Bates was shot through the stomach. Died in the ambulance on his way to Memphis. His widow was also well-provided for, came into eight or ten thousand acres, that's all. She married him on the rebound—never loved her—carried my picture on him the night he died!

And there was that boy that every girl in the Delta had set her cap for! That beautiful, brilliant young Fitzhugh boy from Greene County!

TOM.   What did he leave his widow?

AMANDA.   He never married! Gracious, you talk as though all of my old admirers had turned up their toes to the daisies!

TOM.   Isn't this the first you've mentioned that still survives?

AMANDA.   That Fitzhugh boy went North and made a fortune—came to be known as the Wolf of Wall Street! He had the Midas touch; whatever he touched turned to gold!

And I could have been Mrs. Duncan J. Fitzhugh, mind you! But—I picked your *father!*

LAURA.   (*Rising.*) Mother, let me clear the table.

AMANDA.   No, dear, you go in front and study your typewriter chart. Or practice your shorthand a little. Stay fresh and pretty!—It's almost time for our gentlemen callers to start arriving. (*She flounces girlishly toward the kitchenette.*) How many do you suppose we're going to entertain this afternoon?

(TOM *throws down the paper and jumps up with a groan.*)

LAURA. (*Alone in the dining room.*) I don't believe we're going to receive any, Mother.

AMANDA. (*Reappearing, airily.*) What? No one—not one? You must be joking! (LAURA *nervously echoes her laugh. She slips in a fugitive manner through the half-open portieres and draws them gently behind her. A shaft of very clear light is thrown on her face against the faded tapestry of the curtains.* MUSIC: "THE GLASS MENAGERIE" UNDER FAINTLY. *Lightly.*) Not one gentleman caller? It can't be true! There must be a flood, there must have been a tornado!

LAURA. It isn't a flood, it's not a tornado, Mother. I'm just not popular like you were in Blue Mountain. . . .(TOM *utters another groan.* LAURA *glances at him with a faint, apologetic smile. Her voice catching a little*) Mother's afraid I'm going to be an old maid.

(*The scene dims out with "Glass Menagerie" music*)

SCENE 2

(*The music subsides.*)

LAURA *is seated in the delicate ivory chair at the small claw-foot table.*

She wears a dress of soft violet material for a kimono—her hair tied back from her forehead with a ribbon.

She is washing and polishing her collection of glass.

AMANDA *appears on the fire-escape steps. At the sound of her ascent,* LAURA *catches her breath, thrusts the bowl of ornaments away and seats herself stiffly before the diagram of the typewriter keyboard as though it held her spellbound.*

Something has happened to AMANDA. *It is written in her face as she climbs to the landing: a look that is grim and hopeless and a little absurd.*

She has on one of those cheap or imitation velvety-looking cloth coats with imitation fur collar. Her hat is five or six years old, one of those dreadful cloche hats that were worn in the late twenties and she is clasping an enormous black patent-leather pocketbook with nickel clasps and initials. This is her full-dress outfit, the one she usually wears to the D.A.R.

Before entering she looks through the door.

She purses her lips, opens her eyes very wide, rolls them upward and shakes her head.

Then she slowly lets herself in the door. Seeing her mother's expression, LAURA *touches her lips with a nervous gesture.*

LAURA. Hello, Mother, I was—(*She makes a nervous gesture toward the chart on the wall.* AMANDA *leans against the shut door and stares at* LAURA *with a martyred look.*)

AMANDA. Deception? Deception? (*She slowly removes her hat and gloves, continuing the sweet suffering stare. She lets the hat and gloves fall on the floor—a bit of acting.*)

LAURA. (*Shakily.*) How was the D.A.R. meeting? (AMANDA *slowly opens her purse and removes a dainty white handkerchief which she shakes out delicately and delicately touches to her lips and nostrils.*) Didn't you go to the D.A.R. meeting, Mother?

AMANDA. (*Faintly, almost inaudibly.*) —No.—No. (*Then more forcibly.*) I did not have the strength—to go to the D.A.R. In fact, I did not have the courage! I wanted to find a hole in the ground and hide myself in it forever! (*She crosses slowly to the wall and removes the diagram of the typewritter keyboard. She holds it in front of her for a second, staring at it sweetly and sorrowfully—then bites her lips and tears it in two pieces.*)

LAURA. (*Faintly.*) Why did you do that, Mother? (AMANDA *repeats the same procedure with the chart of the Gregg Alphabet.*) Why are you—

AMANDA. Why? Why? How old are you, Laura?

LAURA. Mother, you know my age.

AMANDA. I thought that you were an adult; it seems that I was mistaken. (*She crosses slowly to the sofa and sinks down and stares at* LAURA.)

LAURA. Please don't stare at me, Mother.

(AMANDA *closes her eyes and lowers her head. Count ten.*)

AMANDA. What are we going to do, what is going to become of us, what is the future?

(*Count ten*)

LAURA. Has something happened, Mother? (AMANDA *draws a long breath and takes out the handkerchief again. Dabbing process.*) Mother, has—something happened?

AMANDA. I'll be all right in a minute, I'm just bewildered—(*Count five.*)—by life. . . .

LAURA. Mother, I wish that you would tell me what's happened!

AMANDA. As you know, I was supposed to be inducted into my office at the D.A.R. this afternoon. But I stopped off at Rubicam's Business College to speak to your teachers about your having a cold and ask them what progress they thought you were making down there.

LAURA. Oh. . . .

AMANDA. I went to the typing instructor and introduced myself as your mother. She didn't know who you were. Wingfield, she said. We don't have any such student enrolled at the school!

I assured her she did, that you had been going to classes since early in January.

"I wonder," she said, "if you could be talking about that terribly shy little girl who dropped out of school after only a few days' attendance?"

"No," I said, "Laura, my daughter, has been going to school every day for the past six weeks!"

"Excuse me," she said. She took the attendance book out and there was your name, unmistakably printed, and all the dates you were absent until they decided that you had dropped out of school.

I still said, "No, there must have been some mistake! There must have been some mix-up in the records!"

And she said, "No—I remember her perfectly now. Her hands shook so that she couldn't hit the right keys! The first time we gave a speed-test, she broke down completely—was sick at the stomach and almost had to be carried into the wash-room! After that morning she never showed up any more. We phoned the house but never got any answer"—while I was working at Famous and Barr, I suppose, demonstrating those— Oh!

I felt so weak I could barely keep on my feet!

I had to sit down while they got me a glass of water!

Fifty dollars' tuition, all of our plans—my hopes and ambitions for you—just gone up the spout, just gone up the spout like that.

(LAURA *draws a long breath and gets awkwardly to her feet. She crosses to the victrola and winds it up.*)

What are you doing?

LAURA. Oh! (*She releases the handle and returns to her seat.*)

AMANDA. Laura, where have you been going when you've gone out pretending that you were going to business college?

LAURA. I've just been going out walking.

AMANDA. That's not true.

LAURA. It is. I just went walking.

AMANDA. Walking? Walking? In winter? Deliberately courting pneumonia in that light coat? Where did you walk to, Laura?

LAURA. All sorts of places—mostly in the park.

AMANDA. Even after you'd started catching that cold?

LAURA. It was the lesser of two evils, Mother. I couldn't go back up. I—threw up—on the floor!

AMANDA. From half past seven till after five every day you mean to tell me you walked around in the park, because you wanted to make me think that you were still going to Rubicam's Business College?

LAURA. It wasn't as bad as it sounds. I went inside places to get warmed up.

AMANDA. Inside, where?

LAURA. I went in the art museum and the bird-houses at the Zoo. I visited the penguins every day! Sometimes I did without lunch and went to the movies. Lately I've been spending most of my afternoons in the Jewel-box, that big glass house where they raise the tropical flowers.

AMANDA. You did all this to deceive me, just for deception? (LAURA *looks down.*) Why?

LAURA. Mother, when you're disappointed, you get that awful suffering look on your face, like the picture of Jesus' mother in the museum!

AMANDA. Hush!

LAURA. I couldn't face it.

(*Pause. A whisper of strings.*)

AMANDA. (*Hopelessly fingering the huge pocketbook.*) So what are we going to do the rest of our lives? Stay home and watch the parades go by? Amuse ourselves with the glass menagerie, darling? Eternally play those worn-out phonograph records your father left as a painful reminder of him?

We won't have a business career—we've given that up because it gave us nervous indigestion! (*Laughs wearily.*) What is there left but dependency all our lives? I know so well what becomes of unmarried women who aren't prepared to occupy a position. I've seen such pitiful cases in the South—barely tolerated spinsters living upon the grudging patronage of sister's husband or brother's wife!—stuck away in some little mouse-trap of a room—encouraged by one in-law to visit another—little birdlike women without any nest—eating the crust of humility all their life!

Is that the future that we've mapped out for ourselves?

I swear it's the only alternative I can think of!

It isn't a very pleasant alternative, is it?

Of course—some girls *do marry.*

(LAURA *twists her hands nervously.*)

Haven't you ever liked some boy?

LAURA. Yes. I liked one once. (*Rises.*) I came across his picture a while ago.

AMANDA. (*With some interest.*) He gave you his picture?

LAURA. No, it's in the year book.

AMANDA. (*Disappointed.*) Oh—a high school boy.

LAURA. Yes. His name was Jim. (LAURA *lifts the heavy annual from the claw-foot table.*) Here he is in *The Pirates of Penzance.*

AMANDA. (*Absently.*) The what?

LAURA. The operetta the senior class put on. He had a wonderful voice and we sat across the aisle from each other Mondays, Wednesdays and Fridays in the Aud. Here he is with the silver cup for debating! See his grin?

AMANDA. (*Absently.*) He must have had a jolly disposition.

LAURA. He used to call me—Blue Roses.

AMANDA. Why did he call you such a name as that?

LAURA. When I had that attack of pleurosis—he asked me what was the matter when I came back. I said—pleurosis—he thought that I said Blue Roses! So that's what he always called me after that. Whenever he saw me, he'd holler, "Hello, Blue Roses!" I didn't care for the girl that he went out with. Emily Meisenbach. Emily was the best-dressed girl at Soldan. She never struck me, though, as being sincere . . . It says in the Personal Section—they're engaged. That's—six years ago! They must be married by now.

AMANDA.   Girls that aren't cut out for business careers usually wind up married to some nice man. (*Gets up with a spark of revival.*) Sister, that's what you'll do!

(LAURA *utters a startled, doubtful laugh. She reaches quickly for a piece of glass.*)

LAURA.   But, Mother—

AMANDA.   Yes? (*Crossing to photograph*)

LAURA.   (*In a tone of frightened apology.*) I'm—crippled!

AMANDA.   Nonsense! Laura, I've told you never, never to use that word. Why, you're not crippled, you just have a little defect—hardly noticeable, even! When people have some slight disadvantage like that, they cultivate other things to make up for it—develop charm—and vivacity—and—*charm!* That's all you have to do! (*She turns again to the photograph.*) One thing your father had *plenty of*—was *charm!*

(TOM *motions to the fiddle in the wings.*)

(*The scene fades out with music.*)

SCENE 3

TOM *speaks from the fire-escape landing.*

TOM.   After the fiasco at Rubicam's Business College, the idea of getting a gentleman caller for Laura began to play a more and more important part in Mother's calculations.

It became an obsession. Like some archetype of the universal unconscious, the image of the gentleman caller haunted our small apartment. . . .

An evening at home rarely passed without some allusion to this image, this spectre, this hope. . . .

Even when he wasn't mentioned, his presence hung in Mother's preoccupied look and in my sister's frightened, apologetic manner —hung like a sentence passed upon the Wingfields!

Mother was a woman of action as well as words.

She began to take logical steps in the planned direction.

Late that winter and in the early spring—realizing that extra money would be needed to properly feather the nest and plume the bird—she conducted a vigorous campaign on the telephone, roping in subscribers to one of those magazines for matrons called *The Home-maker's Companion,* the type of journal that features the serialized sublimations of ladies of letters who think in terms of delicate cup-like breasts, slim, tapering waists, rich, creamy thighs, eyes like wood-smoke in autumn, fingers that soothe and caress like strains of music, bodies as powerful as Etruscan sculpture.

(AMANDA *enters with phone on long extension cord. She is spotted in the dim stage.*)

AMANDA.   Ida Scott? This is Amanda Wingfield!

We *missed* you at the D.A.R. last Monday!

I said to myself: She's probably suffering with that sinus condition! How is that sinus condition?

Horrors! Heaven have mercy!—You're a Christian martyr, yes, that's what you are, a Christian martyr!

Well, I just now happened to notice that your subscription to the *Companion's* about to expire! Yes, it expires with the next issue, honey!—just when that wonderful new serial by Bessie Mae Hopper is getting off to such an exciting start. Oh, honey, it's something that you can't miss! You remember how *Gone With the Wind* took everybody by storm? You simply couldn't go out if you hadn't read it. All everybody *talked* was Scarlett O'Hara. Well, this is a book that critics already compare to *Gone With the Wind*. It's the *Gone With the Wind* of the post-World War generation!— What?—Burning?—Oh, honey, don't let them burn, go take a look in the oven and I'll hold the wire! Heavens—I think she's hung up!

(*Dim out*)

(*Before the stage is lighted, the violent voices of* TOM *and* AMANDA *are heard.*)

(*They are quarreling behind the portieres. In front of them stands* LAURA *with clenched hands and panicky expression.*)

(*A clear pool of light on her figure throughout this scene*)

TOM.   What in Christ's name am I—

AMANDA.   (*Shrilly.*) Don't you use that—

TOM.   Supposed to do!

AMANDA.   Expression! Not in my—

TOM.   Ohhh!

AMANDA.   Presence! Have you gone out of your senses?

TOM.   I have, that's true, *driven* out!

AMANDA.   What is the matter with you, you—big—big—IDIOT!

TOM.   Look!—I've got *no* thing, no single thing—

AMANDA.   Lower your voice!

TOM.   In my life here that I can call my own! Everything is—

AMANDA.   Stop that shouting!

TOM.   Yesterday you confiscated my books! You had the nerve to—

AMANDA.   I took that horrible novel back to the library—yes! That hideous book by that insane Mr. Lawrence. (TOM *laughs wildly.*) I cannot control the output of diseased minds or people who cater to them— (TOM *laughs still more wildly.*) BUT I WON'T ALLOW SUCH FILTH BROUGHT INTO MY HOUSE! No, no, no, no, no!

TOM.   House, house! Who pays rent on it, who makes a slave of him-
self to—
AMANDA.   (*Fairly screeching.*) Don't you DARE to—
TOM.   No, no, I mustn't say things! *I've* got to just—
AMANDA.   Let me tell you—
TOM.   I don't want to hear any more! (*He tears the portieres open.
The upstage area is lit with a turgid smoky red glow.*)

(AMANDA'S *hair is in metal curlers and she wears a very old
bathrobe, much too large for her slight figure, a relic of the faith-
less Mr. Wingfield.*)

(*An upright typewriter and a wild disarray of manuscripts is on
the drop-leaf table. The quarrel was probably precipitated by*
AMANDA'S *interruption of his creative labor. A chair lying over-
thrown on the floor.*)

(*Their gesticulating shadows are cast on the ceiling by the fiery
glow.*)

AMANDA.   You *will* hear more, you—
TOM.   No, I won't hear more, I'm going out!
AMANDA.   You come right back in—
TOM.   Out, out, out! Because I'm—
AMANDA.   Come back here, Tom Wingfield! I'm not through talking
to you!
TOM.   Oh, go—
LAURA.   (*Desperately.*) —Tom!
AMANDA.   You're going to listen, and no more insolence from you!
I'm at the end of my patience!

(*He comes back toward her.*)

TOM.   What do you think I'm at? Aren't I supposed to have any
patience to reach the end of, Mother? I know, I know. It seems
unimportant to you, what I'm *doing*—what I *want* to do—having
a little *difference* between them! You don't think that—
AMANDA.   I think you've been doing things that you're ashamed of.
That's why you act like this. I don't believe that you go every
night to the movies. Nobody goes to the movies night after night.
Nobody in their right minds goes to the movies as often as you
pretend to. People don't go to the movies at nearly midnight, and
movies don't let out at two A.M. Come in stumbling. Muttering to
yourself like a maniac! You get three hours' sleep and then go to
work. Oh, I can picture the way you're doing down there. Moping,
doping, because you're in no condition.
TOM.   (*Wildly.*) No, I'm in no condition!
AMANDA.   What right have you got to jeopardize your job? Jeopardize
the security of us all? How do you think we'd manage if you
were—
TOM.   Listen! You think I'm crazy *about* the *warehouse*? (*He bends
fiercely toward her slight figure.*) You think I'm in love with the

Continental Shoemakers? You think I want to spend fifty-five *years* down there in that—*celotex interior!* With—*fluorescent— tubes!* Look! I'd rather somebody picked up a crowbar and battered out my brains—than go back mornings! I *go!* Every time you come in yelling that God damn *"Rise and Shine!" "Rise and Shine!"* I say to myself, "How *lucky dead* people are!" But I get up. I *go!* For sixty-five dollars a month I give up all that I dream of doing and being *ever!* And you say self—*self's* all I ever think of. Why, listen, if self is what I thought of, Mother, I'd be where he is— GONE! (*Pointing to father's picture.*) As far as the system of transportation reaches! (*He starts past her. She grabs his arm.*) Don't grab at me, Mother!

AMANDA.   Where are you going?

TOM.   I'm going to the *movies!*

AMANDA.   I don't believe that lie!

TOM.   (*Crouching toward her, overtowering her tiny figure. She backs away, gasping.*) I'm going to opium dens! Yes, opium dens, dens of vice and criminals' hang-outs, Mother. I've joined the Hogan gang, I'm a hired assassin, I carry a tommy-gun in a violin case! I run a string of cat-houses in the Valley! They call me Killer, Killer Wingfield, I'm leading a double-life, a simple, honest ware- house worker by day, by night a dynamic *czar* of the *underworld,* Mother. I go to gambling casinos, I spin away fortunes on the roulette table! I wear a patch over one eye and a false mustache, sometimes I put on green whiskers. On those occasions they call me—*El Diablo!* Oh, I could tell you things to make you sleepless! My enemies plan to dynamite this place. They're going to blow us all sky-high some night! I'll be glad, very happy, and so will you! You'll go up, up on a broomstick, over Blue Mountain with seventeen gentlemen callers! You ugly—babbling old—*witch.* . . . (*He goes through a series of violent, clumsy movements, seizing his overcoat, lunging to the door, pulling it fiercely open. The women watch him, aghast. His arm catches in the sleeve of the coat as he struggles to pull it on. For a moment he is pinioned by the bulky garment. With an outraged groan he tears the coat off again, splitting the shoulder of it, and hurls it across the room. It strikes against the shelf of* LAURA'S *glass collection; there is a tinkle of shattering glass.* LAURA *cries out as if wounded.*)

(*Music*)

LAURA.   (*Shrilly.*) My glass!—menagerie. . . . (*She covers her face and turns away.*)

(*But* AMANDA *is still stunned and stupefied by the "ugly witch" so that she barely notices this occurrence. Now she recovers her speech.*)

AMANDA.   (*In an awful voice.*) I won't speak to you—until you apologize! (*She crosses through portieres and draws them together behind her.* TOM *is left with* LAURA. LAURA *clings weakly to the mantel with her face averted. TOM stares at her stupidly for a moment. Then he crosses to shelf. Drops awkwardly on his knees to collect the fallen glass, glancing at LAURA as if he would speak but couldn't.)*

("The Glass Menagerie" steals in as the scene dims out.)

SCENE 4

The interior is dark. Faint light in the alley.

A deep-voiced bell in a church is tolling the hour of five as the scene commences.

TOM appears at the top of the alley. After each solemn boom of the bell in the tower, he shakes a little noise-maker or rattle as if to express the tiny spasm of man in contrast to the sustained power and dignity of the Almighty. This and the unsteadiness of his advance make it evident that he has been drinking.

As he climbs the few steps to the fire-escape landing, light steals up inside. LAURA appears in night-dress, observing TOM'S empty bed in the front room.

TOM fishes in his pockets for door-key, removing a motley assortment of articles in the search, including a perfect shower of movie-ticket stubs and an empty bottle. At last he finds the key, but just as he is about to insert it, it slips from his fingers. He strikes a match and crouches below the door.

TOM   (*Bitterly.*) One crack—and it falls through!

(*LAURA opens the door.*)

LAURA.   Tom! Tom, what are you doing?

TOM.   Looking for a door-key.

LAURA.   Where have you been all this time?

TOM.   I have been to the movies.

LAURA.   All this time at the movies?

TOM.   There was a very long program. There was a Garbo picture and a Mickey Mouse and a travelogue and a newsreel and a preview of coming attractions. And there was an organ solo and a collection for the milk-fund—simultaneously—which ended up in a terrible fight between a fat lady and an usher!

LAURA   (*Innocently.*) Did you have to stay through everything?

TOM.   Of course! And, oh, I forgot! There was a big stage show! The headliner on this stage show was Malvolio the Magician. He performed wonderful tricks, many of them, such as pouring water back and forth between pitchers. First it turned to wine and then it turned to beer and then it turned to whiskey. I know it was whiskey it finally turned into because he needed somebody to come up out of the audience to help him, and I came up—both shows! It was Kentucky Straight Bourbon. A very generous fellow, he gave souvenirs. (*He pulls from his back pocket a shimmering rainbow-colored scarf.*) He gave me this. This is his magic scarf. You can have it, Laura. You wave it over a canary cage and you get a bowl of gold-fish. You wave it over the gold-fish bowl and they fly away canaries. . . . But the wonderfullest trick of all was the coffin trick. We nailed him into a coffin and he got out of the coffin without removing one nail. (*He has come inside.*) There is a trick that would come in handy for me—get me out of this 2 by 4 situation! (*Flops onto bed and starts removing shoes*)

LAURA.   Tom—Shhh!

TOM.   What're you shushing me for?

LAURA.   You'll wake up Mother.

TOM.   Goody, goody! Pay 'er back for all those "Rise an' Shines." (*Lies down, groaning.*) You know it don't take much intelligence to get yourself into a nailed-up coffin, Laura. But who in hell ever got himself out of one without removing one nail?

(*As if in answer, the father's grinning photograph lights up.*)

(*Scene dims out.*)

(*Immediately following: The church bell is heard striking six. At the sixth stroke the alarm clock goes off in AMANDA'S room, and after a few moments we hear her calling: "Rise and Shine! Rise and Shine! Laura, go tell your brother to rise and shine!"*)

TOM.   (*Sitting up slowly.*) I'll rise—but I won't shine.

(*The light increases.*)

AMANDA.   Laura, tell your brother his coffee is ready.

(LAURA *slips into front room.*)

LAURA.   Tom!—It's nearly seven. Don't make Mother nervous. (*He stares at her stupidly. Beseechingly.*) Tom, speak to Mother this morning. Make up with her, apologize, speak to her!

TOM.   She won't to me. It's her that started not speaking.

LAURA.   If you just say you're sorry she'll start speaking.

TOM.   Her not speaking—is that such a tragedy?

LAURA.   Please—please!

AMANDA.   (*Calling from kitchenette.*) Laura, are you going to do what I asked you to do, or do I have to get dressed and go out myself.

LAURA.   Going, going—soon as I get on my coat! (*She pulls on a shapeless felt hat with nervous, jerky movement, pleadingly glancing at* TOM. *Rushes awkwardly for coat. The coat is one of* AMANDA'S, *inaccurately made-over, the sleeves too short for* LAURA.) Butter and what else?

AMANDA.   (*Entering upstage.*) Just butter. Tell them to charge it.

LAURA.   Mother, they make such faces when I do that.

AMANDA.   Sticks and stones can break our bones, but the expression on Mr. Garfinkel's face won't harm us! Tell your brother his coffee is getting cold.

LAURA.   (*At door.*) Do what I asked you, will you, will you, Tom?

(*He looks sullenly away.*)

AMANDA.   Laura, go now or just don't go at all!

LAURA.   (*Rushing out.*) Going—going! (*A second later she cries out. TOM springs up and crosses to door. AMANDA rushes anxiously in. TOM opens the door.*)

TOM.   Laura?

LAURA.   I'm all right. I slipped, but I'm all right.

AMANDA.   (*Peering anxiously after her.*) If anyone breaks a leg on those fire-escape steps, the landlord ought to be sued for every cent he possesses! (*She shuts door. Remembers she isn't speaking and returns to other room.*)

(*As TOM enters listlessly for his coffee, she turns her back to him and stands rigidly facing the window on the gloomy gray vault of the areaway. Its light on her face with its aged but childish features is cruelly sharp, satirical as a Daumier print.*)

(*Music under: "Ave Maria"*)

(*TOM glances sheepishly but sullenly at her averted figure and slumps at the table. The coffee is scalding hot; he sips it and gasps and spits it back in the cup. At his gasp, AMANDA catches her breath and half turns. Then catches herself and turns back to window.*)

(*TOM blows on his coffee, glancing sidewise at his mother. She clears her throat. TOM clears his. He starts to rise. Sinks back down again, scratches his head, clears his throat again. AMANDA coughs. TOM raises his cup in both hands to blow on it, his eyes staring over the rim of it at his mother for several moments. Then he slowly sets the cup down and awkwardly and hesitantly rises from the chair.*)

TOM.   (*Hoarsely.*) Mother. I—I apologize, Mother. (*AMANDA draws a quick, shuddering breath. Her face works grotesquely. She breaks into childlike tears.*) I'm sorry for what I said, for everything that I said, I didn't mean it.

AMANDA.   (*Sobbingly.*) My devotion has made me a witch and so I make myself hateful to my children!

TOM.   No, you *don't*.

AMANDA.   I worry so much, don't sleep, it makes me nervous!

TOM.   (*Gently.*) I understand that.

AMANDA.   I've had to put up a solitary battle all these years. But you're my right-hand bower! Don't fall down, don't fail!

TOM.   (*Gently.*) I try, Mother.

AMANDA.   (*With great enthusiasm.*) Try and you will SUCCEED! (*The notion makes her breathless.*) Why, you—you're just *full* of natural endowments! Both of my children—they're *unusual* children! Don't you think I know it? I'm so—*proud!* Happy and—feel I've—so much to be thankful for but— Promise me one thing, Son!

TOM.   What, Mother?

AMANDA.   Promise, son, you'll—never be a drunkard!
TOM.   (*Turns to her grinning.*) I will never be a drunkard, Mother.
AMANDA.   That's what frightened me so, that you'd be drinking! Eat a bowl of Purina!
TOM.   Just coffee, Mother.
AMANDA.   Shredded wheat biscuit?
TOM.   No. No, Mother, just coffee.
AMANDA.   You can't put in a day's work on an empty stomach. You've got ten minutes—don't gulp! Drinking too-hot liquids makes cancer of the stomach. . . . Put cream in.
TOM.   No, thank you.
AMANDA.   To cool it.
TOM.   No! No, thank you, I want it black.
AMANDA.   I know, but it's not good for you. We have to do all that we can to build ourselves up. In these trying times we live in, all that we have to cling to is—each other. . . . That's why it's so important to— Tom, I— I sent out your sister so I could discuss something with you. If you hadn't spoken, I would have spoken to you. (*Sits down.*)
TOM.   (*Gently.*) What is it, Mother, that you want to discuss?
AMANDA.   *Laura!*

(TOM *put his cup down slowly.*)

(*Music: "The Glass Menagerie"*)

TOM.   —Oh.—Laura . . .
AMANDA.   (*Touching his sleeve.*) You know how Laura is. So quiet but—still water runs deep! She notices things and I think she— broods about them. (TOM *looks up.*) A few days ago I came in and she was crying.
TOM.   What about?
AMANDA.   You.
TOM.   Me?
AMANDA.   She has an idea that you're not happy here.
TOM.   What gave her that idea?
AMANDA.   What gives her any idea? However, you do act strangely. I—I'm not criticizing, understand *that!* I know your ambitions do not lie in the warehouse, that like everybody in the whole wide world—you've had to—make sacrifices, but—Tom—Tom—life's not easy, it calls for—Spartan endurance! There's so many things in my heart that I cannot describe to you! I've never told you but I—*loved* your father. . . .
TOM.   (*Gently.*) I know that, Mother.
AMANDA.   And you—when I see you taking after his ways! Staying out late—and—well, you *had* been drinking the night you were in that—terrifying condition! Laura says that you hate the apartment and that you go out nights to get away from it! Is that true, Tom?
TOM.   No. You say there's so much in your heart that you can't de-

scribe to me. That's true of me, too. There's so much in my heart
that I can't describe to *you!* So let's respect each other's—

AMANDA.   But, why—*why*, Tom—are you always so *restless?* Where
do you *go* to, nights?

TOM.   I—go to the movies.

AMANDA.   Why do you go to the movies so much, Tom?

TOM.   I go to the movies because—I like adventure. Adventure is
something I don't have much of at work, so I go to the movies.

AMANDA.   But, Tom, you go to the movies *entirely* too *much!*

TOM.   I like a lot of adventure.

(AMANDA *looks baffled, then hurt. As the familiar inquisition
resumes, he becomes hard and impatient again.* AMANDA *slips
back into her querulous attitude toward him.*)

AMANDA.   Most young men find adventure in their careers.

TOM.   Then most young men are not employed in a warehouse.

AMANDA.   The world is full of young men employed in warehouses
and offices and factories.

TOM.   Do all of them find adventure in their careers?

AMANDA.   They do or they do without it! Not everybody has a craze
for adventure.

TOM.   Man is by instinct a lover, a hunter, a fighter, and none of
those instincts are given much play at the warehouse!

AMANDA.   Man is by instinct! Don't quote instinct to me! Instinct is
something that people have got away from! It belongs to animals!
Christian adults don't want it!

TOM.   What do Christian adults want, then, Mother?

AMANDA.   Superior things! Things of the mind and the spirit! Only
animals have to satisfy instincts! Surely your aims are somewhat
higher than theirs! Than monkeys—pigs—

TOM.   I reckon they're not.

AMANDA.   You're joking. However, that isn't what I wanted to discuss.

TOM.   (*Rising.*) I haven't much time.

AMANDA.   (*Pushing his shoulders.*) Sit down.

TOM.   You want me to punch in red at the warehouse, Mother?

AMANDA.   You have five minutes. I want to talk about Laura.

TOM.   All right! What about Laura?

AMANDA.   We have to be making some plans and provisions for her.
She's older than you, two years, and nothing has happened. She
just drifts along doing nothing. It frightens me terribly how she
just drifts along.

TOM.   I guess she's the type that people call home girls.

AMANDA.   There's no such type, and if there is, it's a pity! That is
unless the home is hers, with a husband!

TOM.   What?

AMANDA.   Oh, I can see the handwriting on the wall as plain as I
see the nose in front of my face! It's terrifying!
More and more you remind me of your father! He was out all

hours without explanation!—then *left! Good-bye!*

And me with the bag to hold. I saw that letter you got from the Merchant Marine. I know what you're dreaming of. I'm not standing here blindfolded.

Very well, then. Then *do* it!

But not till there's somebody to take your place.

TOM.   What do you mean?

AMANDA.   I mean that as soon as Laura has got somebody to take care of her, married, a home of her own, independent—why, then you'll be free to go wherever you please, on land, on sea, whichever way the wind blows you!

But until that time you've got to look out for your sister. I don't say me because I'm old and don't matter! I say for your sister because she's young and dependent.

I put her in business college—a dismal failure! Frightened her so it made her sick at the stomach.

I took her over to the Young People's League at the church. Another fiasco. She spoke to nobody, nobody spoke to her. Now all she does is fool with those pieces of glass and play those worn-out records. What kind of a life is that for a girl to lead?

TOM.   What can I do about it?

AMANDA.   Overcome selfishness! Self, self, self is all that you ever think of!

(TOM *springs up and crosses to get his coat. It is ugly and bulky. He pulls on a cap with earmuffs.*)

Where is your muffler? Put your wool muffler on!

(*He snatches it angrily from the closet and tosses it around his neck and pulls both ends tight.*)

Tom! I haven't said what I had in mind to ask you.

TOM.   I'm too late to—

AMANDA.   (*Catching his arm—very importunately. Then shyly.*) Down at the warehouse, aren't there some—nice young men?

TOM.   No!

AMANDA.   There *must* be— *some* . . .

TOM.   Mother—

(*Gesture.*)

AMANDA.   Find out one that's clean-living—doesn't drink and—ask him out for sister!

TOM.   What?

AMANDA.   For *sister!* To *meet! Get acquainted!*

TOM.   (*Stamping to door.*) Oh, my *go-osh!*

AMANDA.   Will you? (*He opens door. Imploringly.*) Will you? (*He starts down.*) Will you? *Will* you, dear?

TOM.   (*Calling back.*) Yes!

(AMANDA *closes the door hesitantly and with a troubled but faintly hopeful expression.*)

(*Spot* AMANDA *at phone.*)

AMANDA.   Ella Cartwright? This is Amanda Wingfield! How are you, honey? How is that kidney condition?

(*Count five.*)

   Horrors!

(*Count five.*)

   You're a Christian martyr, yes, honey, that's what you are, a Christian martyr!

   Well, I just now happened to notice in my little red book that your subscription to the *Companion* has just run out! I knew that you wouldn't want to miss out on the wonderful serial starting in this new issue. It's by Bessie Mae Hopper, the first thing she's written since *Honeymoon for Three*.

   Wasn't that a strange and interesting story? Well, this one is even lovelier, I believe. It has a sophisticated, society background. It's all about the horsey set on Long Island!

(*Fade out.*)

SCENE 5

   It is early dusk of a spring evening. Supper has just been finished in the Wingfield apartment. AMANDA *and* LAURA *in light-colored dresses are removing dishes from the table, in the upstage area, which is shadowy, their movements formalized almost as a dance or ritual, their moving forms as pale and silent as moths.*

   TOM, *in white shirt and trousers, rises from the table and crosses toward the fire-escape.*

AMANDA.   (*As he passes her.*) Son, will you do me a favor?

TOM.   What?

AMANDA.   Comb your hair! You look so pretty when your hair is combed! (TOM *slouches on sofa with evening paper.*) There is only one respect in which I would like you to emulate your father.

TOM.   What respect is that?

AMANDA.   The care he always took of his appearance. He never allowed himself to look untidy. (*He throws down the paper and crosses to fire-escape.*) Where are you going?

TOM.   I'm going out to smoke.

AMANDA.   You smoke too much. A pack a day at fifteen cents a pack. How much would that amount to in a month? Thirty times fifteen is how much, Tom? Figure it out and you will be astounded at what you could save. Enough to give you a night-school course in accounting at Washington U! Just think what a wonderful thing that would be for you, Son!

(TOM *is unmoved by the thought.*)

TOM.   I'd rather smoke. (*He steps out on landing, letting the screen door slam.*)

AMANDA.   (*Sharply.*) I know! That's the tragedy of it. . . . (*Alone, she turns to look at her husband's picture.*)

(*Dance music: "All the World Is Waiting for the Sunrise!"*)

TOM.   (*To the audience.*) Across the alley from us was the Paradise Dance Hall. On evenings in spring the windows and doors were open and the music came outdoors. Sometimes the lights were turned out except for a large glass sphere that hung from the ceiling. It would turn slowly about and filter the dusk with delicate rainbow colors. Then the orchestra played a waltz or a tango, something that had a slow and sensuous rhythm. Couples would come outside, to the relative privacy of the alley. You could see them kissing behind ash-pits and telephone poles.

This was the compensation for lives that passed like mine, without any change or adventure.

Adventure and change were imminent in this year. They were waiting around the corner for all these kids.

Suspended in the mist over Berchtesgaden, caught in the folds of Chamberlain's umbrella—

In Spain there was Guernica!

But here there was only hot swing music and liquor, dance halls, bars, and movies, and sex that hung in the gloom like a chandelier and flooded the world with brief, deceptive rainbows. . . .

All the world was waiting for bombardments!

(AMANDA *turns from the picture and comes outside.*)

AMANDA.   (*Sighing.*) A fire-escape landing's a poor excuse for a porch. (*She spreads a newspaper on a step and sits down, gracefully and demurely as if she were settling into a swing on a Mississippi veranda.*) What are you looking at?

TOM.   The moon.

AMANDA.   Is there a moon this evening?

TOM.   It's rising over Garfinkel's Delicatessen.

AMANDA.   So it is! A little silver slipper of a moon. Have you made a wish on it yet?

TOM.   Um-hum.

AMANDA.   What did you wish for?

TOM.   That's a secret.

AMANDA.   A secret, huh? Well, I won't tell mine either. I will be just as mysterious as you.

TOM.   I bet I can guess what yours is.

AMANDA.   Is my head so transparent?

TOM.   You're not a sphinx.

AMANDA.   No, I don't have secrets. I'll tell you what I wished for on the moon. Success and happiness for my precious children! I wish for that whenever there's a moon, and when there isn't a moon, I wish for it, too.

TOM.   I thought perhaps you wished for a gentleman caller.

AMANDA. Why do you say that?
TOM. Don't you remember asking me to fetch one?
AMANDA. I remember suggesting that it would be nice for your
    sister if you brought home some nice young man from the ware-
    house. I think that I've made that suggestion more than once.
TOM. Yes, you have made it repeatedly.
AMANDA. Well?
TOM. We are going to have one.
AMANDA. *What?*
TOM. A gentleman caller!

(*The annunciation is celebrated with music.*)

(AMANDA *rises.*)

AMANDA. You mean you have asked some nice young man to come
    over?
TOM. Yep. I've asked him to dinner.
AMANDA. You really did?
TOM. I did!
AMANDA. You did, and did he—*accept?*
TOM. He did!
AMANDA. Well, well—well, well! That's—lovely!
TOM. I thought that you would be pleased.
AMANDA. It's definite, then?
TOM. Very definite.
AMANDA. Soon?
TOM. Very soon.
AMANDA. For heaven's sake, stop putting on and tell me some
    things, will you?
TOM. What things do you want me to tell you?
AMANDA. *Naturally* I would like to know when he's *coming!*
TOM. He's coming tomorrow.
AMANDA. *Tomorrow?*
TOM. Yep. Tomorrow.
AMANDA. But, Tom!
TOM. Yes, Mother?
AMANDA. Tomorrow gives me no time!
TOM. Time for what?
AMANDA. Preparations! Why didn't you phone me at once, as soon
    as you asked him, the minute that he accepted? Then, don't you
    see, I could have been getting ready!
TOM. You don't have to make any fuss.
AMANDA. Oh, Tom, Tom, Tom, of course I have to make a fuss! I
    want things nice, not sloppy! Not thrown together. I'll certainly
    have to do some fast thinking, won't I?
TOM. I don't see why you have to think at all.
AMANDA. You just don't know. We can't have a gentleman caller
    in a pig-sty! All my wedding silver has to be polished, the mono-
    grammed table linen ought to be laundered! The windows have to

be washed and fresh curtains put up. And how about clothes? We
have to *wear* something, don't we?

TOM.   Mother, this boy is no one to make a fuss over!

AMANDA.   Do you realize he's the first young man we've introduced
to your sister?

It's terrible, dreadful, disgraceful that poor little sister has never
received a single gentleman caller! Tom, come inside! (*She opens
the screen door.*)

TOM.   What for?

AMANDA.   I want to ask you some things.

TOM.   If you're going to make such a fuss, I'll call it off, I'll tell him
not to come!

AMANDA.   You certainly won't do anything of the kind. Nothing of-
fends people worse than broken engagements. It simply means
I'll have to work like a Turk! We won't be brilliant, but we will
pass inspection. Come on inside. (*TOM follows, groaning.*) Sit
down.

TOM.   Any particular place you would like me to sit?

AMANDA.   Thank heavens I've got that new sofa! I'm also making
payments on a floor lamp I'll have sent out! And put the chintz
covers on, they'll brighten things up! Of course I'd hoped to have
these walls re-papered. . . . What is the young man's name?

TOM.   His name is O'Connor.

AMANDA.   That, of course, means fish—tomorrow is Friday! I'll have
that salmon loaf—with Durkee's dressing! What does he do? He
works at the warehouse?

TOM.   Of course! How else would I—

AMANDA.   Tom, he—doesn't drink?

TOM.   Why do you ask me that?

AMANDA.   Your father *did!*

TOM.   Don't get started on that!

AMANDA.   He *does* drink, then?

TOM.   Not that I know of!

AMANDA.   Make sure, be certain! The last thing I want for my
daughter's a boy who drinks!

TOM.   Aren't you being a little bit premature? Mr. O'Connor has not
yet appeared on the scene!

AMANDA.   But will tomorrow. To meet your sister, and what do I
know about his character? Nothing! Old maids are better off than
wives of drunkards!

TOM.   Oh, my God!

AMANDA.   Be still!

TOM.   (*Leaning forward to whisper.*) Lots of fellows meet girls whom
they don't marry!

AMANDA.   Oh, talk sensibly, Tom—and don't be sarcastic! (*She has
gotten a hairbrush.*)

TOM.   What are you doing?

AMANDA.   I'm brushing that cow-lick down! What is this young man's position at the warehouse?

TOM.   (*Submitting grimly to the brush and the interrogation.*) This young man's position is that of a shipping clerk, Mother.

AMANDA.   Sounds to me like a fairly responsible job, the sort of a job *you* would be in if you just had more *get-up*.
    What is his salary? Have you any idea?

TOM.   I would judge it to be approximately eighty-five dollars a month.

AMANDA.   Well—not princely, but—

TOM.   Twenty more than I make.

AMANDA.   Yes, how well I know! But for a family man, eighty-five dollars a month is not much more than you can just get by on. . . .

TOM.   Yes, but Mr. O'Connor is not a family man.

AMANDA.   He might be, mightn't he? Some time in the future?

TOM.   I see. Plans and provisions.

AMANDA.   You are the only young man that I know of who ignores the fact that the future becomes the present, the present the past, and the past turns into everlasting regret if you don't plan for it!

TOM.   I will think that over and see what I can make of it.

AMANDA.   Don't be supercilious with your mother! Tell me some more about this—what do you call him?

TOM.   James D. O'Connor. The D. is for Delaney.

AMANDA.   Irish on *both* sides! *Gracious!* And doesn't drink?

TOM.   Shall I call him up and ask him right this minute?

AMANDA.   The only way to find out about those things is to make discreet inquiries at the proper moment. When I was a girl in Blue Mountain and it was suspected that a young man drank, the girl whose attentions he had been receiving, if any girl *was*, would sometimes speak to the minister of his church, or rather her father would if her father was living, and sort of feel him out on the young man's character. That is the way such things are discreetly handled to keep a young woman from making a tragic mistake!

TOM.   Then how did you happen to make a tragic mistake?

AMANDA.   That innocent look of your father's had everyone fooled! He *smiled*—the world was *enchanted!*
    No girl can do worse than put herself at the mercy of a handsome appearance!
    I hope that Mr. O'Connor is not too good-looking.

TOM.   No, he's not too good-looking. He's covered with freckles and hasn't too much of a nose.

AMANDA.   He's not right-down homely, though?

TOM.   Not right-down homely. Just medium homely, I'd say.

AMANDA.   Character's what to look for in a man.

TOM.   That's what I've always said, Mother.

AMANDA.   You've never said anything of the kind and I suspect you would never give it a thought.

TOM.   Don't be so suspicious of me.

AMANDA.   At least I hope he's the type that's up and coming.

TOM.   I think he really goes in for self-improvement.

AMANDA.   What reason have you to think so?

TOM.   He goes to night school.

AMANDA.   (*Beaming.*) Splendid! What does he do, I mean study?

TOM.   Radio engineering and public speaking!

AMANDA.   Then he has visions of being advanced in the world!
Any young man who studies public speaking is aiming to have an executive job some day!
And radio engineering? A thing for the future!
Both of these facts are very illuminating. Those are the sort of things that a mother should know concerning any young man who comes to call on her daughter. Seriously or—not.

TOM.   One little warning. He doesn't know about Laura. I didn't let on that we had dark ulterior motives. I just said, why don't you come and have dinner with us? He said okay and that was the whole conversation.

AMANDA.   I bet it was! You're eloquent as an oyster.
However, he'll know about Laura when he gets here. When he sees how lovely and sweet and pretty she is, he'll thank his lucky stars he was asked to dinner.

TOM.   Mother, you mustn't expect too much of Laura.

AMANDA.   What do you mean?

TOM.   Laura seems all those things to you and me because she's ours and we love her. We don't even notice she's crippled any more.

AMANDA.   Don't say crippled! You know that I never allow that word to be used!

TOM.   But face facts, Mother. She is and—that's not all—

AMANDA.   What do you mean "not all"?

TOM.   Laura is very different from other girls.

AMANDA.   I think the difference is all to her advantage.

TOM.   Not quite all—in the eyes of others—strangers—she's terribly shy and lives in a world of her own and those things make her seem a little peculiar to people outside the house.

AMANDA.   Don't say peculiar.

TOM.   Face the facts. She is.

(*The dance-hall music changes to a tango that has a minor and somewhat ominous tone.*)

AMANDA.   In what way is she peculiar—may I ask?

TOM.   (*Gently.*) She lives in a world of her own—a world of—little glass ornaments, Mother. . . . (*Gets up.* AMANDA *remains, holding brush, looking at him, troubled.*) She plays old phonograph records and—that's about all— (*He glances at himself in the mirror and crosses to door.*)

AMANDA.   (*Sharply.*) Where are you going?

TOM.   I'm going to the movies. (*Out screen door.*)

AMANDA.   Not to the movies, every night to the movies! (*Follows*

quickly to screen door.) I don't believe you always go to the movies!
(*He is gone.* AMANDA *looks worriedly after him for a moment.
Then vitality and optimism return and she turns from the door.
Crossing to portieres.*) Laura! Laura! (LAURA *answers from
kitchenette.*)

LAURA.   Yes, Mother.

AMANDA.   Let those dishes go and come in front! (LAURA *appears
with dish towel. Gaily.*) Laura, come here and make a wish on the
moon!

LAURA.   (*Entering.*) Moon—moon?

AMANDA.   A little silver slipper of a moon. Look over your left
shoulder, Laura, and make a wish!

(LAURA *looks faintly puzzled as if called out of sleep.* AMANDA
seizes her shoulders and turns her at an angle by the door.)

Now! Now, darling, *wish!*

LAURA.   What shall I wish for, Mother?

AMANDA.   (*Her voice trembling and her eyes suddenly filling with
tears.*) Happiness! Good fortune!

(*The violin rises and the stage dims out.*)

CURTAIN

SCENE 6

TOM.   And so the following evening I brought Jim home to dinner. I
had known Jim slightly in high school. In high school Jim was a
hero. He had tremendous Irish good nature and vitality with the
scrubbed and polished look of white chinaware. He seemed to
move in a continual spotlight. He was a star in basketball, captain
of the debating club, president of the senior class and the glee
club and he sang the male lead in the annual light operas. He was
always running or bounding, never just walking. He seemed always at the point of defeating the law of gravity. He was shooting
with such velocity through his adolescence that you would logically
expect him to arrive at nothing short of the White House by the
time he was thirty. But Jim apparently ran into more interference
after his graduation from Soldan. His speed had definitely slowed.
Six years after he left high school he was holding a job that
wasn't much better than mine.

He was the only one at the warehouse with whom I was on
friendly terms. I was valuable to him as someone who could remember his former glory, who had seen him win basketball games
and the silver cup in debating. He knew of my secret practice of
retiring to a cabinet of the wash-room to work on poems when
business was slack in the warehouse. He called me Shakespeare.
And while the other boys in the warehouse regarded me with
suspicious hostility, Jim took a humorous attitude toward me.

Gradually his attitude affected the others, their hostility wore off
and they also began to smile at me as people smile at an oddly
fashioned dog who trots across their path at some distance.

I knew that Jim and Laura had known each other at Soldan,
and I had heard Laura speak admiringly of his voice. I didn't know
if Jim remembered her or not. In high school Laura had been as
unobtrusive as Jim had been astonishing. If he did remember
Laura, it was not as my sister, for when I asked him to dinner, he
grinned and said, "You know, Shakespeare, I never thought of
you as having folks!"

He was about to discover that I did. . . .

(*Light up stage.*)

(*Friday evening. It is about five o'clock of a late spring evening
which comes "scattering poems in the sky."*)

(*A delicate lemony light is in the Wingfield apartment.*)

(*AMANDA has worked like a Turk in preparation for the gentleman caller. The results are astonishing. The new floor lamp with
its rose-silk shade is in place, a colored paper lantern conceals
the broken light fixture in the ceiling, new billowing white curtains are at the windows, chintz covers are on chairs and sofa, a
pair of new sofa pillows make their initial appearance.*)

(*Open boxes and tissue paper are scattered on the floor.*)

(*LAURA stands in the middle with lifted arms while AMANDA
crouches before her, adjusting the hem of the new dress, devout
and ritualistic. The dress is colored and designed by memory. The
arrangement of LAURA'S hair is changed; it is softer and more
becoming. A fragile, unearthly prettiness has come out in LAURA:
she is like a piece of translucent glass touched by light, given a
momentary radiance, not actual, not lasting.*)

AMANDA.   (*Impatiently.*) Why are you trembling?
LAURA.   Mother, you've made me so nervous!
AMANDA.   How have I made you nervous?
LAURA.   By all this fuss! You make it seem so important!
AMANDA.   I don't understand you, Laura. You couldn't be satisfied
with just sitting home, and yet whenever I try to arrange some-
thing for you, you seem to resist it.

(*She gets up.*)

Now take a look at yourself.

No, wait! Wait just a moment—I have an idea!
LAURA.   What is it now?

(*AMANDA produces two powder puffs which she wraps in handkerchiefs and stuffs in LAURA'S bosom.*)

LAURA.   Mother, what are you doing?
AMANDA.   They call them "Gay Deceivers"!
LAURA.   I won't wear them!
AMANDA.   You will!

LAURA.   Why should I?
AMANDA.   Because, to be painfully honest, your chest is flat.
LAURA.   You make it seem like we were setting a trap.
AMANDA.   All pretty girls are a trap, a pretty trap, and men expect
them to be.
    Now look at yourself, young lady. This is the prettiest you will
ever be!
    I've got to fix myself now! You're going to be surprised by your
mother's appearance! (*She crosses through portieres, humming
gaily.*)
    (LAURA *moves slowly to the long mirror and stares solemnly at
herself.*)
    (*A wind blows the white curtains inward in a slow, graceful mo-
tion and with a faint, sorrowful sighing.*)
AMANDA.   (*Off stage.*) It isn't dark enough yet. (LAURA *turns slowly
before the mirror with a troubled look.*)
AMANDA.   (*Laughing, off.*) I'm going to show you something. I'm
going to make a spectacular appearance!
LAURA.   What is it, Mother?
AMANDA.   Possess your soul in patience—you will see!
    Something I've resurrected from that old trunk! Styles haven't
changed so terribly much after all. . . .
(*She parts the portieres.*)
    Now just look at your mother!
(*She wears a girlish frock of yellowed voile with a blue silk sash.
She carries a bunch of jonquils—the legend of her youth is nearly
revived. Feverishly.*)
    This is the dress in which I led the cotillion. Won the cakewalk
twice at Sunset Hill, wore one spring to the Governor's ball in
Jackson!
    See how I sashayed around the ballroom, Laura?
(*She raises her skirt and does a mincing step around the room.*)
    I wore it on Sundays for my gentlemen callers! I had it on the
day I met your father—
    I had malaria fever all that spring. The change of climate
from East Tennessee to the Delta—weakened resistance—I had
a little temperature all the time—not enough to be serious—just
enough to make me restless and giddy!—Invitations poured in—
parties all over the Delta!—"Stay in bed," said Mother, "you have
fever!"—but I just wouldn't.—I took quinine but kept on going,
going!—Evenings, dances!—Afternoons, long, long rides! Picnics
—lovely!—So lovely, that country in May.—All lacy with dogwood,
literally flooded with jonquils!—That was the spring I had the
craze for jonquils. Jonquils became an absolute obsession. Mother
said, "Honey, there's no more room for jonquils." And still I kept
on bringing in more jonquils. Whenever, wherever I saw them, I'd

say, "Stop! Stop! I see jonquils!" I made the young men help me gather the jonquils! It was a joke, Amanda and her jonquils! Finally there were no more vases to hold them, every available space was filled with jonquils. No vases to hold them? All right, I'll hold them myself! And then I—(*She stops in front of the picture. Music.*) met your father!

Malaria fever and jonquils and then—this—boy. . . .

(*She switches on the rose-colored lamp.*)

I hope they get here before it starts to rain.

(*She crosses upstage and places the jonquils in bowl on table.*)

I gave your brother a little extra change so he and Mr. O'Connor could take the service car home.

LAURA.   (*With altered look.*) What did you say his name was?

AMANDA.   O'Connor.

LAURA.   What is his first name?

AMANDA.   I don't remember. Oh, yes, I do. It was—Jim!

(LAURA *sways slightly and catches hold of a chair.*)

LAURA.   (*Faintly.*) Not—Jim!

AMANDA.   Yes, that was it, it was Jim! I've never known a Jim that wasn't nice!

(*Music: Ominous*)

LAURA.   Are you sure his name is Jim O'Connor?

AMANDA.   Yes. Why?

LAURA.   Is he the one that Tom used to know in high school?

AMANDA.   He didn't say so. I think he just got to know him at the warehouse.

LAURA.   There was a Jim O'Connor we both knew in high school —(*Then, with effort.*) If that is the one that Tom is bringing to dinner—you'll have to excuse me, I won't come to the table.

AMANDA.   What sort of nonsense is this?

LAURA.   You asked me once if I'd ever liked a boy. Don't you remember I showed you this boy's picture?

AMANDA.   You mean the boy you showed me in the year book?

LAURA.   Yes, that boy.

AMANDA.   Laura, Laura, were you in love with that boy?

LAURA.   I don't know, Mother. All I know is I couldn't sit at the table if it was him!

AMANDA.   It won't be him! It isn't the least bit likely. But whether it is or not, you will come to the table. You will not be excused.

LAURA.   I'll have to be, Mother.

AMANDA.   I don't intend to humor your silliness, Laura. I've had too much from you and your brother, both!

So just sit down and compose yourself till they come. Tom has forgotten his key so you'll have to let them in, when they arrive.

LAURA.   (*Panicky.*) Oh, Mother—*you* answer the door!

AMANDA.   (*Lightly.*) I'll be in the kitchen—busy!

LAURA.   Oh, Mother, please answer the door, don't make me do it!

AMANDA.　(*Crossing into kitchenette.*) I've got to fix the dressing for the salmon. Fuss, fuss—silliness!—over a gentleman caller!

(*Door swings shut. LAURA is left alone.*)

(*She utters a low moan and turns off the lamp, sits stiffly on the edge of the sofa, knotting her fingers together.*)

(*TOM and* JIM *appear on the fire-escape steps and climb to landing. Hearing their approach, LAURA rises with a panicky gesture. She retreats to the portieres.*)

(*The doorbell. LAURA catches her breath and touches her throat. Low drums.*)

AMANDA.　(*Calling.*) Laura, sweetheart! The door!

(*LAURA stares at it without moving.*)

JIM.　I think we just beat the rain.

TOM.　Uh-huh. (*He rings again, nervously. JIM whistles and fishes for a cigarette.*)

AMANDA.　(*Very, very gaily.*) Laura, that is your brother and Mr. O'Connor! Will you let them in, darling?

(*LAURA crosses toward kitchenette door.*)

LAURA　(*Breathlessly.*) Mother—you go to the door!

(*AMANDA steps out of kitchenette and stares furiously at LAURA. She points imperiously at the door.*)

LAURA.　Please, please!

AMANDA.　(*In a fierce whisper.*) What is the matter with you, you silly thing?

LAURA.　(*Desperately.*) Please, you answer it, *please!*

AMANDA.　I told you I wasn't going to humor you, Laura. Why have you chosen this moment to lose your mind?

LAURA.　Please, please, please, you go!

AMANDA.　You'll have to go to the door because I can't!

LAURA.　(*Despairingly.*) I can't either!

AMANDA.　Why?

LAURA.　I'm *sick!*

AMANDA.　I'm sick, too—of your nonsense! Why can't you and your brother be normal people? Fantastic whims and behavior!

(*TOM gives a long ring.*)

Preposterous goings on! Can you give me one reason—(*Calls out lyrically.*) COMING! JUST ONE SECOND!—why you should be afraid to open a door? Now you answer it, Laura!

LAURA.　Oh, oh, oh . . . (*She returns through the portieres. Darts to the victrola and winds it frantically and turns it on.*)

AMANDA.　Laura Wingfield, you march right to that door!

LAURA.　Yes—yes, Mother!

(*A faraway, scratchy rendition of "Dardanella" softens the air and gives her strength to move through it. She slips to the door and draws it cautiously open.*)

(*TOM enters with the caller, JIM O'CONNOR.*)

TOM.   Laura, this is Jim. Jim, this is my sister, Laura.

JIM.   (*Stepping inside.*) I didn't know that Shakespeare had a sister!

LAURA.   (*Retreating stiff and trembling from the door.*) How—how do you do?

JIM.   (*Heartily extending his hand.*) Okay!

(*LAURA touches it hesitantly with hers.*)

JIM.   Your hand's *cold*, Laura!

LAURA.   Yes, well—I've been playing the victrola. . . .

JIM.   Must have been playing classical music on it! You ought to play a little hot swing music to warm you up!

LAURA.   Excuse me—I haven't finished playing the victrola. . . .

(*She turns awkwardly and hurries into the front room. She pauses a second by the victrola. Then catches her breath and darts through the portieres like a frightened deer.*)

JIM.   (*Grinning.*) What was the matter?

TOM.   Oh—with Laura? Laura is—terribly shy.

JIM.   Shy, huh? It's unusual to meet a shy girl nowadays. I don't believe you ever mentioned you had a sister.

TOM.   Well, now you know. I have one. Here is the *Post Dispatch.* You want a piece of it?

JIM.   Uh-huh.

TOM.   What piece? The comics?

JIM.   Sports! (*Glances at it*) Ole Dizzy Dean is on his bad behavior.

TOM.   (*Disinterest.*) Yeah? (*Lights cigarette and crosses back to fire-escape door.*)

JIM.   Where are *you* going?

TOM.   I'm going out on the terrace.

JIM.   (*Goes after him.*) You know, Shakespeare—I'm going to sell you a bill of goods!

TOM.   What goods?

JIM.   A course I'm taking.

TOM.   Huh?

JIM.   In public speaking! You and me, we're not the warehouse type.

TOM.   Thanks—that's good news.

But what has public speaking got to do with it?

JIM.   It fits you for—executive positions!

TOM.   Awww.

JIM.   I tell you it's done a helluva lot for me.

TOM.   In what respect?

JIM.   In every! Ask yourself what is the difference between you an' me and men in the office down front? Brains?—No!—Ability?—No! Then what? Just one little thing—

TOM.   What is that one little thing?

JIM.   Primarily it amounts to—social poise! Being able to square up to people and hold your own on any social level!

AMANDA.   (*Off stage.*) Tom?

TOM.   Yes, Mother?

AMANDA. Is that you and Mr. O'Connor?
TOM. Yes, Mother.
AMANDA. Well, you just make yourselves comfortable in there.
TOM. Yes, Mother.
AMANDA. Ask Mr. O'Connor if he would like to wash his hands.
JIM. Aw, no—no—thank you—I took care of that at the warehouse.
    Tom—
TOM. Yes.
JIM. Mr. Mendoza was speaking to me about you.
TOM. Favorably?
JIM. What do you think?
TOM. Well—
JIM. You're going to be out of a job if you don't wake up.
TOM. I am waking up—
JIM. You show no signs.
TOM. The signs are interior. I'm planning to change. (*He leans
    over the rail speaking with quiet exhilaration. The incandescent
    marquees and signs of the first-run movie houses light his face
    from across the alley. He looks like a voyager.*) I'm right at the
    point of committing myself to a future that doesn't include the
    warehouse and Mr. Mendoza or even a night-school course in
    public speaking.
JIM. What are you gassing about?
TOM. I'm tired of the movies.
JIM. Movies!
TOM. Yes, movies! Look at them— (*A wave toward the marvels of
    Grand Avenue*) All of those glamorous people—having adventures
    —hogging it all, gobbling the whole thing up! You know what
    happens? People go to the *movies* instead of *moving!* Hollywood
    characters are supposed to have all the adventures for everybody
    in America, while everybody in America sits in a dark room and
    watches them have them! Yes, until there's a war. That's when
    adventure becomes available to the masses! *Everyone's* dish, not
    only Gable's! Then the people in the dark room come out of the
    dark room to have some adventures themselves—Goody, goody!
    —It's our turn now, to go to the South Sea Island—to make a
    safari—to be exotic, far-off!—But I'm not patient. I don't want
    to wait till then. I'm tired of the *movies* and I am *about to move!*
JIM. (*Incredulously.*) Move?
TOM. Yes.
JIM. When?
TOM. Soon!
JIM. Where? Where?

(*Theme Three music seems to answer the question, while* TOM
thinks it over. He searches among his pockets.)

TOM. I'm starting to boil inside. I know I seem dreamy, but inside—
    well, I'm boiling!—Whenever I pick up a shoe, I shudder a little

thinking how short life is and what I am doing!—Whatever that means, I know it doesn't mean shoes—except as something to wear on a traveler's feet! (*Finds paper.*) Look—

JIM.   What?

TOM.   I'm a member.

JIM.   (*Reading.*) The Union of Merchant Seamen.

TOM.   I paid my dues this month, instead of the light bill.

JIM.   You will regret it when they turn the lights off.

TOM.   I won't be here.

JIM.   How about your mother?

TOM.   I'm like my father. The bastard son of a bastard! See how he grins? And he's been absent going on sixteen years!

JIM.   You're just talking, you drip. How does your mother feel about it?

TOM.   Shhh!—Here comes Mother! Mother is not acquainted with my plans!

AMANDA.   (*Enters portieres.*) Where are you all?

TOM.   On the terrace, Mother.

(*They start inside. She advances to them.* TOM *is distinctly shocked at her appearance. Even* JIM *blinks a little. He is making his first contact with girlish Southern vivacity and in spite of the night-school course in public speaking is somewhat thrown off the beam by the unexpected outlay of social charm.*)

(*Certain responses are attempted by* JIM *but are swept aside by* AMANDA'S *gay laughter and chatter.* TOM *is embarrassed but after the first shock* JIM *reacts very warmly. Grins and chuckles, is altogether won over.*)

AMANDA.   (*Coyly smiling, shaking her girlish ringlets.*) Well, well, well, so this is Mr. O'Connor. Introductions entirely unnecessary. I've heard so much about you from my boy. I finally said to him, Tom—good gracious!—why don't you bring this paragon to supper? I'd like to meet this nice young man at the warehouse!—Instead of just hearing him sing your praises so much!

I don't know why my son is so stand-offish—that's not Southern behavior!

Let's sit down and—I think we could stand a little more air in here! Tom, leave the door open. I felt a nice fresh breeze a moment ago. Where has it gone to?

Mmm, so warm already! And not quite summer, even. We're going to burn up when summer really gets started.

However, we're having—we're having a very light supper. I think light things are better fo' this time of year. The same as light clothes are. Light clothes an' light food are what warm weather calls fo'. You know our blood gets so thick during th' winter—it takes a while fo' us to *adjust* ou'selves!—when the season changes . . .

It's come so quick this year. I wasn't prepared. All of a sudden—heavens! Already summer!—I ran to the trunk an' pulled out this

light dress— Terribly old! Historical almost! But feels so good
—so good an' co-ol, y' know. . . .

TOM.   Mother—

AMANDA.   Yes, honey?

TOM.   How about—supper?

AMANDA.   Honey, you go ask Sister if supper is ready! You know that
     Sister is in full charge of supper!

     Tell her you hungry boys are waiting for it.

     (*To* JIM.)

     Have you met Laura?

JIM.   She—

AMANDA.   Let you in? Oh, good, you've met already! It's rare for a
     girl as sweet an' pretty as Laura to be domestic! But Laura is,
     thank heavens, not only pretty, but also very domestic. I'm not at
     all. I never was a bit. I never could make a thing but angel-food
     cake. Well, in the South we had so many servants. Gone, gone,
     gone. All vestige of gracious living! Gone completely! I wasn't
     prepared for what the future brought me. All of my gentlemen
     callers were sons of planters and so of course I assumed that I
     would be married to one and raise my family on a large piece of
     land with plenty of servants. But man proposes—and woman ac-
     cepts the proposal!—To vary that old, old saying a little bit—I
     married no planter! I married a man who worked for the telephone
     company!—That gallantly smiling gentleman over there! (*Points
     to the picture.*) A telephone man who—fell in love with long-
     distance!—Now he travels and I don't even know where!—But
     what am I going on for about my—tribulations?

     Tell me yours—I hope you don't have any!

     Tom?

TOM.   (*Returning.*) Yes, Mother?

AMANDA.   Is supper nearly ready?

TOM.   It looks to me like supper is on the table.

AMANDA.   Let me look— (*She rises prettily and looks through por-
     tieres.*) Oh, lovely!—But where is Sister?

TOM.   Laura is not feeling well and she says that she thinks she'd
     better not come to the table.

AMANDA.   What?—Nonsense!—Laura? Oh, Laura!

LAURA.   (*Off stage, faintly.*) Yes, Mother.

AMANDA.   You really must come to the table. We won't be seated
     until you come to the table!

     Come in, Mr. O'Connor. You sit over there, and I'll—

     Laura? Laura Wingfield!

     You're keeping us waiting, honey! We can't say grace until you
     come to the table!

(*The back door is pushed weakly open and* LAURA *comes in. She
is obviously quite faint, her lips trembling, her eyes wide and staring. She moves unsteadily toward the table.*)

(*Outside a summer storm is coming abruptly. The white curtains billow inward at the windows and there is a sorrowful murmur and deep blue dusk.*)

(LAURA *suddenly stumbles—she catches at a chair with a faint moan.*)

TOM.   Laura!

AMANDA.   Laura!

(*There is a clap of thunder.*)

(*Despairingly.*)

Why, Laura, you *are* sick, darling! Tom, help your sister into the living room, dear!

Sit in the living room, Laura—rest on the sofa.

Well!

(*To the gentleman caller.*)

Standing over the hot stove made her ill!—I told her that it was just too warm this evening, but—

(TOM *comes back in.* LAURA *is on the sofa.*)

Is Laura all right now?

TOM.   Yes.

AMANDA.   What *is* that? Rain? A nice cool rain has come up!

(*She gives the gentleman caller a frightened look.*)

I think we may—have grace—now . . .

(TOM *looks at her stupidly.*)

Tom, honey—you say grace!

TOM.   Oh . . .

"For these and all thy mercies—"

(*They bow their heads,* AMANDA *stealing a nervous glance at* JIM. *In the living room* LAURA, *stretched on the sofa, clenches her hands to her lips, to hold back a shuddering sob.*)

God's Holy Name be praised—

(*The scene dims out.*)

SCENE 7

Half an hour later. Dinner is just being finished in the upstage area which is concealed by the drawn portieres.

As the curtain rises LAURA *is still huddled upon the sofa, her feet drawn under her, her head resting on a pale blue pillow, her eyes wide and mysteriously watchful. The new floor lamp with its shade of rose-colored silk gives a soft, becoming light to her face, bringing out the fragile, unearthly prettiness which usually escapes attention. There is a steady murmur of rain, but it is slackening and stops soon after the scene begins; the air outside becomes pale and luminous as the moon breaks out.*

A moment after the curtain rises, the lights in both rooms flicker and go out.

JIM.   Hey, there, Mr. Light Bulb!

(AMANDA *laughs nervously.*)

AMANDA.   Where was Moses when the lights went out? Ha-ha. Do you know the answer to that one, Mr. O'Connor?

JIM.   No, Ma'am, what's the answer?

AMANDA.   In the dark!

(JIM *laughs appreciatively.*)

Everybody sit still. I'll light the candles. Isn't it lucky we have them on the table? Where's a match? Which of you gentlemen can provide a match?

JIM.   Here.

AMANDA.   Thank you, sir.

JIM.   Not at all, Ma'am!

AMANDA.   I guess the fuse has burnt out. Mr. O'Connor, can you tell a burnt-out fuse? I know I can't and Tom is a total loss when it comes to mechanics.

(*Sound: Getting up: Voices recede a little to kitchenette.*)

Oh, be careful you don't bump into something. We don't want our gentleman caller to break his neck. Now wouldn't that be a fine howdy-do?

JIM.   Ha-ha!

Where is the fuse box?

AMANDA.   Right here next to the stove. Can you see anything?

JIM.   Just a minute.

AMANDA.   Isn't electricity a mysterious thing?

Wasn't it Benjamin Franklin who tied a key to a kite?

We live in such a mysterious universe, don't we? Some people say that science clears up all the mysteries for us. In my opinion it only creates more!

Have you found it yet?

JIM.   No, Ma'am. All these fuses look okay to me.

AMANDA.   Tom!

TOM.   Yes. Mother?

AMANDA.   That light bill I gave you several days ago. The one I told you we got the notices about?

TOM.   Oh.—Yeah.

AMANDA.   You didn't neglect to pay it by any chance?

TOM.   Why, I—

AMANDA.   Didn't! I might have known it!

JIM.   Shakespeare probably wrote a poem on that light bill, Mrs. Wingfield.

AMANDA.   I might have known better than to trust him with it! There's such a high price for negligence in this world!

JIM.   Maybe the poem will win a ten-dollar prize.

AMANDA.   We'll just have to spend the remainder of the evening in
the nineteenth century, before Mr. Edison made the Mazda lamp!
JIM.   Candlelight is my favorite kind of light.
AMANDA.   That shows you're romantic! But that's no excuse for Tom.
Well, we got through dinner. Very considerate of them to let
us get through dinner before they plunged us into everlasting dark-
ness, wasn't it, Mr. O'Connor?
JIM.   Ha-ha!
AMANDA.   Tom, as a penalty for your carelessness you can help me
with the dishes.
JIM.   Let me give you a hand.
AMANDA.   Indeed you will not!
JIM.   I ought to be good for something.
AMANDA.   Good for something? (*Her tone is rhapsodic.*)
You? Why, Mr. O'Connor, nobody, *nobody's* given me this much
entertainment in years—as you have!
JIM.   Aw, now, Mrs. Wingfield!
AMANDA.   I'm not exaggerating, not one bit! But Sister is all by her
lonesome. You go keep her company in the parlor!
I'll give you this lovely old candelabrum that used to be on the
altar at the Church of the Heavenly Rest. It was melted a little
out of shape when the church burnt down. Lightning struck it one
spring. Gypsy Jones was holding a revival at the time and he
intimated that the church was destroyed because the Episcopalians
gave card parties.
JIM.   Ha-ha.
AMANDA.   And how about you coaxing Sister to drink a little wine?
I think it would be good for her! Can you carry both at once?
JIM.   Sure. I'm Superman!
AMANDA.   Now, Thomas, get into this apron!
(*The door of kitchenette swings closed on* AMANDA'S *gay
laughter; the flickering light approaches the portieres.*)
(LAURA *sits up nervously as he enters. Her speech at first is low
and breathless from the almost intolerable strain of being alone
with a stranger.*)
(*In her first speeches in this scene, before* JIM'S *warmth over-
comes her paralyzing shyness,* LAURA'S *voice is thin and breath-
less as though she has just run up a steep flight of stairs.*)
(JIM'S *attitude is gently humorous. In playing this scene it should
be stressed that while the incident is apparently unimportant, it
is to* LAURA *the climax of her secret life.*)
JIM.   Hello, there, Laura.
LAURA.   (*Faintly.*) Hello. (*She clears her throat.*)
JIM.   How are you feeling now? Better?
LAURA.   Yes. Yes, thank you.
JIM.   This is for you. A little dandelion wine. (*He extends it toward
her with extravagant gallantry.*)

LAURA.   Thank you.

JIM.   Drink it—but don't get drunk!

(*He laughs heartily.* LAURA *takes the glass uncertainly; laughs shyly.*)

Where shall I set the candles?

LAURA.   Oh—oh, anywhere . . .

JIM.   How about here on the floor? Any objections?

LAURA.   No.

JIM.   I'll spread a newspaper under to catch the drippings. I like to sit on the floor. Mind if I do?

LAURA.   Oh, no.

JIM.   Give me a pillow?

LAURA.   What?

JIM.   A pillow!

LAURA.   Oh . . .(*Hands him one quickly*)

JIM.   How about you? Don't you like to sit on the floor?

LAURA.   Oh—yes.

JIM.   Why don't you, then?

LAURA.   I—will.

JIM.   Take a pillow! (LAURA *does. Sits on the other side of the candelabrum.* JIM *crosses his legs and smiles engagingly at her.*) I can't hardly see you sitting way over there.

LAURA.   I can—see you.

JIM.   I know, but that's not fair, I'm in the limelight. (LAURA *moves her pillow closer.*) Good! Now I can see you! Comfortable?

LAURA.   Yes.

JIM.   So am I. Comfortable as a cow! Will you have some gum?

LAURA.   No, thank you.

JIM.   I think that I will indulge, with your permission. (*Musingly unwraps it and holds it up.*) Think of the fortune made by the guy that invented the first piece of chewing gum. Amazing, huh? The Wrigley Building is one of the sights of Chicago.—I saw it summer before last when I went to the Century of Progress. Did you take in the Century of Progress?

LAURA.   No, I didn't.

JIM.   Well, it was quite a wonderful exposition. What impressed me most was the Hall of Science. Gives you an idea of what the future will be in America, even more wonderful than the present time is! (*Pause. Smiling at her.*) Your brother tells me you're shy. Is that right, Laura?

LAURA.   I—don't know.

JIM.   I judge you to be an old-fashioned type of girl. Well, I think that's a pretty good type to be. Hope you don't think I'm being too personal—do you?

LAURA.   (*Hastily, out of embarrassment.*) I believe I *will* take a piece of gum, if you—don't mind. (*Clearing her throat.*) Mr. O'Connor, have you—kept up with your singing?

JIM.   Singing? Me?

LAURA.   Yes. I remember what a beautiful voice you had.

JIM.   When did you hear me sing?

(*Voice off stage in the pause*)

VOICE   (*Off stage.*)

> O blow, ye winds, heigh-ho
> A-roving I will go!
>   I'm off to my love
>   With a boxing glove—
> Ten thousand miles away!

JIM.   You say you've heard me sing?

LAURA.   Oh, yes! Yes, very often . . . I—don't suppose—you remember me—at all?

JIM.   (*Smiling doubtfully.*) You know I have an idea I've seen you before. I had that idea soon as you opened the door. It seemed almost like I was about to remember your name. But the name that I started to call you—wasn't a name! And so I stopped myself before I said it.

LAURA.   Wasn't it—Blue Roses?

JIM.   (*Springs up. Grinning.*) Blue Roses!—My gosh, yes—Blue Roses!

 That's what I had on my tongue when you opened the door!

 Isn't it funny what tricks your memory plays? I didn't connect you with high school somehow or other.

 But that's where it was; it was high school. I didn't even know you were Shakespeare's sister!

 Gosh, I'm sorry.

LAURA.   I didn't expect you to. You—barely knew me!

JIM.   But we did have a speaking acquaintance, huh?

LAURA.   Yes, we—spoke to each other.

JIM.   When did you recognize me?

LAURA.   Oh, right away!

JIM.   Soon as I came in the door?

LAURA.   When I heard your name I thought it was probably you. I knew that Tom used to know you a little in high school. So when you came in the door—

 Well, then I was—sure.

JIM.   Why didn't you *say* something, then?

LAURA.   (*Breathlessly.*) I didn't know what to say, I was—too surprised!

JIM.   For goodness' sakes! You know, this sure is funny!

LAURA.   Yes! Yes, isn't it, though . . .

JIM.   Didn't we have a class in something together?

LAURA.   Yes, we did.

JIM.   What class was that?

LAURA.   It was—singing—Chorus!

JIM.   Aw!

LAURA.   I sat across the aisle from you in the Aud.

JIM.   Aw.

LAURA.   Mondays, Wednesdays and Fridays.

JIM.   Now I remember—you always came in late.

LAURA.   Yes, it was so hard for me, getting upstairs. I had that brace on my leg—it clumped so loud!

JIM.   I never heard any clumping.

LAURA.   (*Wincing at the recollection.*) To me it sounded like—thunder!

JIM.   Well, well, well, I never even noticed.

LAURA.   And everybody was seated before I came in. I had to walk in front of all those people. My seat was in the back row. I had to go clumping all the way up the aisle with everyone watching!

JIM.   You shouldn't have been self-conscious.

LAURA.   I know, but I was. It was always such a relief when the singing started.

JIM.   Aw, yes, I've placed *you* now! I used to call you Blue Roses. How was it that I got started calling you that?

LAURA.   I was out of school a little while with pleurosis. When I came back you asked me what was the matter. I said I had pleurosis—you thought I said Blue Roses. That's what you always called me after that!

JIM.   I hope you didn't mind.

LAURA.   Oh, no—I liked it. You see, I wasn't acquainted with many —people. . . .

JIM.   As I remember you sort of stuck by yourself.

LAURA.   I—I—never had much luck at—making friends.

JIM.   I don't see why you wouldn't.

LAURA.   Well, I—started out badly.

JIM.   You mean being—

LAURA.   Yes, it sort of—stood between me—

JIM.   You shouldn't have let it!

LAURA.   I know, but it did, and—

JIM.   You were shy with people!

LAURA.   I tried not to be but never could—

JIM.   Overcome it?

LAURA.   No, I—I never could!

JIM.   I guess being shy is something you have to work out of kind of gradually.

LAURA   (*sorrowfully*). Yes—I guess it—

JIM.   Takes time!

LAURA.   Yes—

JIM.   People are not so dreadful when you know them. That's what you have to remember! And everybody has problems, not just you, but practically everybody has got some problems.

You think of yourself as having the only problems, as being the only one who is disappointed. But just look around you and you will see lots of people as disappointed as you are. For instance, I hoped when I was going to high school that I would be further along at this time, six years later, than I am now— You remember that wonderful write-up I had in *The Torch?*

LAURA.   Yes! (*She rises and crosses to table.*)

JIM.   It said I was bound to succeed in anything I went into! (LAURA *returns with the annual.*) Holy Jeez! *The Torch!* (*He accepts it reverently. They smile across it with mutual wonder.* LAURA *crouches beside him and they begin to turn through it.* LAURA'S *shyness is dissolving in his warmth.*)

LAURA.   Here you are in *The Pirates of Penzance!*

JIM.   (*Wistfully.*) I sang the baritone lead in that operetta.

LAURA.   (*Raptly.*) So—*beautifully!*

JIM.   (*Protesting.*) Aw—

LAURA.   Yes, yes—beautifully—beautifully!

JIM.   You heard me?

LAURA.   All three times!

JIM.   No!

LAURA.   Yes!

JIM.   All three performances?

LAURA.   (*Looking down.*) Yes.

JIM.   Why?

LAURA.   I—wanted to ask you to—autograph my program.

JIM.   Why didn't you ask me to?

LAURA.   You were always surrounded by your own friends so much that I never had a chance to.

JIM.   You should have just—

LAURA.   Well, I—thought you might think I was—

JIM.   Thought I might think you was—what?

LAURA.   Oh—

JIM.   (*With reflective relish.*) I was beleaguered by females in those days.

LAURA.   You were terribly popular!

JIM.   Yeah—

LAURA.   You had such a—friendly way—

JIM.   I was spoiled in high school.

LAURA.   Everybody— liked you!

JIM.   Including you?

LAURA.   I—yes, I—I did, too— (*She gently closes the book in her lap.*)

JIM.   Well, well, well!—Give me that program, Laura. (*She hands it to him. He signs it with a flourish.*) There you are—better late than never!

LAURA.   Oh, I—what a—surprise!

JIM.   My signature isn't worth very much right now.

But some day—maybe—it will increase in value!

Being disappointed is one thing and being discouraged is something else. I am disappointed but I am not discouraged.

I'm twenty-three years old.
How old are you?

LAURA.   I'll be twenty-four in June.

JIM.   That's not old age!

LAURA.   No, but—

JIM.   You finished high school?

LAURA.   (*With difficulty.*) I didn't go back.

JIM.   You mean you dropped out?

LAURA.   I made bad grades in my final examinations. (*She rises and replaces the book and the program. Her voice strained.*) How is— Emily Meisenbach getting along?

JIM.   Oh, that kraut-head!

LAURA.   Why do you call her that?

JIM.   That's what she was.

LAURA.   You're not still—going with her?

JIM.   I never see her.

LAURA.   It said in the Personal Section that you were—engaged!

JIM.   I know, but I wasn't impressed by that—propaganda!

LAURA.   It wasn't—the truth?

JIM.   Only in Emily's optimistic opinion!

LAURA.   Oh—

(JIM *lights a cigarette and leans indolently back on his elbows smiling at* LAURA *with a warmth and charm which lights her inwardly with altar candles. She remains by the table and turns in her hands a piece of glass to cover her tumult.*)

JIM.   (*After several reflective puffs on a cigarette.*) What have you done since high school? (*She seems not to hear him.*) Huh? (LAURA *looks up.*) I said what have you done since high school, Laura?

LAURA.   Nothing much.

JIM.   You must have been doing something these six long years.

LAURA.   Yes.

JIM.   Well, then, such as what?

LAURA.   I took a business course at business college—

JIM.   How did that work out?

LAURA.   Well, not very—well—I had to drop out, it gave me—in-digestion—

(JIM *laughs gently.*)

JIM.   What are you doing now?

LAURA.   I don't do anything—much. Oh, please don't think I sit around doing nothing! My glass collection takes up a good deal of time. Glass is something you have to take good care of.

JIM.   What did you say—about glass?

LAURA.   Collection I said—I have one— (*She clears her throat and turns away again, acutely shy.*)

JIM.   (*Abruptly.*) You know what I judge to be the trouble with you?

Inferiority complex! Know what that is? That's what they call it when someone low-rates himself!

I understand it because I had it, too. Although my case was not so aggravated as yours seems to be. I had it until I took up public speaking, developed my voice, and learned that I had an aptitude for science. Before that time I never thought of myself as being outstanding in any way whatsoever!

Now I've never made a regular study of it, but I have a friend who says I can analyze people better than doctors that make a profession of it. I don't claim that to be necessarily true, but I can sure guess a person's psychology, Laura! (*Takes out his gum.*) Excuse me, Laura. I always take it out when the flavor is gone. I'll use this scrap of paper to wrap it in. I know how it is to get it stuck on a shoe.

Yep—that's what I judge to be your principal trouble. A lack of confidence in yourself as a person. You don't have the proper amount of faith in yourself. I'm basing that fact on a number of your remarks and also on certain observations I've made. For instance that clumping you thought was so awful in high school. You say that you even dreaded to walk into class. You see what you did? You dropped out of school, you gave up an education because of a clump, which as far as I know was practically nonexistent! A little physical defect is what you have. Hardly noticeable even! Magnified thousands of times by imagination!

You know what my strong advice to you is? Think of yourself as *superior* in some way!

LAURA.   In what way would I think?

JIM.   Why, man alive, Laura! Just look about you a little. What do you see? A world full of common people! All of 'em born and all of 'em going to die!

Which of them has one-tenth of your good points! Or mine! Or anyone else's, as far as that goes—Gosh!

Everybody excels in some one thing. Some in many!

(*Unconsciously glances at himself in the mirror.*)

All you've got to do is discover in *what!*

Take me, for instance.

(*He adjusts his tie at the mirror.*)

My interest happens to lie in electro-dynamics. I'm taking a course in radio engineering at night school, Laura, on top of a fairly responsible job at the warehouse. I'm taking that course and studying public speaking.

LAURA.   Ohhhh.

JIM.   Because I believe in the future of television!

(*Turning back to her.*)

I wish to be ready to go up right along with it. Therefore I'm planning to get in on the ground floor. In fact I've already made

the right connections and all that remains is for the industry itself
to get under way! Full steam—

(*His eyes are starry.*)

Knowledge—Zzzzzp! *Money*—Zzzzzzp!—*Power!*
That's the cycle democracy is built on!

(*His attitude is convincingly dynamic.* LAURA *stares at him, even
her shyness eclipsed in her absolute wonder. He suddenly grins.*)

I guess you think I think a lot of myself!

LAURA.   No—o-o-o, I—

JIM.   Now how about you? Isn't there something you take more interest in than anything else?

LAURA.   Well, I do—as I said—have my—glass collection—

(*A peal of girlish laughter from the kitchen.*)

JIM.   I'm not right sure I know what you're talking about.
What kind of glass is it?

LAURA.   Little articles of it, they're ornaments mostly!
Most of them are little animals made out of glass, the tiniest
little animals in the world. Mother calls them a glass menagerie!
Here's an example of one, if you'd like to see it!
This one is one of the oldest. It's nearly thirteen.

(*Music: "The Glass Menagerie"*)

(*He stretches out his hand.*)

Oh, be careful—if you breathe, it breaks!

JIM.   I'd better not take it. I'm pretty clumsy with things.

LAURA.   Go on, I trust you with him!

(*Places it in his palm.*)

There now—you're holding him gently!
Hold him over the light, he loves the light! You see how the
light shines through him?

JIM.   It sure does shine!

LAURA.   I shouldn't be partial, but he is my favorite one.

JIM.   What kind of a thing is this one supposed to be?

LAURA.   Haven't you noticed the single horn on his forehead?

JIM.   A unicorn, huh?

LAURA.   Mmm-hmmm!

JIM.   Unicorns, aren't they extinct in the modern world?

LAURA.   I know!

JIM.   Poor little fellow, he must feel sort of lonesome.

LAURA.   (*Smiling.*) Well, if he does he doesn't complain about it. He
stays on a shelf with some horses that don't have horns and all
of them seem to get along nicely together.

JIM.   How do you know?

LAURA.   (*Lightly.*) I haven't heard any arguments among them!

JIM.   (*Grinning.*) No arguments, huh? Well, that's a pretty good sign!
Where shall I set him?

LAURA.   Put him on the table. They all like a change of scenery once in a while!

JIM.   (*Stretching.*) Well, well, well, well—
Look how big my shadow is when I stretch!

LAURA.   Oh, oh, yes—it stretches across the ceiling!

JIM.   (*Crossing to door.*) I think it's stopped raining. (*Opens fire-escape door.*) Where does the music come from?

LAURA.   From the Paradise Dance Hall across the alley.

JIM.   How about cutting the rug a little, Miss Wingfield?

LAURA.   Oh, I—

JIM.   Or is your program filled up? Let me have a look at it. (*Grasps imaginary card.*) Why, every dance is taken! I'll just have to scratch some out. (*Waltz music: "La Golondrina."*) Ahhh, a waltz! (*He executes some sweeping turns by himself, then holds his arms toward LAURA.*)

LAURA.   (*Breathlessly.*) I—can't dance!

JIM.   There you go, that inferiority stuff!

LAURA.   I've never danced in my life!

JIM.   Come on, try!

LAURA.   Oh, but I'd step on you!

JIM.   I'm not made out of glass.

LAURA.   How—how—how do we start?

JIM.   Just leave it to me. You hold your arms out a little.

LAURA.   Like this?

JIM.   A little bit higher. Right. Now don't tighten up, that's the main thing about it—relax.

LAURA.   (*Laughing breathlessly.*) It's hard not to.

JIM.   Okay.

LAURA.   I'm afraid you can't budge me.

JIM.   What do you bet I can't? (*He swings her into motion.*)

LAURA.   Goodness, yes, you can!

JIM.   Let yourself go, now, Laura, just let yourself go.

LAURA.   I'm—

JIM.   Come on!

LAURA.   Trying!

JIM.   Not so stiff— Easy does it!

LAURA.   I know but I'm—

JIM.   Loosen th' backbone! There now, that's a lot better.

LAURA.   Am I?

JIM.   Lots, lots better! (*He moves her about the room in a clumsy waltz.*)

LAURA.   Oh, my!

JIM.   Ha-ha!

LAURA.   Oh, my goodness!

JIM.   Ha-ha-ha! (*They suddenly bump into the table. JIM stops.*) What did we hit on?

LAURA.   Table.

JIM.   Did something fall off it? I think—

LAURA.   Yes.
JIM.   I hope that it wasn't the little glass horse with the horn!
LAURA.   Yes.
JIM.   Aw, aw, aw. Is it broken?
LAURA.   Now it is just like all the other horses.
JIM.   It's lost its—
LAURA.   Horn!

It doesn't matter. Maybe it's a blessing in disguise.
JIM.   You'll never forgive me. I bet that that was your favorite piece of glass.
LAURA.   I don't have favorites much. It's no tragedy, Freckles. Glass breaks so easily. No matter how careful you are. The traffic jars the shelves and things fall off them.
JIM.   Still I'm awfully sorry that I was the cause.
LAURA.   (*Smiling.*) I'll just imagine he had an operation. The horn was removed to make him feel less—freakish!

(*They both laugh.*)

Now he will feel more at home with the other horses, the ones that don't have horns . . .
JIM.   Ha-ha, that's very funny!

(*Suddenly serious.*)

I'm glad to see that you have a sense of humor. You know— you're—well—very different! Surprisingly different from anyone else I know!

(*His voice becomes soft and hesitant with a genuine feeling.*)

Do you mind me telling you that?

(LAURA *is abashed beyond speech.*)

I mean it in a nice way . . .

(LAURA *nods shyly, looking away.*)

You make me feel sort of—I don't know how to put it!
I'm usually pretty good at expressing things, but—
This is something that I don't know how to say!

(LAURA *touches her throat and clears it—turns the broken unicorn in her hands.*)

(*Even softer.*)

Has anyone ever told you that you were pretty?

(*Pause: Music.*)

(LAURA *looks up slowly, with wonder, and shakes her head.*)

Well, you are! In a very different way from anyone else.
And all the nicer because of the difference, too.

(*His voice becomes low and husky.* LAURA *turns away, nearly faint with the novelty of her emotions.*)

I wish that you were my sister. I'd teach you to have some confidence in yourself. The different people are not like other people, but being different is nothing to be ashamed of. Because other people are not such wonderful people. They're one hundred times one thousand. You're one times one! They walk all over the earth. You just stay here. They're common as—weeds, but—you—well, you're —*Blue Roses!*

(*Music changes.*)

LAURA.   But blue is wrong for—roses . . .

JIM.   It's right for you!—You're—pretty!

LAURA.   In what respect am I pretty?

JIM.   In all respects—believe me! Your eyes—your hair—are pretty! Your hands are pretty!

(*He catches hold of her hand.*)

You think I'm making this up because I'm invited to dinner and have to be nice. Oh, I could do that! I could put on an act for you, Laura, and say lots of things without being very sincere. But this time I am. I'm talking to you sincerely. I happened to notice you had this inferiority complex that keeps you from feeling comfortable with people. Somebody needs to build your confidence up and make you proud instead of shy and turning away and—blushing—

Somebody—ought to—

Ought to—*kiss* you, Laura!

(*His hand slips slowly up her arm to her shoulder.*)

(*Music swells tumultuously.*)

(*He suddenly turns her about and kisses her on the lips.*)

(*When he releases her,* LAURA *sinks on the sofa with a bright, dazed look.*)

(JIM *backs away and fishes in his pocket for a cigarette.*)

Stumble-john!

(*He lights the cigarette, avoiding her look.*)

(*There is a peal of girlish laughter from* AMANDA *in the kitchen.*)

(LAURA *slowly raises and opens her hand. It still contains the little broken glass animal. She looks at it with a tender, bewildered expression.*)

Stumble-john!

I shouldn't have done that— That was way off the beam.

You don't smoke, do you?

(*She looks up, smiling, not hearing the question.*)

(*He sits beside her a little gingerly. She looks at him speechlessly —waiting.*)

(*He coughs decorously and moves a little farther aside as he considers the situation and senses her feelings, dimly, with perturbation.*)

(*Gently.*)

Would you—care for a—mint?

(*She doesn't seem to hear him but her look grows brighter even.*)

Peppermint—Life-Saver?

My pocket's a regular drug store—wherever I go . . .

(*He pops a mint in his mouth. Then gulps and decides to make a clean breast of it. He speaks slowly and gingerly.*)

Laura, you know, if I had a sister like you, I'd do the same thing as Tom. I'd bring out fellows and—introduce her to them. The right type of boys of a type to—appreciate her.

Only—well—he made a mistake about me.

Maybe I've got no call to be saying this. That may not have been the idea in having me over. But what if it was?

There's nothing wrong about that. The only trouble is that in my case—I'm not in a situation to—do the right thing.

I can't take down your number and say I'll phone.

I can't call up next week and—ask for a date.

I thought I had better explain the situation in case you—misunderstood it and—hurt your feelings. . . .

(*Pause.*)

(*Slowly, very slowly, LAURA'S look changes, her eyes returning slowly from his to the ornament in her palm.*)

(*AMANDA utters another gay laugh in the kitchen.*)

LAURA.   (*Faintly.*) You—won't—call again?

JIM.   No, Laura, I can't.

(*He rises from the sofa.*)

As I was just explaining, I've—got strings on me.

Laura, I've—been going steady!

I go out all of the time with a girl named Betty. She's a home-girl like you, and Catholic, and Irish, and in a great many ways we —get along fine.

I met her last summer on a moonlight boat trip up the river to Alton, on the *Majestic.*

Well—right away from the start it was—love!

(*LAURA sways slightly forward and grips the arm of the sofa. He fails to notice, now enrapt in his own comfortable being.*)

Being in love has made a new man of me!

(*Leaning stiffly forward, clutching the arm of the sofa, LAURA struggles visibly with her storm. But JIM is oblivious, she is a long way off.*)

The power of love is really pretty tremendous!

Love is something that—changes the whole world, Laura!

(*The storm abates a little and LAURA leans back. He notices her again.*)

It happened that Betty's aunt took sick; she got a wire and had to go to Centralia. So Tom—when he asked me to dinner—I naturally just accepted the invitation, not knowing that you—that he—that I—

(*He stops awkwardly.*)

Huh—I'm a stumble-john!

(*He flops back on the sofa.*)

(*The holy candles in the altar of LAURA'S face have been snuffed out. There is a look of almost infinite desolation.*)

(JIM *glances at her uneasily.*)

I wish that you would—say something. (*She bites her lip which was trembling and then bravely smiles. She opens her hand again on the broken glass ornament. Then she gently takes his hand and raises it level with her own. She carefully places the unicorn in the palm of his hand, then pushes his fingers closed upon it.*) What are you—doing that for? You want me to have him?—Laura? (*She nods.*) What for?

LAURA.   A—souvenir . . .

(*She rises unsteadily and crouches beside the victrola to wind it up.*)

(*At this moment AMANDA rushes brightly back in the front room. She bears a pitcher of fruit punch in an old-fashioned cut-glass pitcher and a plate of macaroons. The plate has a gold border and poppies painted on it.*)

AMANDA.   Well, well, well! Isn't the air delightful after the shower? I've made you children a little liquid refreshment.

(*Turns gaily to the gentleman caller.*)

Jim, do you know that song about lemonade?

"Lemonade, lemonade
Made in the shade and stirred with a spade—
Good enough for any old maid!"

JIM.   (*Uneasily.*) Ha-ha! No—I never heard it.

AMANDA.   Why, Laura! You look so serious!

JIM.   We were having a serious conversation.

AMANDA.   Good! Now you're better acquainted!

JIM.   (*Uncertainly.*) Ha-ha! Yes.

AMANDA.   You modern young people are much more serious-minded than my generation. I was so gay as a girl!

JIM.   You haven't changed, Mrs. Wingfield.

AMANDA.   Tonight I'm rejuvenated! The gaiety of the occasion, Mr. O'Connor!

(*She tosses her head with a peal of laughter. Spills lemonade.*)

Oooo! I'm baptizing myself!

JIM.   Here—let me—

AMANDA.   (*Setting the pitcher down.*) There now. I discovered we had some maraschino cherries. I dumped them in, juice and all!

JIM.   You shouldn't have gone to that trouble, Mrs. Wingfield.

AMANDA.   Trouble, trouble? Why, it was loads of fun!
Didn't you hear me cutting up in the kitchen? I bet your ears

were burning! I told Tom how outdone with him I was for keeping you to himself so long a time! He should have brought you over much, much sooner! Well, now that you've found your way, I want you to be a very frequent caller! Not just occasional but all the time.

Oh, we're going to have a lot of gay times together! I see them coming!

Mmm, just breathe that air! So fresh, and the moon's so pretty!

I'll skip back out—I know where my place is when young folks are having a—serious conversation!

JIM.   Oh, don't go out, Mrs. Wingfield. The fact of the matter is I've got to be going.

AMANDA.   Going, now? You're joking! Why, it's only the shank of the evening, Mr. O'Connor!

JIM.   Well, you know how it is.

AMANDA.   You mean you're a young workingman and have to keep workingmen's hours. We'll let you off early tonight. But only on the condition that next time you stay later.

What's the best night for you? Isn't Saturday night the best night for you workingmen?

JIM.   I have a couple of time-clocks to punch, Mrs. Wingfield. One at morning, another one at night!

AMANDA.   My, but you *are* ambitious! You work at night, too?

JIM.   No, Ma'am, not work but—Betty! (*He crosses deliberately to pick up his hat. The band at the Paradise Dance Hall goes into a tender waltz.*)

AMANDA.   Betty? Betty? Who's—Betty!

(*There is an ominous cracking sound in the sky.*)

JIM.   Oh, just a girl. The girl I go steady with! (*He smiles charmingly. The sky falls.*)

AMANDA.   (*A long-drawn exhalation.*) Ohhhh . . . Is it a serious romance, Mr. O'Connor?

JIM.   We're going to be married the second Sunday in June.

AMANDA.   Ohhhh—how nice!

Tom didn't mention that you were engaged to be married.

JIM.   The cat's not out of the bag at the warehouse yet.

You know how they are. They call you Romeo and stuff like that.

(*He stops at the oval mirror to put on his hat. He carefully shapes the brim and the crown to give a discreetly dashing effect.*)

It's been a wonderful evening, Mrs. Wingfield. I guess this is what they mean by Southern hospitality.

AMANDA.   It really wasn't anything at all.

JIM.   I hope it don't seem like I'm rushing off. But I promised Betty I'd pick her up at the Wabash depot, an' by the time I get my jalopy down there her train'll be in. Some women are pretty upset if you keep 'em waiting.

AMANDA.   Yes, I know— The tyranny of women!

>   (*Extends her hand.*)

>   Good-bye, Mr. O'Connor.

>   I wish you luck—and happiness—and success! All three of them, and so does Laura!—Don't you, Laura?

LAURA.   Yes!

JIM.   (*Taking her hand.*) Good-bye, Laura. I'm certainly going to treasure that souvenir. And don't forget the good advice I gave you.

>   (*Raises his voice to a cheery shout.*)

>   So long, Shakespeare!

>   Thanks again, ladies— Good night!

>   (*He grins and ducks jauntily out.*)

>   (*Still bravely grimacing,* AMANDA *closes the door on the gentleman caller. Then she turns back to the room with a puzzled expression. She and* LAURA *don't dare to face each other.* LAURA *crouches beside the victrola to wind it.*)

AMANDA.   (*Faintly.*) Things have a way of turning out so badly. I don't believe that I would play the victrola.

>   Well, well—well—

>   Our gentleman caller was engaged to be married!

>   Tom!

TOM.   (*From back.*) Yes, Mother?

AMANDA.   Come in here a minute. I want to tell you something awfully funny.

TOM.   (*Enters with macaroon and a glass of the lemonade.*) Has the gentleman caller gotten away already?

AMANDA.   The gentleman caller has made an early departure.

>   What a wonderful joke you played on us!

TOM.   How do you mean?

AMANDA.   You didn't mention that he was engaged to be married.

TOM.   Jim? Engaged?

AMANDA.   That's what he just informed us.

TOM.   I'll be jiggered! I didn't know about that.

AMANDA.   That seems very peculiar.

TOM.   What's peculiar about it?

AMANDA.   Didn't you call him your best friend down at the warehouse?

TOM.   He is, but how did I know?

AMANDA.   It seems extremely peculiar that you wouldn't know your best friend was going to be married!

TOM.   The warehouse is where I work, not where I know things about people!

AMANDA.   You don't know things anywhere! You live in a dream; you manufacture illusions!

>   (*He crosses to door.*)

Where are you going?

TOM.　I'm going to the movies.

AMANDA.　That's right, now that you've had us make such fools of ourselves. The effort, the preparations, all the expense! The new floor lamp, the rug, the clothes for Laura! All for what? To entertain some other girl's fiancé!

Go to the movies, go! Don't think about us, a mother deserted, an unmarried sister who's crippled and has no job! Don't let anything interfere with your selfish pleasure!

Just go, go, go—to the movies!

TOM.　All right, I will! The more you shout about my selfishness to me the quicker I'll go, and I won't go to the movies!

AMANDA.　Go, then! Then go to the moon—you selfish dreamer!

(*Tom smashes his glass on the floor. He plunges out on the fire-escape, slamming the door. LAURA screams—cut by door.*)

(*Dance-hall music up. TOM goes to the rail and grips it desperately, lifting his face in the chill white moonlight penetrating the narrow abyss of the alley.*)

(*TOM'S closing speech is timed with the interior pantomime. The interior scene is played as though viewed through soundproof glass. AMANDA appears to be making a comforting speech to LAURA who is huddled upon the sofa. Now that we cannot hear the mother's speech, her silliness is gone and she has dignity and tragic beauty. LAURA'S dark hair hides her face until at the end of the speech she lifts it to smile at her mother. AMANDA'S gestures are slow and graceful, almost dance-like, as she comforts the daughter. At the end of her speech she glances a moment at the father's picture—then withdraws through the portieres. At close of TOM'S speech, LAURA blows out the candles, ending the play.*)

TOM.　I didn't go to the moon, I went much further—for time is the longest distance between two places—

Not long after that I was fired for writing a poem on the lid of a shoe-box.

I left Saint Louis. I descended the steps of this fire-escape for a last time and followed, from then on, in my father's footsteps, attempting to find in motion what was lost in space—

I traveled around a great deal. The cities swept about me like dead leaves, leaves that were brightly colored but torn away from the branches.

I would have stopped, but I was pursued by something.

It always came upon me unawares, taking me altogether by surprise. Perhaps it was a familiar bit of music. Perhaps it was only a piece of transparent glass—

Perhaps I am walking along a street at night, in some strange city, before I have found companions. I pass the lighted window of a shop where perfume is sold. The window is filled with pieces of colored glass, tiny transparent bottles in delicate colors, like bits of a shattered rainbow.

Then all at once my sister touches my shoulder. I turn around and look into her eyes . . .

Oh, Laura, Laura, I tried to leave you behind me, but I am more faithful than I intended to be!

I reach for a cigarette, I cross the street, I run into the movies or a bar, I buy a drink, I speak to the nearest stranger—anything that can blow your candles out!

(LAURA *bends over the candles.*)

—for nowadays the world is lit by lightning! Blow out your candles, Laura—and so good-bye. . . .

(*She blows the candles out.*)

(*The Scene Dissolves*)

QUESTIONS

1. Most play readers skip rapidly through stage directions, anxious to get to the dialogue. That's a mistake anytime, but especially with this play. The playwright describes the setting of the Wingfield apartment with unusual deliberation and detail. He calls the interior "dim and poetic," "unrealistic," yet he gives more details of layout than are found in most stage directions. Read the introductory comments aloud, to a group or to yourself. What general feeling or impression do you get? One commentator has said that "the hopelessness of the characters' plight is emphasized by the enveloping tenement framework of their lives—oppressively urban, glaringly modern." Is this the feeling you get? If not, what? What impression would you want to give if you were the set designer or director? Sketch a set arrangement for the scenes.

2. Tom calls the play "a memory play." Since it's his memory that generates the episodes, what is it that he is remembering and why is he doing so? In a sense he's confronting himself in his role as narrator. What do his opening comments tell us about him, about his attitude toward himself and toward the world in general? What is the *tone* of his remarks?

3. How may it be said that in other less obvious ways this is a memory play? Consider what keeps Amanda going, what preys on Laura, what gives Jim doubts about himself. How may it be said that the past (the remembered past) has its hand on the present?

4. How, specifically, does the opening scene define the relationships in the family? Characterize Amanda as she reveals herself here. What is distasteful about her behavior? What is attractive? Characterize Tom and Laura. What is attractive or unattractive about them? What basic conflicts in the play are set in motion in this scene?

5. What purposes are served by Scene 2, the second "episode" in the play? What is added to our understanding of the relationship between Laura and her mother? Is it surprising that six weeks have gone by without Amanda's having any inkling of what Laura's been doing? Why or why not? Why is Amanda so anxious for Laura to have a job or to have "gentlemen callers"? Is it just a matter of caring about her "future"? Amanda does most of the talking in this scene, as she does in the first. What advice would you give to the actress playing Laura in responding, verbally and physically, to what Amanda says?

6. Scene 3, or episode 3, is an explosive confrontation between Amanda and Tom. How does it fill in the suggestions about their relationship already touched on in Tom's opening comments and Scene 1? What contrast is there between his detached, sardonic opening soliloquy, Amanda's abortive sales talk, and the burst of recriminations that follow hard after? Why is there a "clear pool of light on [Laura's] figure" throughout the scene? In what sense is she the main focus of the scene even though she utters only a few words?

7. Scene 4 opens with the third pairing of the play's principals, this time Laura and Tom. How would you characterize their relationship as revealed so far in the play and in this brief encounter? What does Tom mean when in his final soliloquy he says, "Oh, Laura, Laura, I tried to leave you behind me, but I am more faithful than I intended to be"? In what ways are they two of a kind? In what ways different? How does what happens at the very end of this scene point up their samenesses and differences?

8. How do Scenes 5 and 6 fill out the portraits of the three Wingfields that have already been sketched? How does Jim O'Connor play off against all three in Scenes 5 through 7? What is his dramatic function in the play?

9. Tom calls Jim O'Connor "the most realistic character in the play." Do you agree? Why or why not? Williams has described him simply as a "nice, ordinary, young man." What do you think of his advice to Laura? Of his treatment of her? Of his plans for himself? Why hasn't he "done better" since getting out of high school?

10. Who's at fault in this family entrapment? Any of them? All of them? Or isn't such a question relevant here at all? What do you take the playwright to be trying to say through the obviously sympathetic treatment of all three of the family's members.

11. If you were directing the play, how would you handle the narrator's presence? Would he be on-stage all the time, even when he's not a character and not actually talking to the audience? Explain.

12. In pairs, prepare readings for all or parts of several scenes (possibilities: the first confrontation between Tom and Amanda [Scene 1], the first between Laura and Amanda [Scene 2], the one between Laura and Jim [Scene 7]). Have several pairs do the same scene back-to-back and ask class members to keep notes on the various interpretations. In preparing for the reading, put yourself in the role; have an attitude toward the "self" you are playing and try to convey that attitude consistently. Pay attention to what the playwright says about the characters in his general introduction and in the stage directions.

13. Williams keeps insisting that the play is not "realistic." What grounds can you find in it for agreeing with him? Can it be argued simultaneously that in some ways the play is highly realistic? In what ways? For what purposes would you say the playwright has created this contradiction?

14. A number of mentions are made of the political events of the time, particularly of the growing power of fascism in Europe and of the prolonged depression in the United States. How important is this historical framework to the play? Could it just as easily be set in pre-World War I times or in the late '60s, say? Why or why not?

ESSAY QUESTIONS

Take as your lead either of the following comments on *The Glass Menagerie* and write a paper developing the idea, or qualifying it, or refuting it—or a combination of all three:

1. "*The Glass Menagerie* ends on a note of futility and leaves a sensitive audience depressed. Though we sympathize deeply with all the characters, they lack the stature for tragedy. Their problems are not presented as great and universal, Amanda's being rooted in an effete tradition, Laura's in a physical deformity. . . . We feel no great relief in the escape of Tom, because it is a flight from responsibility that settles nothing."

2. "Tom is the archetypal American rebel—the articulate, weary drifter, ultimately damned not so much by the circumstances of his life as by his relentless insight."

The Infernal Machine

The French playwright Jean Cocteau (1889–1963) was an unusually versatile and original artist, successful as a poet, novelist, essayist, librettist, screenwriter, dramatist, painter, and stage and film director. As playwright and director, he was an experimenter who tried to find new forms to replace the popular realistic theater, at that time as commercially successful and artistically impoverished in France as elsewhere in the Western world. *The Infernal Machine* is a brilliant example of the boldness of approach to new forms (in many cases the return to old forms) that a number of playwrights—Brecht, Eliot, Yeats, Beckett, Pirandello, Albee, to name some—have adopted in the past four or five decades.

The Infernal Machine is not a wholly new departure. Many of the conventions of the realistic theater are evident: straightforward, ordinary, up-to-date language in the dialogue; reference to the kind of "real" world readily recognizable by a modern audience, despite the subject matter and locale; ordinary people behaving for the most part like ordinary people with problems; carefully delineated sets and lighting effects.

But Cocteau takes great liberties with the conventions of realism. Most obviously, he uses as subject matter a well-known Greek myth and retells it, not in a modern equivalent form, but in its own terms and setting, no matter how modern the ideas and dialogue are. His Thebans are real twentieth-century Parisians who move in a world with real ghosts and sphinxes. The settings are localized and realistic: "A patrol path round the ramparts of Thebes"; "An unpeopled spot on a hill overlooking Thebes." But the scene of the action—"a little platform in the center of the stage"—is surrounded by "nocturnal curtains" and the acts are "flooded in the livid mythical light of quicksilver." Throughout the play the surrounding darkness comments on the futility—absurdity even—of the human assertiveness that acts itself out on the "little platform."

The Infernal Machine

JEAN COCTEAU
(1891–1963)

Translated by
Carl Wildman

CHARACTERS
(in order of appearance)

THE VOICE
THE YOUNG SOLDIER
THE SOLDIER
THE CAPTAIN
JOCASTA, *the queen, widow of Laïus*
TIRESIAS, *a soothsayer, nearly blind*
THE GHOST OF LAIUS, *dead king*
THE SPHINX
ANUBIS, *Egyptian God of the Dead*
THE THEBAN MATRON
A LITTLE BOY
A LITTLE GIRL
OEDIPUS, *son of Laïus*
CREON, *brother of Jocasta*
THE MESSENGER FROM CORINTH
THE SHEPHERD OF LAIUS
ANTIGONE, *daughter of Oedipus*

ACT I
THE GHOST OF LAIUS

THE VOICE.

> *'He will kill his father. He will marry his mother.'*

To thwart this oracle of Apollo, Jocasta, Queen of Thebes, leaves her son on the mountain side with his feet pierced and bound. A shepherd of Corinth finds the nursling and carries it to Polybius. Polybius and Merope, king and queen of Corinth, were bemoaning

196

a sterile marriage. The child, Oedipus, or *Pierced-feet*, respected by bears and wolves, is to them a heaven-sent gift. They adopt him.

When a young man, Oedipus questions the oracle of Delphi.

The god speaks: *You will murder your father and marry your mother.* He must therefore fly from Polybius and Merope. The fear of parricide and incest drives him on towards his fate.

One evening, arriving at the crossroads of Delphi and Daulis, he meets an escort. A horse jostles him; a quarrel starts; a servant threatens him; he replies with a blow from his stick. The blow misses the servant and kills the master. This dead man is Laïus, the old king of Thebes. Parricide!

The escort, fearing an ambush, took to its heels. Oedipus, unsuspecting, passed on. Besides, he is young, enthusiastic; this accident is soon forgotten.

During one of his halts he learns of the scourge of the Sphinx. The Sphinx, 'the winged Virgin,' 'the Singing Bitch,' is killing off the young men of Thebes. This monster asks a riddle and kills those who do not guess it. Queen Jocasta, widow of Laïus, offers her hand and her crown to the conqueror of the Sphinx.

Like the young Siegfried to come, Oedipus hurries on. He is consumed with curiosity and ambition. The meeting takes place. What was the nature of this meeting? Mystery. Be that as it may, Oedipus enters Thebes a conqueror, he marries the queen. Incest!

For the gods really to enjoy themselves, their victim must fall from a great height. Years come and go in prosperity. Two daughters and two sons complicate the monstrous union. The people love their king. But the plague suddenly descends upon them. The gods accuse an anonymous criminal of infecting the country and demand that he shall be driven out. Going from one discovery to another, and as if intoxicated by misfortune, Oedipus, in the end, finds himself cornered. The trap shuts. All becomes clear. With her red scarf Jocasta hangs herself. With the golden brooch of the hanging woman Oedipus puts out his eyes.

Spectator, this machine, you see here wound up to the full in such a way that the spring will slowly unwind the whole length of a human life, is one of the most perfect constructed by the infernal gods for the mathematical destruction of a mortal.

A patrol path round the ramparts of Thebes. High walls. A stormy night. Summer lightning. The din and bands of the popular district can be heard.[1]

(Editor's note: The numbered footnotes are Cocteau's; those with an ° have been added.)

1 The four scenes should be planted on a little platform in the center of the stage, surrounded by nocturnal curtains. The slope of the platform varies according to the requirements of the scenes. Besides the lighting of details, the four acts should be flooded in the livid mythical light of quicksilver.

YOUNG SOLDIER.   They're having a good time!

SOLDIER.   Trying to.

YOUNG SOLDIER.   Well, anyway, they dance all night.

SOLDIER.   They can't sleep, so they dance.

YOUNG SOLDIER.   Never mind, they're getting tight and going with women, and spending their nights in all sorts of dives, while I am here tramping up and down with you. Well I, for one, can't stick it any longer! I can't stick it! I can't! That's clear enough, isn't it? I've had my bellyful!

SOLDIER.   Desert then.

YOUNG SOLDIER.   Oh, no! I've made up my mind. I'm going to put my name down for the Sphinx.

SOLDIER.   What for?

YOUNG SOLDIER.   What for? Why, to do something, of course. To put an end to all this creepy business and ghastly hanging about.

SOLDIER.   You wouldn't get scared, though?

YOUNG SOLDIER.   Scared? How d'you mean?

SOLDIER.   Oh, just scared, you know! I've seen brighter and tougher lads than you who got the wind up. Unless this gent is going to kill the Sphinx and draw the first prize.

YOUNG SOLDIER.   And why not? Oh, I know the only man who came back alive from the Sphinx had become a gibbering idiot. But supposing what he gibbers is true? What if it is a riddle? What if I guess the answer? What——

SOLDIER.   Now listen here, you poor bastard. Don't you realize that hundreds upon hundreds of chaps who've been to the stadium and college and everything have left their carcasses behind there, and you, a poor little private soldier like you wants to——

YOUNG SOLDIER.   I shall go! I shall, because I can't bear any longer counting the stones of this wall, hearing that band, and seeing your rotten mug, and—— (*He stamps.*)

SOLDIER.   That's the stuff, my hero! I was waiting for this explosion. I like it better that way. Now . . . now . . . enough blubbering. . . . Take it easy . . . there, there, there . . .

YOUNG SOLDIER.   To hell with you!

(*The* SOLDIER *bangs his spear against the wall behind the* YOUNG SOLDIER *who becomes rigid.*)

SOLDIER.   What's up?

YOUNG SOLDIER.   Didn't you hear anything?

SOLDIER.   No . . . where?

YOUNG SOLDIER.   Ah! . . . I seemed to . . . I thought for a moment—

SOLDIER.   You're like a sheet. . . . What's the matter? Are you going to pass out?

YOUNG SOLDIER.   It's silly . . . I seemed to hear a knock. I thought it was him!

SOLDIER.   The Sphinx!

YOUNG SOLDIER.   No, him, the ghost, the phantom, you know!

SOLDIER. The ghost? Our dear old ghost of Laïus? And is that what turns your stomach over? Really!

YOUNG SOLDIER. I'm sorry.

SOLDIER. You're sorry, mate? What are you talking about? To start with, there's a good chance that our ghost will not appear again after last night's business. So that's that. And besides, what are you sorry about? Look at things squarely. We can hardly say this ghost scared us. Oh, well . . . the first time perhaps! . . . But, after that, eh? . . . He was a decent old ghost, almost a pal, a relief. Well, if the idea of this ghost makes you jumpy, it's because you're in a real state of nerves, like me, like everybody in Thebes, rich or poor alike, except a few big pots who make something out of everything. There's not much fun in war, anyway, but we don't know a blind thing about the enemy we're up against. We're beginning to get fed up with oracles, happy deaths, and heroic mothers. Do you think I should pull your leg as I do if my nerves weren't on edge, and do you think you'd start blubbering, and that lot over there'd get tight and dance? No, they'd be in bed and fast asleep, and we'd be playing dice while waiting for friend phantom.

YOUNG SOLDIER. I say . . .

SOLDIER. Well? . . .

YOUNG SOLDIER. What d'you think it's like . . . the Sphinx?

SOLDIER. Oh! give the Sphinx a rest. If I knew what it was like I shouldn't be here doing guard duty with you tonight.

YOUNG SOLDIER. Some make out it's no bigger than a hare, and is timid, and has a tiny little face, like a woman's. But I think it has a woman's head and breasts, and sleeps with the young men.

SOLDIER. Oh, turn it up! Shut up and forget it!

YOUNG SOLDIER. Perhaps it doesn't ask anything and doesn't even touch you. You meet it, look at it, and die of love.

SOLDIER. All we needed was for you to go and fall in love with the public scourge. After all, public scourge . . . between ourselves, do you know what I think about this public scourge? . . . It's a vampire! Yes, a common or garden vampire! Someone in hiding from the police, and who they can't lay their hands on.

YOUNG SOLDIER. A vampire with a woman's head?

SOLDIER. Can't you turn it up? No, not him! A real old vampire with a beard and moustache, and a belly. He sucks your blood and that's how it is they bring corpses back home, all with the same wound in the same place: the back of the neck! And now, go and see for yourself if you're still keen.

YOUNG SOLDIER. You say that . . .

SOLDIER. I say that . . . I say that . . . Hi! . . . The captain.

(*They stand up to attention. The* CAPTAIN *enters and folds his arms.*)

CAPTAIN. Easy! . . . Well, my lads. . . . Is this where we see ghosts?

SOLDIER. Sir——

CAPTAIN.   Silence! You will speak when I ask you. Which of you two
has dared——
YOUNG SOLDIER.   I did, sir!
CAPTAIN.   Good Lord! Whose turn to speak is it? Are you going to
keep quiet? I was asking: which of you two has dared to make a
report about a service matter, without it passing through the normal channels? Right over my head. Answer.
SOLDIER.   It wasn't his fault, sir, he knew——
CAPTAIN.   Was it you or him?
YOUNG SOLDIER.   Both of us, but I——
CAPTAIN.   Silence! I want to know how the high priest came to hear
of what happens at night at this post, while I myself heard nothing.
YOUNG SOLDIER.   It's my fault, sir, my fault. My comrade here didn't
want to say anything about it. But I thought I ought to speak and,
as this incident didn't concern the service . . . and, well . . . I told
his uncle everything; because his uncle's wife is sister to one of
the queen's linen-maids, and his brother-in-law is in Tiresias's
temple.
SOLDIER.   That's why I said it was my fault, sir.
CAPTAIN.   All right! Don't burst my eardrums. So . . . this incident
doesn't concern the service. Very good, oh, very good! . . . And
it seems . . . this famous incident which doesn't concern the service
is a ghost story?
YOUNG SOLDIER.   Yes, sir.
CAPTAIN.   A ghost appeared to you one night when you were on guard
duty, and this ghost said to you . . . Just what did this ghost say
to you?
YOUNG SOLDIER.   He told us, sir, he was the specter of King Laïus,
and he had tried to appear several times since his murder, and he
begged us to find some way of warning Queen Jocasta and Tiresias
with all speed.
CAPTAIN.   With all speed! Fancy that! What a nice old ghost he must
be! And . . . didn't you ask him, say, why *you* had the honor of
this visit and why he doesn't appear directly before the queen or
Tiresias?
SOLDIER.   Yes, sir, I asked him, I did. His answer was that he wasn't
free to put in an appearance anywhere, and that the ramparts
were the most favorable spot for people who had died violent
deaths, because of the drains.
CAPTAIN.   Drains?
SOLDIER.   Yes, sir. He said drains, meaning because of the fumes
which rise there.
CAPTAIN.   Hoho! A very learned specter, and he doesn't hide his light
under a bushel. Did he scare you much? And what did he look
like? What was his face like? What clothes did he wear? Where
did he stand, and what language did he speak? Are his visits long
or short? Have you seen him on different occasions? Although this
business doesn't concern the service, I must say I am curious to

learn from your lips a few details about the manners and customs of ghosts.

YOUNG SOLDIER. Well, he did scare us a bit the first night, I admit. You see, sir, he appeared very suddenly, like a lamp lighting up, there in the thickness of the wall.

SOLDIER. We both saw him.

YOUNG SOLDIER. It was hard to make out the face and the body; the mouth, when it was open, was clearer, and a white tuft of his beard, and a large red stain, bright red, near the right ear. He spoke with difficulty and couldn't somehow manage to get out more than one sentence at a time. But you'd better ask my comrade here about that, sir. He explained to me how it was the poor fellow couldn't manage to get it over.

SOLDIER. Oh! you know, sir, there's nothing very complicated about it! He spent all his energy in the effort to appear, that is, in leaving his new shape and taking on the old, so that we could see him. That's the reason why each time he spoke a little better, he began to disappear, became transparent like, and you could see the wall through him.

YOUNG SOLDIER. And as soon as he spoke badly you could see him very well. But you saw him badly as soon as he spoke well, and began saying the same thing over again. 'Queen Jocasta. You must . . . you must . . . Queen . . . Queen . . . Queen Jocasta. . . . You must warn the queen. . . . You must warn Queen Jocasta. . . . I ask you, gentlemen, I ask you, I . . . I . . . Gentlemen . . . I ask . . . you must . . . you must . . . I ask you, gentlemen, to warn . . . I ask you . . . The queen . . . Queen Jocasta . . . to warn, gentlemen, to warn . . . Gentlemen . . . Gentlemen . . .' That's how he went on.

SOLDIER. And you could see he was afraid of disappearing before he'd said his piece right to the end.

YOUNG SOLDIER. Oh yes, and then, you know, remember, eh? Every time the same business. The red stain went last. Just like a ship's light on the wall, it was, sir.

SOLDIER. But the whole thing was over in a minute!

YOUNG SOLDIER. He has appeared in the same place five times, every night, a little before dawn.

SOLDIER. But last night it was different, we . . . well, we had a bit of a fight, and my comrade here decided to tell the royal house everything.

CAPTAIN. Well! Well! And how was this night 'different,' which, if I'm not mistaken, caused a dispute between you . . .?

SOLDIER. It was like this, sir. . . . You know, guard duty isn't exactly all beer and skittles.

YOUNG SOLDIER. So really we were waiting for the ghost to turn up, like.

SOLDIER. And we laid the odds.

YOUNG SOLDIER.   Will come . . .

SOLDIER.   Won't . . .

YOUNG SOLDIER.   Will come . . .

SOLDIER.   Won't . . . and it may seem a funny thing to say, but it was a comfort to see him.

YOUNG SOLDIER.   A habit, as you might say.

SOLDIER.   We ended by imagining we saw him when he wasn't there. We'd say to each other: 'It's moving! The wall is lighting up. Don't you see anything? No. But you must do. Over there, I tell you. . . . The wall isn't the same. Don't you see, look, look!'

YOUNG SOLDIER.   And we looked and stared our eyes out. We didn't dare move.

SOLDIER.   We watched for the least change.

YOUNG SOLDIER.   And when, at last, he turned up, we could breathe again, and weren't the least bit afraid.

SOLDIER.   The other night we watched and watched and stared ourselves nearly blind; we thought he'd never show up, but he appeared stealthily . . . not at all quickly like on the first nights. And once he was visible, he said new things and told us as well as he could that something fearful had happened, a thing of death which he couldn't explain to the living. He spoke of places where he could go and places where he couldn't go, and that he had been where he shouldn't and knew a secret which he shouldn't know, and that he would be discovered and punished, and afterwards he wouldn't be allowed to appear, he wouldn't be able to appear any more. (*Solemn voice.*) 'I shall die my last death,' he said, 'and it will be finished, finished. You see, gentlemen, there is not a moment to lose. Run! Warn the queen! Find Tiresias! Gentlemen! Gentlemen, have pity! . . .' He was begging away and day was breaking. And there he stuck!

YOUNG SOLDIER.   Suddenly we thought he'd go mad.

SOLDIER.   We understood from sentences without beginning or end that he had left his post, as it were, . . . didn't know how to disappear, and was lost. We saw him going through the same performance to disappear as to appear, and he couldn't manage it. So then he asked us to swear at him, because, he said, swearing at ghosts is the way to make them go. The silliest thing about it was that we hadn't the guts to do it. The more he repeated: 'Come on young men, insult me! Let yourselves go, do your best. . . . Oh, come on!'—the softer we looked.

YOUNG SOLDIER.   And the less we could lay our tongue to! . . .

SOLDIER.   Yes, that was the limit! And yet, it's not for lack of blackguarding our superiors.

CAPTAIN.   Very nice of you, men, I'm sure! Thank you on behalf of the superiors.

SOLDIER.   Oh! I didn't mean that, sir. . . . I meant . . . I meant the princes, crowned heads, ministers, the government, what . . . the powers that be. In fact, we'd often talked over wrongs which are done. . . . But he was such a decent sort, the ghost of poor old King Laïus, the swearwords wouldn't come. There he was, urging us on and we kept dithering: 'Go on then! Buzz off, you old bastard!' In short, we gave him bouquets!

YOUNG SOLDIER.   Because, you see, sir, 'you old bastard' is a kind of friendly way of speaking among soldiers.

CAPTAIN.   It's as well to know.

SOLDIER.   Go on! Go on then! . . . you bleeding . . . you old . . . Poor ghost. He hung there between life and death and he was beside himself with fear because of the cocks and the sun. When, all of a sudden, we saw the wall become the wall again, and the red stain go out. We were dog-tired.

YOUNG SOLDIER.   It was after that night that I decided to speak to his uncle as he refused to speak himself.

CAPTAIN.   Your ghost doesn't seem to be very punctual.

SOLDIER.   Oh, you know, sir, he may not show himself again.

CAPTAIN.   I am in his way, no doubt.

SOLDIER.   No, sir, I mean after last night . . .

CAPTAIN.   But I understand from what you say that your ghost is very polite. He will appear, I'm quite sure. In the first place, the politeness of kings is punctuality, and the politeness of ghosts consists in taking on human form, according to your ingenious theory.

SOLDIER.   Possibly, sir, but it's also possible that with ghosts there are no more kings, and they may mistake a century for a minute. So if the ghost appears in a thousand years instead of this evening . . .

CAPTAIN.   You're a clever sort of chap, but patience has its limits. I tell you this ghost will appear. I tell you my presence is upsetting him, and I tell you that no one outside the service must come along this patrol path.

SOLDIER.   Yes, sir.

CAPTAIN.   (*In an outburst.*) So, ghost or no ghost, you are to stop anyone turning up here without the password. Those are orders. Is that clear?

SOLDIER.   Yes, sir.

CAPTAIN.   And don't forget to patrol. Dismiss! (*The two soldiers stand stiffly at the slope.*) (*False exit.*) Don't try any clever tricks! I've got my eye on you. (*He disappears. Long silence.*)

SOLDIER.   As you were!

YOUNG SOLDIER.   He thought we were trying to pull his leg.

SOLDIER.   Don't you believe it! He thought someone was trying to pull ours.

YOUNG SOLDIER.   Ours?

SOLDIER.   Yes, chum. I get to know lots of things, I do, through my uncle. The queen is nice, you know, but she isn't really liked; they think she's . . . (*He taps his head.*) They say she is eccentric and has a foreign accent, and is under the influence of Tiresias. This Tiresias advises the queen to do everything that will harm her. Do this . . . and do that. . . . She tells him her dreams, and asks him if she ought to get up right foot or left foot first; he leads her by the nose and licks her brother's boots, and plots with him against his sister. They are a low lot there. I wouldn't mind betting the captain thought our ghost was out of the same bag as the Sphinx. A priest's trick to attract Jocasta and make her believe anything they want.

YOUNG SOLDIER.   No?

SOLDIER.   Shakes you, doesn't it? But that's how it is. . . . (*In a very low voice.*) Listen, I believe in the ghost myself, take it from me. But, for that very reason, because I believe in him and they don't, I advise you to keep your mouth shut. You've already succeeded in making a fine hash of things. Take down this report: 'Has given proof of an intelligence well above his rank. . . .'

YOUNG SOLDIER.   Still, if our king . . .

SOLDIER.   Our king! . . . Our king! . . . Steady on! . . . A dead king isn't a living king. It's like this, if King Laïus were living, well, between ourselves, he would manage on his own and wouldn't come looking for us to act as his A.D.C.° (*They move off towards the right by the patrol path.*)

VOICE OF JOCASTA.   (*At the bottom of the steps. She has a very strong accent: the international accent of royalty.*) Still another flight! I hate steps! We can see nothing! Where are we?

VOICE OF TIRESIAS.   But, Majesty, you know what I think of this escapade, and *I* didn't— —

VOICE OF JOCASTA.   Stop it, Zizi. You only open your mouth to say silly things. This is not the time for moral lessons.

VOICE OF TIRESIAS.   You should have taken another guide. I am nearly blind.

VOICE OF JOCASTA.   What is the use of being a soothsayer, I wonder! Why, you don't even know where the steps are. I shall break my leg! It will be your fault, Zizi, your fault, as usual.

VOICE OF TIRESIAS.   My fleshly eyes have gone out to the advantage of an inner eye which has other uses than counting steps.

VOICE OF JOCASTA.   And now he's cross all over his eye! There, there! We love you, Zizi; but these flights of steps upset me so. We had to come, Zizi, we simply had to!

VOICE OF TIRESIAS.   Majesty— —

VOICE OF JOCASTA.   Don't be obstinate. I had no idea there were all these wretched steps. I am going to go up backwards. You will steady me. Don't be afraid. *I* am leading you. But if I looked at the steps, I should fall. Take my hands. Forward! (*They appear on the set.*) There . . . there . . . there . . . four, five, six, seven

---

° A.D.C.: aide-de-camp.

. . . (JOCASTA *arrives on the platform and moves to the right.* TIRESIAS *treads on the end of her scarf. She utters a cry.*)

TIRESIAS. What is it?

JOCASTA. It's your foot, Zizi! You're walking on my scarf.

TIRESIAS. Forgive me . . .

JOCASTA. Ah! he's cross! But it isn't you that I am annoyed with, it's the scarf! I am surrounded by objects which hate me! All day long this scarf is strangling me. At one time it catches in the branches, at another it gets wound on to the hub of a carriage, another time you tread on it. It's a positive fact. And I am afraid of it, but I dare not be separated from it! Awful! It will be the death of me.

TIRESIAS. Look what a state your nerves are in.

JOCASTA. And what is the use of your third eye, I should like to know? Have you found the Sphinx? Have you found the murderers of Laïus? Have you calmed the people? Guards are stationed at my door and I am left with things that hate me, that want my death!

TIRESIAS. From mere hearsay——

JOCASTA. I feel things. I feel things better than all of you! (*She puts her hand on her belly.*) I feel them there! Was every possible effort made to discover the murderers of Laïus?

TIRESIAS. Majesty, you know very well the Sphinx made further searches impossible.

JOCASTA. Well, I for one don't care a jot about your fowls' entrails. . . . I feel, there . . . that Laïus is suffering and wants to be heard. I am determined to get to the bottom of this story, and to hear this young guard for myself; and I *shall* hear him. I am your queen, Tiresias, don't you forget it.

TIRESIAS. My dear child, you must try and understand a poor blind man who adores you, watches over you, and wishes you were sleeping in your room instead of running after a shadow on the ramparts.

JOCASTA. (*With mystery.*) I do not sleep.

TIRESIAS. You don't sleep?

JOCASTA. No. Zizi, I don't sleep. The Sphinx and the murder of Laïus have put my nerves all on edge. You were right there. And I am glad in a way, because if I fall asleep for so much as a minute I have a dream, always the same, and I am ill for the whole day.

TIRESIAS. Isn't it my business to interpret dreams? . . .

JOCASTA. The place of the dream is rather like this platform, so I'll tell you. I am standing in the night, cradling a kind of nursling. Suddenly this nursling becomes a sticky paste which runs through my fingers. I shriek and try to throw this paste away, but . . . oh! Zizi . . . if only you knew, it's foul. . . . This thing, this paste stays hanging on to me, and when I think I'm free of it the paste flies back and strikes me across the face. And this paste is living. It has a kind of mouth which fixes itself on mine. And it creeps everywhere, it feels after my belly, and my thighs. Oh! Horrible!

TIRESIAS.   Calm yourself.

JOCASTA.   I don't want to sleep any more, Zizi . . . I don't want to sleep any more. Listen to that music. Where is it? They don't sleep either. It's lucky for them they have that music. They are afraid, Zizi . . . and rightly. They must dream horrible things, and they don't want to sleep. And while I think of it, why this music? Why is it allowed? Do I have music to keep me from sleeping? I didn't know these places stayed open all night. How is it there is this scandal, Zizi? Creon must send out orders! This music must be forbidden! This scandal must stop at once.

TIRESIAS.   Majesty, I implore you to calm yourself and to give up this idea. You're beside yourself for lack of sleep. We have authorized these bands so that the people don't become demoralized, to keep up their courage. There would be crimes . . . and worse than that if there were no dancing in the crowded parts of the town.

JOCASTA.   Do I dance?

TIRESIAS.   That's different. You are in mourning for Laïus.

JOCASTA.   So are they all, Zizi. All of them! Every one! And yet they can dance and I can't. It's too unfair . . . I shall——

TIRESIAS.   Someone coming, madam.

JOCASTA   I say, Zizi, I'm shaking. I have come out with all my jewels.

TIRESIAS.   There's nothing to fear. You won't meet prowlers on the patrol path. It must be the guards.

JOCASTA.   Perhaps the soldier I am looking for?

TIRESIAS.   Don't move. We'll find out.

The soldiers enter. They see JOCASTA *and* TIRESIAS.

YOUNG SOLDIER.   Steady, looks like somebody.

SOLDIER.   Where have they sprung from? (*Aloud.*) Who goes there?

TIRESIAS.   (*To the queen.*) This is going to be awkward. . . . (*Aloud.*) Listen, my good men . . .

YOUNG SOLDIER.   Password.

TIRESIAS.   You see, madam, we ought to have the password. You're getting us into an awful mess.

JOCASTA.   Password? Why? What password? How silly, Zizi. I shall go and speak to him myself.

TIRESIAS.   Madam, I implore you. They have instructions. These guards might not recognize you, nor believe me. It's very dangerous.

JOCASTA.   How romantic you are! You see dramas everywhere.

SOLDIER.   They're whispering together. Perhaps they're going to spring on us.

TIRESIAS.   (*To the soldiers.*) You have nothing to fear. I am old and nearly blind. Let me explain my presence on these ramparts, and the presence of the person who accompanies me.

SOLDIER.   No speeches. The password!

TIRESIAS.   One moment. Just a moment. Listen, my good men, have you seen any gold coins?

SOLDIER.   Attempted bribery. (*He goes towards the right to guard the patrol path and leaves the* YOUNG SOLDIER *opposite* TIRESIAS.)

TIRESIAS.   You're wrong. I meant: have you seen the queen's portrait on a gold coin?

YOUNG SOLDIER.   Yes!

TIRESIAS.   (*Stepping aside and showing the queen, who is counting the stars, in profile.*) And . . . don't you recognize . . .?

YOUNG SOLDIER.   If you're trying to make out there's a connection, I don't get it. The queen is so young, and this . . . 'er . . . lady . . . well! . . .

JOCASTA.   What does he say?

TIRESIAS.   He says he finds madam very young to be the queen. . . .

JOCASTA.   How entertaining!

TIRESIAS.   (*To the* SOLDIER.) Fetch your officer.

SOLDIER.   No need. I have my orders. Clear off! Look sharp!

TIRESIAS.   You'll hear more of this!

JOCASTA.   Zizi, what is it now? What does he say?

The CAPTAIN *enters.*

CAPTAIN.   What's going on here?

YOUNG SOLDIER.   Two people without the password, sir.

CAPTAIN.   (*Going towards* TIRESIAS.) Who are you? (*He suddenly recognizes* TIRESIAS.) My lord! (*He bows.*) My profoundest apologies.

TIRESIAS.   Phew! Thanks, Captain. I thought this young warrior was going to run us through.

CAPTAIN.   I am extremely sorry, my lord! (*To the* YOUNG SOLDIER.) Idiot! Leave us.

(*The* YOUNG SOLDIER *goes to his comrade on the extreme right.*)

SOLDIER.   (*To the* YOUNG SOLDIER.) What a brick!

TIRESIAS.   Don't scold him! He was obeying orders. . . .

CAPTAIN.   Such a visit . . . in such a place! What can I do for your lordship?

TIRESIAS.   (*Standing back to show the queen.*) Her Majesty!

(*The* CAPTAIN *starts back.*)

CAPTAIN.   (*Bows at a respectful distance.*) Majesty! . . .

JOCASTA.   No ceremony, please! I should like to know which guard saw the ghost.

CAPTAIN.   Oh, the sorry young specimen who ill-used my lord Tiresias, and if Your Majesty . . .

JOCASTA.   See, Zizi. What luck! I was right in coming. . . (*To the* CAPTAIN.) Tell him to approach.

CAPTAIN.   (*To* TIRESIAS.) My lord, I don't know if the queen fully realizes that this young soldier would explain himself better through his officer; and that, if he speaks for himself, Her Majesty will be in danger of——

JOCASTA.   What now, Zizi? . . .

TIRESIAS.   The Captain was pointing out that he is used to the men and he might serve as a kind of interpreter.

JOCASTA.   Send the Captain away! Has the boy a tongue, or not? Let him come near.

TIRESIAS.   (*Aside to the* CAPTAIN.) Don't insist, the queen is over-wrought. . . .

CAPTAIN.   Very well. . . (*He goes to his soldiers. To the* YOUNG SOLDIER.) The queen wants to speak to you. And control your tongue. I'll pay you out for this, young fellow-me-lad.

JOCASTA.   Come here!

(*The* CAPTAIN *pushes the* YOUNG SOLDIER *forward.*)

CAPTAIN.   Go along then! Go on, booby, forward. You won't be eaten. Excuse him, Your Majesty. Our lads are scarcely familiar with court ways.

JOCASTA.   Ask that man to leave us alone with the soldier.

TIRESIAS.   But, Majesty——

JOCASTA.   And no 'but Majestys.' . . . If this Captain stays a moment longer I shall kick him.

TIRESIAS.   Listen, officer. (*He leads him aside.*) The queen wants to be alone with the guard who has seen something. She has her whims. She might have your record blotted for you, you know, and I couldn't do anything about it.

CAPTAIN.   Right. I'll leave you. . . . If I stayed it was because . . . well . . . I don't mean to give you advice, my lord. . . . But, between you and me, be on your guard about this ghost story. (*He bows.*) My lord. . . . (*A long salute to the queen. He passes near the* SOLDIER.) Hi! The queen wishes to stay alone with your comrade.

JOCASTA.   Who is the other soldier? Has he seen the ghost?

YOUNG SOLDIER.   Yes, Your Majesty, we were on guard duty together.

JOCASTA.   Then let him stop. Let him stay there! I'll call him if I want him. Good evening, Captain, that will be all.

CAPTAIN.   (*To the* SOLDIER.) We'll have this out later. (*He goes out.*)

TIRESIAS.   (*To the queen.*) You have mortally offended that officer.

JOCASTA.   About time, too! Generally it's the men who are mortally offended and never the officers. (*To the* YOUNG SOLDIER.) How old are you?

YOUNG SOLDIER.   Nineteen.

JOCASTA.   Exactly his age! He would be his age. . . . He looks splendid! Come nearer. Look, Zizi, what muscles! I adore knees. You can tell the breed by the knees. He would look like that too. . . . Isn't he fine, Zizi. Feel those biceps, like iron. . . .

TIRESIAS.   I am sorry, madam, but you know . . . I'm no authority. I can scarcely see what they're like.

JOCASTA.   Then feel . . . Test them. Thighs like a horse! He steps away! Don't be afraid. . . . The old grandpa is blind. Heaven knows what he's imagining, poor lad! He's quite red! He's adorable! And nineteen!

YOUNG SOLDIER.   Yes, Your Majesty!

JOCASTA.   (*Mocking him.*) Yes, Your Majesty! Isn't he just too delicious! Ah! what a shame! Perhaps he doesn't even know he's handsome. (*As one speaks to a child.*) Well . . . did you see the ghost?

YOUNG SOLDIER.   Yes, Your Majesty!

JOCASTA.   The ghost of King Laïus?

YOUNG SOLDIER.   Yes, Your Majesty! The king told us he was the king.

JOCASTA.   Zizi . . . what do you know with all your fowls and stars? Listen to this boy. . . . And what did the king say?

TIRESIAS.   (*Leading the queen away.*) Majesty! Be careful. These young people are hotheaded, credulous . . . pushful. . . . Be on your guard. Are you certain this boy has seen the ghost, and, even if he has seen it, was it really the ghost of your husband?

JOCASTA.   Gods! How unbearable you are! Unbearable and a spoilsport. Every time you come and break the spell you stop miracles with your intelligence and incredulity. Please let me question this boy on my own. You can preach afterwards. (*To the* YOUNG SOLDIER.) Listen. . . .

YOUNG SOLDIER.   Your Majesty! . . .

JOCASTA.   (*To* TIRESIAS.) I'll find out straight away whether he has seen Laïus. (*To the* YOUNG SOLDIER.) How did he speak?

YOUNG SOLDIER.   He spoke quickly and a lot, Your Majesty, ever such a lot, and he got mixed up, and he didn't manage to say what he wanted to.

JOCASTA.   That's he! Poor dear! But why on these ramparts? The stench. . . .

YOUNG SOLDIER.   That's it, Your Majesty. . . . The ghost said it was because of the swamps and the rising fumes that he could appear.

JOCASTA.   How interesting! Tiresias, you would never learn that from your birds. And what did he say?

TIRESIAS.   Madam, madam, you must at least question him with some order. You'll muddle this youngster's head completely.

JOCASTA.   Quite right, Zizi, quite right. (*To the* YOUNG SOLDIER.) What was he like? How did you see him?

YOUNG SOLDIER.   In the wall, Your Majesty. A sort of transparent statue, as you might say. You could see the beard most clearly, and the black hole of the mouth as he spoke, and a red stain on the temple, bright red.

JOCASTA.   That's blood!

YOUNG SOLDIER.   Fancy! We didn't think of that.

JOCASTA.   It's a wound! How dreadful! (LAIUS *appears.*) And what did he say? Did you understand anything?

YOUNG SOLDIER.   It wasn't easy, Your Majesty. My comrade noticed that he had to make a big effort to appear, and each time he made an effort to express himself clearly he disappeared; then he was puzzled as to how to set about it.

JOCASTA.   Poor dear!

GHOST.   Jocasta! Jocasta! My wife! Jocasta! (*They neither hear nor see him during the whole of the scene.*)

TIRESIAS.   (*Addressing the* SOLDIER.) And were you not able to grasp anything intelligible?

GHOST.   Jocasta!

SOLDIER.   Well, yes, my lord. We understood he wanted to warn you of a danger, put you on your guard, both the queen and you, but that's all. The last time he explained he knew some secrets he ought not to have known, and if he was discovered he would not be able to appear again.

GHOST.   Jocasta! Tiresias! Can't you see me? Can't you hear me?

JOCASTA.   And didn't he say anything else? Didn't he say anything particular?

SOLDIER.   Ah, well, Your Majesty! Perhaps he didn't want to say anything particular in our presence. He was asking for you. That is why my comrade tried to let you know about it.

JOCASTA.   Dear boys! And I have come. I knew it all the time. I felt it there! You see, Zizi, with all your doubts. And tell us, Young Soldier, where the ghost appeared. I want to touch the exact spot.

GHOST.   Look at me! Listen to me, Jocasta! Guards, you always saw me before. Why not see me now? This is torture! Jocasta! Jocasta!

(*While these words are being uttered the* SOLDIER *goes to the place where the* GHOST *is. He touches it with his hand.*)

SOLDIER.   There. (*He strikes the wall.*) There, in the wall.

YOUNG SOLDIER.   Or in front of the wall. It was difficult to make out.

JOCASTA.   But why doesn't he appear tonight? Do you think he will still be able to appear?

GHOST.   Jocasta! Jocasta! Jocasta!

SOLDIER.   I am sorry, Your Majesty, I don't think so, after what happened last night. I'm afraid there was a spot of bother and Her Majesty may be too late.

JOCASTA.   What a shame! Always too late. Zizi, I am always the last person in the whole kingdom to be informed. Think of the time we have wasted with your fowls and oracles! We ought to have run, to have guessed. We shall learn absolutely nothing! And there will be disasters, terrible disasters. And it will be your fault, Zizi, your fault, as usual.

TIRESIAS.   Madam, the queen is speaking in front of these men.

JOCASTA.   Yes, I am speaking in front of these men! I suppose I ought to restrain myself? When King Laïus, the dead King Laïus, has spoken in front of these men. But he has not spoken to you, Zizi, nor to Creon. He hasn't been to the temple to show himself. He showed himself on the patrol path to these men, to this boy of nineteen who is so handsome and looks like—

TIRESIAS.   I implore you——

JOCASTA.   Yes, I am overwrought, you must try to understand. These dangers, this specter, this music, this pestilential smell. . . . And there's a storm about. I can feel it in my shoulder. I am stifling, Zizi, stifling.

GHOST.   Jocasta! Jocasta!

JOCASTA.   I think I hear my name. Didn't you hear anything?

TIRESIAS.   My poor lamb. You're worn out. Day is breaking. You are dreaming where you stand. Are you even sure this ghost business hasn't come from the fatigue of these young men on the watch who force themselves not to sleep and who live in this depressing, swampy atmosphere?

GHOST.   Jocasta! For pity's sake, listen to me! Look at me! Gentlemen, you are kind. Keep the queen. Tiresias! Tiresias!

TIRESIAS.   (*To the* YOUNG SOLDIER.) Step aside a moment, I want to speak to the queen.

(*The* YOUNG SOLDIER *goes to his comrade.*)

SOLDIER.   Well, old son! You've clicked! She's fallen for you! Petted by the queen, eh!

YOUNG SOLDIER.   Look here! . . .

SOLDIER.   You're made for life. Don't forget your pals.

TIRESIAS.   . . . Listen! Cockcrow. The ghost will not return. Let us go home.

JOCASTA.   Did you see how handsome he is?

TIRESIAS.   Don't recall those sad things, my lamb. If you had a son . . .

JOCASTA.   If I had a son, he would be handsome, brave, he would guess the riddle and kill the Sphinx. He would return victor.

TIRESIAS.   And you would go without a husband.

JOCASTA.   Little boys always say: 'I want to become a man so that I can marry mother.' It's not such a bad idea, you know, Tiresias. Is there a sweeter union, a union that is sweeter and more cruel, and prouder, than that couple: a son and a young mother? Listen, Zizi, just now, when I touched that young guard, heaven alone knows what he must have thought, the poor lad, and I myself nearly fainted. He would be nineteen, Tiresias, nineteen! The same age as this soldier. Can we be sure Laïus did not appear to him because of this likeness?

(*Cock crows.*)

GHOST.   Jocasta! Jocasta! Jocasta! Tiresias! Jocasta!

TIRESIAS.   (*To the soldiers.*) My friends, do you think it is any use waiting?

GHOST.   For pity's sake!

SOLDIER.   Frankly, no, my lord. The cocks are crowing. He will not appear now.

GHOST.   Gentlemen! Mercy! Am I invisible? Can't you hear me?

JOCASTA.   Come along! I will be obedient. But I am very glad I questioned the boy. You must find out his name and where he lives. (*She goes towards the steps.*) I had forgotten these steps, Zizi!

. . . That band is making me ill. Listen, we can go back through the higher town by the side streets, and we can see the night life.

TIRESIAS.   Madam, you don't mean it.

JOCASTA.   Oh! now he's beginning again! He'll send me simply raving! Mad and off my head. I've got my veils on, Zizi, how do you expect I should be recognized?

TIRESIAS.   My child, you said yourself you have come out wearing all your jewels. Your brooch alone has pearls as large as an egg.

JOCASTA.   I am a martyr! Others can laugh and dance and amuse themselves. Do you imagine I am going to leave this brooch at the palace where it's simply asking to be taken? Call the guard. Tell him to help me down these steps. And you can follow us.

TIRESIAS.   But, madam, since the presence of this young man affects you so strongly . . .

JOCASTA.   He is young and strong. He will help me, and I shan't break my neck. Obey your queen for once, at least.

TIRESIAS.   Hi! . . . No, he. . . . Yes, you . . . Help the queen down the steps. . . .

SOLDIER.   You see, old man!

YOUNG SOLDIER.   (*Approaching.*) Yes, my lord.

GHOST.   Jocasta! Jocasta! Jocasta!

JOCASTA.   He's shy! And flights of steps hate me. Steps, hooks, and scarves. Oh! yes, they do, they hate me! They're after my death. (*A cry.*) Ho!

YOUNG SOLDIER.   Has the queen hurt herself?

TIRESIAS.   No, silly! Your foot! Your foot!

YOUNG SOLDIER.   What foot?

TIRESIAS.   Your foot on the end of the scarf. You nearly strangled the queen.

YOUNG SOLDIER.   Ye gods!

JOCASTA.   Zizi, you are utterly ridiculous. Poor darling. There you go calling him a murderer because he walks, as you did, on this scarf. Don't upset yourself, my boy. My lord is absurd. He never misses an opportunity of hurting people's feelings.

TIRESIAS.   But, madam——

JOCASTA.   You are the one who is clumsy. Come along. Thank you, my boy. Send your name and address to the temple. One, two, three, four. . . . Marvelous! Zizi! Do you see how well I'm getting down. Eleven, twelve. . . . Zizi, are you following? Two more steps. (*To the* SOLDIER.) Thank you. I can manage now. Help grandpa! (JOCASTA *disappears left, with* TIRESIAS. *Cocks are heard.*)

VOICE OF JOCASTA.   Through your fault I shall never know what my poor Laïus wanted.

GHOST.   Jocasta!

VOICE OF TIRESIAS.   That story is all very vague.

VOICE OF JOCASTA.   What? very vague? What do you mean, vague? It's you who are vague with your third eye. That boy knows what he has seen, and he has seen the king. Have you seen the king?

VOICE OF TIRESIAS.   But——

VOICE OF JOCASTA.   Have you seen him? . . . No. . . . Well . . . It's amazing . . . it's like . . . (*The voices die away.*)

GHOST.   Jocasta! Tiresias! Have pity!

(*The two soldiers turn to each other and see the* GHOST.)

THE SOLDIERS.   Oh! the Ghost!

GHOST.   Gentlemen, at last! I am saved! I kept calling, begging. . . .

SOLDIER.   You were there?

GHOST.   During the whole of your talk with the queen and Tiresias. Then why was I invisible?

YOUNG SOLDIER.   I'll run and fetch them!

SOLDIER.   Halt!

GHOST.   What? You stop him?

YOUNG SOLDIER.   Let me go . . .

SOLDIER.   When the joiner comes the chair stops wobbling; when you get to the shoemender your sandal stops hurting you; when you get to the doctor you no longer feel the pain. Fetch them! That would only make him disappear.

GHOST.   Alas! Do these simple souls then know what the priests cannot divine?

YOUNG SOLDIER.   I shall go.

GHOST.   Too late. . . . Stay. It is too late. I am discovered. They are coming; they are going to take me. Ah! they're here! Help! Help! Quick! Tell the queen a young man is approaching Thebes, and on no account . . . No! No! Mercy! Mercy! They've got me! Help! Ended! I . . . I. . . . Mercy . . . I . . . I . . .

(*Long silence. The two soldiers, back to the audience, contemplate endlessly the place in the wall where the* GHOST *disappeared.*)

SOLDIER.   Good God!

YOUNG SOLDIER.   Poor devil!

SOLDIER.   These things are beyond us, old man.

YOUNG SOLDIER.   But it's clear that, in spite of death, that fellow wanted, at all costs, to warn his wife of a danger which is threatening her. My duty is to overtake the queen and the high priest and repeat to them word for word what we have just heard.

SOLDIER.   You want the queen badly, don't you? (*The* YOUNG SOLDIER *shrugs his shoulders.*) Well . . . he only had to appear to them and talk to them, they were there. We saw him all right ourselves and they didn't. But, to crown all, they even prevented *us* from seeing him. So there you have it! Dead kings become ordinary people. Poor Laïus! Now he knows how easy it is to get into touch with the great of the earth.

YOUNG SOLDIER.   But us?

SOLDIER.   Oh, us! It's easy enough to get into touch with men, you coon. . . . But, when it comes to officers, queens, and high priests . . . they always go before it happens, or come when it's all over.

YOUNG SOLDIER.   What's 'it'?

SOLDIER.   How should I know? . . . I understand myself, that's the chief thing.

YOUNG SOLDIER.   And you wouldn't go and warn the queen?

SOLDIER.   A word of advice: let princes deal with princes, ghosts with ghosts, and soldiers with soldiers. (*Flourish.*)

END OF   ACT I

ACT II
THE MEETING OF OEDIPUS AND THE SPHINX

THE VOICE.

Spectators, let us imagine we can recall the minutes we have just lived through together and relive them elsewhere. For, while the Ghost of Laïus was trying to warn Jocasta on the ramparts of Thebes, the Sphinx and Oedipus met on a hill overlooking the town. The bugle calls, moon, stars, and crowing cocks will be the same.

THE SCENERY

An unpeopled spot on a hill overlooking Thebes, by moonlight. The road to Thebes (from right to left) passes over the forestage. It gives the impression of rounding a high leaning stone whose base is fixed at the lower end of the platform and forms the support for the wings on the right. Behind the ruins of a little temple is a broken wall. In the middle of the wall stands a complete pedestal which used to indicate the entrance to the temple and bears the trace of a chimera: a wing, a foot, a haunch.

Broken and overturned columns. For the Shades of Anubis and Nemesis at the end, a record by the actors can declaim the dialogue, while the actress mimes the part of the dead girl with the head of a jackal.

When the curtain rises a girl in a white dress is seen sitting among the ruins. The head of a jackal lies in her lap, its body remaining hidden behind her. Distant bugle calls.

SPHINX. Listen.

JACKAL. Well?

SPHINX. That's the last call. We're free.

(ANUBIS *gets up, and the jackal's head is seen to belong to him.*)

JACKAL, ANUBIS. It's the first. There'll be two more before the gates are closed.

SPHINX. It's the last. I'm quite sure it's the last.

ANUBIS. You're sure because you want the gates closed, but I'm sorry duty forces me to contradict you; we're not free. That was the first bugle call. We'll wait.

SPHINX. I may have been mistaken, but——

ANUBIS. May have been mistaken! You were. . . .

SPHINX. Anubis!

ANUBIS. Sphinx?

SPHINX. I've had enough of killing, enough of dealing out death.

ANUBIS. We must obey. There are mysteries within mystery, gods above gods. We have our gods and they have theirs. That's what is called infinity.

SPHINX. You see, Anubis, there is no second call. It's you who are mistaken, let us go. . . .

ANUBIS.   Do you mean you would like this night to pass without any
deaths?

SPHINX.   Yes! I do, indeed! Yes! Although it's growing late, I tremble
to think someone may still come by.

ANUBIS.   You're getting sensitive.

SPHINX.   That's my business.

ANUBIS.   Don't get cross.

SPHINX.   Why must we always be acting without aim, without end,
without understanding? Why, for example, should you have a dog's
head, Anubis? Why have the god of the dead in the shape given
to him by credulous people? Why must we have an Egyptian god
in Greece and why must he have a dog's head?

ANUBIS.   It's marvelous, how like a woman you look when it comes
to asking questions.

SPHINX.   That is no answer!

ANUBIS.   Well, my answer is: that logic forces us to appear to men in
the shape in which they imagine us; otherwise, they would see only
emptiness. Moreover, neither Egypt nor Greece nor death, neither
the past nor the future has any meaning for us. Further, you know
only too well to what use I must put this jaw. And finally, our
masters prove their wisdom by giving me a material form which is
not human and so preventing me from losing my head, however
beastly it may be; for I am your keeper, remember. I can see that
if they had given you a mere watchdog we should already be in
Thebes with me on a leash and you sitting in the middle of a band
of young men.

SPHINX.   How stupid you are!

ANUBIS.   Then try and remember that these victims who touch the
girl-figure you have assumed are no more than noughts wiped off
a slate, even if each of these noughts were an open mouth calling
for help.

SPHINX.   That may be. But here the calculations of gods are hard to
follow. . . . Here we kill. Here the dead really die. Here I do kill.
(*While the* SPHINX *was speaking with her eyes on the ground*
ANUBIS *pricked up his ears, looked round, and moved silently off
over the ruins where he disappears. When the* SPHINX *raises her
eyes, she looks for* ANUBIS, *and finds herself face to face with a
small group of people who enter downstage right, and whom*
ANUBIS *has scented. The group is composed of a* THEBAN
MATRON, *her little boy and girl. The* MATRON *is dragging her
daughter along. The boy is walking ahead.*)

MATRON.   Look where you're going! Get along now! Don't look behind
you! Leave your sister alone! Go on. . . . (*She sees the* SPHINX *as
the little boy stumbles into her.*) Look out! I told you to look where
you're going! Oh! I'm so sorry, miss. . . . He never looks where he's
going. . . . He hasn't hurt you, has he?

SPHINX.   No! not at all.

MATRON.   I didn't expect to meet anyone on my path at such an hour.

SPHINX.   I'm new to these parts, I haven't been long in Thebes; I was on my way to a relative who lives in the country and got lost.

MATRON.   Poor dear! And where does your relative live?

SPHINX.   . . . Near the twelfth milestone.

MATRON.   The very part I come from! I had lunch with my family, at my brother's place, you know. He made me stay to dinner. And then, you know, you begin gossiping and don't notice the time, and so here I am going home after curfew with my brats half asleep already.

SPHINX.   Good night.

MATRON.   Good night. (*She makes to go.*) And . . . I say . . . don't linger on the way. I know the likes of you and me haven't much to fear . . . but I wouldn't be too bold, if I were you, till I was inside the walls.

SPHINX.   Are you afraid of thieves?

MATRON.   Thieves! Ye gods, what could they get out of me? Oh, no, my dear! Where *do* you come from? Anyone can see you're not from the town. Thieves! I should think so! I mean the Sphinx!

SPHINX.   Do you really, honestly and truly, believe in that nonsense yourself?

MATRON.   That nonsense indeed! How young you are. Young people are so disbelieving these days. Oh, yes, they are! That's how disasters happen. Let alone the Sphinx, I'll give you a case from my family. . . . My brother that I've just left. . . . (*She sits down and lowers her voice.*) He married a beautiful tall blonde from the north. One night he wakes up and what does he find? His wife in bed without head or entrails. She was a vampire. When he'd got over the first fright what does my brother do? without a moment's hesitation he finds an egg and lays it on the pillow in the place of his wife's head. That's how you stop vampires getting back into their body. All at once he hears a moaning. It was the head and entrails flying wildly across the room and begging my brother to take away the egg. My brother wouldn't, and the head went from moans to anger, from anger to tears, from tears to kisses. To cut a long story short, my idiot brother takes away the egg and lets his wife get back into her body. Now he knows his wife is a vampire and my sons make fun of their uncle. They maintain that he made up this entire vampire story to disguise the fact that his wife really did go out, but with her body, and that he let her come back, and that he's a coward and ashamed of himself. But *I* know very well my sister-in-law is a vampire. . . . And my sons are in danger of marrying fiends from the underworld, all because they are obstinate and *disbelieving*.

    And the same with the Sphinx—I'm sorry if I hurt your feelings, but it's only the likes of my sons and you who don't believe in it.

SPHINX.   Your sons . . . ?

MATRON.   Not the little brat who just bumped into you. I mean my
boy of seventeen. . . .

SPHINX.   You have several sons, have you?

MATRON.   I had four. Now I have three. Seven, sixteen, and seventeen.
And I can tell you ever since that wicked beast appeared the house
has been impossible.

SPHINX.   Your sons quarrel . . . ?

MATRON.   I mean, my dear, that it's impossible to live under the same
roof. The one who's sixteen is only interested in politics. According to him the Sphinx is a bugbear used to scare the poor and to
impose on them. There may have been something like your old
Sphinx at one time—that's how my son speaks—but now the old
Sphinx is dead; and he's merely a priests' demon and an excuse for
police jobbery.° They fleece and loot and terrorize the masses,
and then blame it all on the Sphinx. It's a good thing the Sphinx
has broad shoulders. Whose fault is it that we starve to death, that
prices go up, and that bands of looters swarm over the country-
side? Why, the Sphinx's, of course. And the Sphinx is to blame
because business is bad, and the government's weak and one crash
follows another; because the temples are glutted with rich offerings
while mothers and wives are losing the bare necessities of life, and
because foreigners with money to spend are leaving the town. . . .
Ah, you should see him, miss, how he gets up on the table, shouting, waving his arms, and stamping his feet; and then he de-
nounces those who are responsible for it all, preaches revolt, eggs
on the anarchists, shouting at the top of his voice names that are
enough to get us all hanged. And between ourselves, miss . . . I
know . . . you can take it from me . . . the Sphinx exists all right,
but they're making the most of it. You can be sure of that. What
we want is a man, a dictator!

SPHINX.   And . . . what about the brother of your young dictator?

MATRON.   Oh! he's another kettle of fish. He despises his brother, he
despises me, he despises the gods, he despises everything. He makes
you wonder where he can get hold of all he comes out with. He
says, if you please, that the Sphinx would interest him if it killed
for killing's sake, but that this Sphinx of ours is in league with the
oracles, and so it doesn't interest him.

SPHINX.   And your fourth son? When was it . . . ?

MATRON.   I lost him nearly a year ago. He was just nineteen.

SPHINX.   Poor woman. . . . What did he die of?

MATRON.   Sphinx.

SPHINX.   (*Gloomily.*) Ah! . . .

MATRON.   It's all very well for his younger brother to maintain he was
a victim of police intrigues. . . . Oh, no! There's no mistake, he died
through the Sphinx. Ah, my dear! . . . if I live to a hundred I'll

---

° **jobbery:** corruption.

never forget that scene. One morning (he hadn't been home that night) I thought I heard him knock; I opened the front door and saw the underneath of his poor feet and then there followed a long way off, ever so far away, his poor little face, and in the back of his neck—look, just here—a large wound from which the blood had already stopped flowing. They brought him to me on a stretcher. Then I went: Ho! and fell, all of a heap. . . . A blow like that, you know, you don't get over in a hurry. You may be thankful you don't come from Thebes, thankful if you have no brothers. . . . You're lucky. . . . My other boy, the orator, wants to avenge him. What's the good? But he hates the priests, and my poor son was one of a series of human offerings.

SPHINX.   Human offerings?

MATRON.   To be sure. During the first months of the Sphinx the soldiers were sent to avenge the fine young men who were found dead all over the place, and they returned empty-handed. The Sphinx couldn't be found. Then, as there was a rumor that the Sphinx asked riddles, young people from the schools were sacrificed; and then the priests stated that the Sphinx demanded human offerings. At that, the youngest and weakest and fairest were chosen.

SPHINX.   Poor woman!

MATRON.   I tell you, my dear, what we want is a man of action. Queen Jocasta is still young. At a distance you would say she was twenty-nine or thirty. What we want is a ruler to fall from the sky, marry her, and kill the beast; someone to make an end of corruption, lock up Creon and Tiresias, improve the state of finance and liven up the people, someone who would care for the people and save us, yes, that's it, save us. . . .

SON.   Mummy!

MATRON.   Sh!

SON.   Mummy . . . I say, mummy, what does the Sphinx look like?

MATRON.   I don't know. (*To the* SPHINX.) And what d'you think is the latest? They're asking us to contribute our last farthings for a monument to those killed by the Sphinx! Will that bring them back to us, I should like to know?

SON.   Mummy . . . what is the Sphinx like?

SPHINX.   Poor little chap! His sister's asleep. Come along. . . .

(*The son clings to the skirt of the* SPHINX.)

MATRON.   Now don't worry the lady.

SPHINX.   He's all right. (*She strokes his neck.*)

SON.   I say, mummy, is this lady the Sphinx?

MATRON.   Little silly. (*To the* SPHINX.) I hope you don't mind. At that age children don't know what they're saying. . . . (*She gets up.*) Oh my! (*She takes the little girl who is asleep in her arms.*) Come along now! Off we go, lazybones!

SON.   Mummy, is that lady the Sphinx? I say, mummy, is the Sphinx
that lady? Is that the Sphinx, mummy?

MATRON.   Sh! Don't be silly. (*To the* SPHINX.) Well, good evening.
Excuse my gossiping to you. I was glad to stop for a breather. . . .
And . . . take care. (*Fanfare.*) Quickly. There's the second bugle.
After the third we'll be shut out.

SPHINX.   Go along, quickly. I'll hurry my way. You've put me on my
guard.

MATRON.   Believe me, we'll not feel safe until there comes a man who
will rid us of this scourge. (*She goes out left.*)

SON'S VOICE.   I say, mummy, what's the Sphinx look like? Why wasn't
it that lady? Then what's he like?

SPHINX.   A scourge!

ANUBIS.   (*Coming from among the ruins.*) That woman *would* have
to come along here just now.

SPHINX.   I've been unhappy for the past two days, for two days now
I've been carrying on in this miserable way in the hope that this
massacre would come to an end.

ANUBIS.   Don't worry. You're all right.

SPHINX.   Listen. This is my secret wish and these the circumstances
which would allow me to mount my pedestal for a last time. A
young man will climb the hill, I shall fall in love with him. He'll
have no fear. And when I ask my question he will answer as to
an equal. He will give *the answer*, d'you hear, Anubis, and I shall
fall dead.

ANUBIS.   Make no mistake: only your mortal form will fall dead.

SPHINX.   And isn't that the form I should want to live in to make him
happy!

ANUBIS.   It's nice to see that human form doesn't make a great goddess become a little woman.

SPHINX.   You see how right I was. That bugle we heard was the last
after all!

ANUBIS.   Daughter of men! One is never finished with you. I tell you
no! No! (*He leaves her side and mounts an overturned column.*)
That was the second. When I've heard another one you can go. Oh!

SPHINX.   What is it?

ANUBIS.   Bad news.

SPHINX.   Someone coming?

ANUBIS.   Yes.

(*The* SPHINX *gets up beside* ANUBIS *and looks into the wings,
right.*)

SPHINX.   I can't! I can't and I won't question this young man. You
needn't ask me to.

ANUBIS.   I should say, if you're like a young mortal, he's like a young
god.

SPHINX.   What grace, Anubis, and what shoulders! He's coming.

ANUBIS. I'll hide. Don't forget you are the Sphinx. I'm keeping my eye on you. I'll be with you at the first sign.

SPHINX. Anubis, listen . . . quickly. . . .

ANUBIS. Sh! . . . He's here. (*ANUBIS hides.*)

(*OEDIPUS enters upstage right. He is walking along with his eyes on the ground. He starts.*)

OEDIPUS. Oh! I'm sorry. . . .

SPHINX. I startled you.

OEDIPUS. Well . . . no . . . I was dreaming, I was miles away, and suddenly, before me——

SPHINX. You took me for an animal.

OEDIPUS. Almost.

SPHINX. Almost? Almost an animal, that's the Sphinx.

OEDIPUS. Yes, I know.

SPHINX. You admit you took me for the Sphinx. Thank you.

OEDIPUS. Oh! I soon realized my mistake.

SPHINX. Too kind. The truth of the matter is it can't be so amusing to find yourself suddenly face to face with the Sphinx, if you're a young man.

OEDIPUS. And . . . if you're a girl?

SPHINX. He doesn't attack girls.

OEDIPUS. Because girls avoid his haunts and are not supposed to go out alone when the light is failing.

SPHINX. You'd do well to mind your own business, young man, and let me go my way.

OEDIPUS. Which way?

SPHINX. You're simply amazing. Must I give my reasons for being out to a complete stranger?

OEDIPUS. And suppose I guessed your reason?

SPHINX. You amuse me.

OEDIPUS. Aren't you moved by curiosity, the curiosity which is raging amongst all modern young women, the curiosity to know what the Sphinx looks like? If he has claws, or a beak, or wings, and whether he takes after the tiger or the vulture?

SPHINX. Oh, come, come!

OEDIPUS. The Sphinx is the criminal of the day. Who's seen him? No one. Fabulous rewards are promised to the first person who discovers him. The faint of heart tremble. Young men die. . . . But a girl, couldn't she venture into the forbidden area, setting orders at defiance, and dare what no reasonable person would dare, to unearth the monster, surprise him in his lair, get a view of him?

SPHINX. You're on the wrong tack, I tell you. I'm going back to a relative who lives in the country, and as I had forgotten the very existence of a Sphinx and that the outskirts of Thebes are not safe, I was resting a moment on the stones of these old ruins. You see how far you're out.

OEDIPUS.   What a pity! For some time now I've only run across people as dull as ditch water; so I hoped for something more unusual. Pardon me.

SPHINX.   Good evening!

OEDIPUS.   Good evening! (*They pass each other. But* OEDIPUS *turns back.*) I say! I may appear unpleasant, but I honestly can't bring myself to believe you. Your presence in these ruins still intrigues me enormously.

SPHINX.   You're simply incredible.

OEDIPUS.   Because if you were like other girls you would already have made off as fast as your legs would carry you.

SPHINX.   My dear boy, you're quite absurd.

OEDIPUS.   It seemed to me so marvelous to find in a girl a worthy competitor.

SPHINX.   A competitor? Then you are looking for the Sphinx?

OEDIPUS.   Looking for him? Let me tell you, I've been on the march for a whole month. Probably that's why I appeared ill-mannered just now. I was so wild with excitement as I drew near Thebes that I could have shouted my enthusiasm to the nearest block of stone, when, instead of a block of stone, what stands in my path but a girl in white? So I couldn't help talking to her about what was uppermost in my mind and thinking she must have the same purpose as myself.

SPHINX.   But surely, a moment ago, when you saw me spring out of the shadow, you didn't seem to me very much on the alert for a man who wants to measure his strength with the enemy.

OEDIPUS.   That is true. I was dreaming of fame, and the beast would have caught me unawares. Tomorrow in Thebes I shall equip myself and the hunt will begin.

SPHINX.   You love fame?

OEDIPUS.   I'm not sure about that. I like trampling crowds, trumpet calls, flying banners, waving palm branches, the sun, gold and purple, happiness, luck—you know, to live!

SPHINX.   Is that what you call living?

OEDIPUS.   Don't you?

SPHINX.   No, I must say I have quite a different idea of life.

OEDIPUS.   What's that?

SPHINX.   To love. To be loved by the one you love.

OEDIPUS.   I shall love my people and they me.

SPHINX.   The public square is not a home.

OEDIPUS.   The public square has nothing to do with it. The people of Thebes are looking for a man. If I kill the Sphinx I shall be that man. Queen Jocasta is a widow; I shall marry her. . . .

SPHINX.   A woman who might be your mother!

OEDIPUS.   The main thing is that she is not.

SPHINX.   Do you imagine that a queen and her people would give themselves up to the first comer?

OEDIPUS.   Would you call the vanquisher of the Sphinx a first comer?
I know the promised reward is the queen. Don't laugh at me. Please
listen. You must. I must prove that my dream isn't merely a dream.
My father is King of Corinth. My father and mother were already
old when I was born and I lived in a court of gloom. Too much
fuss and comfort produced in me a feverish longing for adventure. I began to pine and waste away, when one evening a drunk
shouted at me that I was a bastard and that I was usurping the
place of a legitimate son. Blows and abuse followed, and the next
day, despite the tears of Merope and Polybius, I decided to visit
the sanctuaries and question the gods. They all replied with the
same oracle: You will murder your father and marry your mother.
SPHINX.   What?
OEDIPUS.   Yes, I mean it. At first this oracle fills you with horror, but
I'm not so easily imposed on! I soon saw how nonsensical the whole
thing was. I took into account the ways of the gods and the priests,
and I came to this conclusion: either the oracle hid a less serious
meaning which had to be discovered, or the priests who communicate from temple to temple by means of birds found it perhaps to
their advantage to put this oracle into the mouth of the gods and
to weaken my chances of coming into power. Briefly, I soon forgot
my fears, and, I may say, used this threat of parricide and incest
as an excuse to flee the court and satisfy my thirst for the
unknown.
SPHINX.   Now it's my turn to feel dazed. I'm sorry I rather made fun
of you. Will you forgive me, prince?
OEDIPUS.   Give me your hand. May I ask your name? Mine is Oedipus;
I'm nineteen.
SPHINX.   Oh, what does it matter about mine, Oedipus? You must like
illustrious names. . . . That of a little girl of seventeen wouldn't
interest you.
OEDIPUS.   That's unkind.
SPHINX.   You adore fame. Yet I should have thought the surest way
of foiling the oracle would be to marry a woman younger than
yourself.
OEDIPUS.   That doesn't sound like you. That's more like a mother of
Thebes where marriageable young men are few.
SPHINX.   And that's not like you either. That was a gross, common
thing to say.
OEDIPUS.   So, I shall have walked the roads past mountain and stream
merely to take a wife who will quickly become a Sphinx, worse
than that, a Sphinx with breasts and claws!
SPHINX.   Oedipus. . . .
OEDIPUS.   No, thank you! I prefer to try my luck. Take this belt: with
that you will be able to get to me when I have killed the beast.
(*Business.*)
SPHINX.   Have you ever killed?

OEDIPUS.   Yes, once. At the crossroads of Delphi and Daulis. I was walking along like a moment ago. A carriage was approaching driven by an old man with an escort of four servants. When I was on a level with the horses one of them reared and knocked me into one of these servants. The fool tried to strike me, I aimed a blow at him with my stick, but he dodged down and I caught the old man on the temple. He fell and the horses bolted, dragging him along. I ran after them, the servants were terrified and fled; I found myself alone with the bleeding body of the old man and the horses who screamed as they rolled about entangled, and broke their legs. It was dreadful . . . dreadful. . . .

SPHINX.   Yes, isn't it . . . it's dreadful to kill.

OEDIPUS.   Oh, well, it wasn't my fault and I think no more about it. The thing is to clear all obstacles, to wear blinkers, and not to give way to self-pity. Besides, there is my star.

SPHINX.   Then farewell, Oedipus. I am of the sex which is disturbing to heroes. Let us go our ways, we can have little in common.

OEDIPUS.   Disturbing to heroes, eh! You have a high opinion of your sex.

SPHINX.   And . . . supposing the Sphinx killed you?

OEDIPUS.   His death depends, if I'm not mistaken, on questions which I must answer. If I guess right he won't even touch me, he'll just die.

SPHINX.   And if you do not guess right?

OEDIPUS.   Thanks to my unhappy childhood I have pursued studies which give me a great start over the riffraff of Thebes.

SPHINX.   I'm glad to hear it.

OEDIPUS.   And I don't think this simple-minded monster is expecting to be confronted by a pupil of the best scholars of Corinth.

SPHINX.   You have an answer to everything. A pity, for, I own, Oedipus, I have a soft spot for weak people, and I should like to have found you wanting.

OEDIPUS.   Farewell.

(*The* SPHINX *makes one step as if to rush in pursuit of* OEDIPUS, *stops, but cannot resist the call. Until her 'I! I!' the* SPHINX *does not take her eyes off those of* OEDIPUS; *she moves as it were round this immobile, steady, vast gaze under eyelids which do not flicker.*)

SPHINX.   Oedipus!

OEDIPUS.   Did you call me?

SPHINX.   One last word. For the moment does nothing else occupy your mind, nothing else fire your heart, nothing stir your spirit save the Sphinx?

OEDIPUS.   Nothing else, for the moment.

SPHINX.   And he . . . or she who brought you into his presence. . . . I mean who would help you. . . . I mean who may perhaps know something to help bring about this meeting . . . would he or she

in your eyes assume such prestige that you would be touched and
moved?

OEDIPUS.   Naturally, but what does all this mean?

SPHINX.   And supposing I, I myself, were to divulge a secret, a
tremendous secret?

OEDIPUS.   You're joking!

SPHINX.   A secret which would allow you to enter into contact with
the enigma of enigmas, with the human beast, with the singing
bitch, as it is called, with the Sphinx?

OEDIPUS.   What! You? You? Did I guess aright, and has your curiosity
led you to discover . . .? No! How stupid of me. This is a woman's
trick to make me turn back.

SPHINX.   Good-bye.

OEDIPUS.   Oh! Forgive me! . . .

SPHINX.   Too late.

OEDIPUS.   I'm kneeling; a simple fool who begs forgiveness.

SPHINX.   You're a fatuous young man who is sorry to have lost his
chance and is trying to get it back.

OEDIPUS.   I am and I'm ashamed. Look, I believe you, I'll listen. But
if you have played me a trick I shall drag you by the hair and grip
you till the blood flows.

SPHINX.   Come here. (*She leads him opposite the pedestal.*) Shut your
eyes. Don't cheat. Count up to fifty.

OEDIPUS.   (*With his eyes shut.*) Take care!

SPHINX.   It's your turn to do that.

(*OEDIPUS counts. One feels that something extraordinary is happening. The* SPHINX *bounds across the ruins, disappears behind a
wall and reappears in the real pedestal, that is, she seems to be
fastened on to the pedestal, the bust resting on the elbows and
looking straight ahead, whereas the actress is really standing, and
only lets her bust appear and her arms in spotted gloves with her
hands grasping the edge; out of the broken wing suddenly grow
two immense, pale, luminous wings and the fragment of statue
completes her, prolonging her, and appearing to belong to her.*
OEDIPUS *is heard counting:* 'Forty-seven, forty-eight, forty-nine,'
then he makes a pause and shouts: 'Fifty.' *He turns round.*)

OEDIPUS.   You!

SPHINX.   (*In a high distant voice, joyous and terrible.*) Yes, I! I, the
Sphinx!

OEDIPUS.   I'm dreaming!

SPHINX.   You are no dreamer, Oedipus. You know what you want, and
did want. Silence. Here I command. Approach. (OEDIPUS, *with
his arms held stiffly by his body as if paralyzed, tries frantically to
free himself.*) Come forward. (OEDIPUS *falls on his knees.*) As
your legs refuse their help, jump, hop. . . . It's good for a hero to
make himself ridiculous. Come along! Move yourself! Don't worry,

there's nobody to see you. (OEDIPUS, *writing with anger, moves forward on his knees.*) That's it. Stop! And now. . . .

OEDIPUS.   And now, I'm beginning to understand your methods, what moves you make to lure and slay.

SPHINX.   . . . And now, I am going to give you a demonstration, I'm going to show you what would happen in this place, Oedipus, if you were any ordinary handsome youth from Thebes, and if you hadn't the privilege of pleasing me.

OEDIPUS.   I know what your pleasantries are worth. (*He knits up all the muscles of his body. It is obvious he is struggling against a charm.*)

SPHINX.   Yield! Don't try to screw up your muscles and resist. Relax! If you resist you will only make my task more delicate and I might hurt you.

OEDIPUS.   I shall resist! (*He shuts his eyes and turns his head away.*)

SPHINX.   You need not shut your eyes or turn away your head. For it is not by my look nor by my voice that I work. A blind man is not so dexterous, the net of a gladiator not so swift, nor lightning so fine, nor a coachman so stiff, nor a cow so weighty, nor a schoolboy working at his sums with his tongue out so good, nor a ship so hung with rigging, so spread with sails, secure and buoyant; a judge is not so incorruptible, insects so voracious, birds so bloodthirsty, the egg so nocturnal, Chinese executioners so ingenious, the heart so fitful, the trickster's hand so deft, the stars so fateful, the snake moistening its prey with saliva so attentive. I secrete, I spin, I pay out, I wind, I unwind, I rewind, in such a way that it is enough for me to desire these knots for them to be made, to think about them for them to be pulled tight or slackened. My thread is so fine it escapes the eye, so fluid you might think you were suffering from a poison, so hard a quiver on my part would break your limbs, so highly strung a bow stroked between us would make music in the air; curled like the sea, the column, and the rose, muscled like the octopus, contrived like the settings of our dreams, above all invisible, unseen, and majestic like the blood circulating in statues, my thread coils round you in fantastic patterns with the volubility of honey falling upon honey.

OEDIPUS.   Let me go!

SPHINX.   And I speak, I work, I wind, I unwind, I calculate, I meditate, I weave, I winnow, I knit, I plait, I cross, I go over it again and again, I tie and untie and tie again, retaining the smallest knots that I shall later on have to untie for you on pain of death; I pull tight, I loosen, I make mistakes and go back, I hesitate, I correct, entangle and disentangle, unlace, lace up and begin afresh; and I adjust, I agglutinate, I pinion, I strap, I shackle, I heap up my effects, till you feel that from the tip of your toes to the top of your head you are wrapped round by all the muscles of a reptile whose slightest breath constricts yours and makes you inert like the arm on which you fall asleep.

OEDIPUS. (*In a weak voice.*) Let me be! Mercy!...

SPHINX. And you will cry for mercy, and you won't have to be ashamed of that, for you won't be the first. I have heard prouder than you call for their mothers, and I have seen more insolent than you burst into tears; and the more silent are even weaker than the rest: they faint before the end and I have to minister to them after the fashion of embalmers in whose hands the dead are drunk men no longer able to stand on their feet!

OEDIPUS. Merope!... Mother!

SPHINX. Then I should command you to advance a little closer, and I should help you by loosening your limbs. So! And I should question you. I should ask you, for example: What animal is it that goes on four legs in the morning, in the afternoon on two, and in the evening on three? And you would cudgel your brains, till in the end your mind would settle on a little medal you won as a child, or you would repeat a number, or count the stars between these two broken columns; and I should make you return to the point by revealing the enigma.

Man is the animal who walks on four legs when he is a child, on two when he is full-grown, and when he is old with the help of a stick as a third leg.

OEDIPUS. How idiotic!

SPHINX. You would shout: How idiotic! You all say that. Then, since that cry only confirms your failure, I should call my assistant, Anubis. Anubis!

(ANUBIS *appears and stands on the right of the pedestal with folded arms; and his head turned to one side.*)

OEDIPUS. Oh, miss!... Oh, Sphinx!... Oh, Sphinx, please don't! No! No!

SPHINX. And I should make you go down on your knees. Go on.... Go on ... that's right.... Do as you're told. And you'd bend your head ... and Anubis would bound forward. He would open his wolf-like jaws! (OEDIPUS *utters a cry.*) I said: *would* bend, *would* bound forward, *would* open.... Haven't I always been careful to express myself in that mood? Why that cry? Why that horrified expression? It was a demonstration, Oedipus, simply a demonstration. You're free.

OEDIPUS. Free! (*He moves an arm, a leg.... He gets up, he reels, he puts his hand to his head.*)

ANUBIS. Pardon me, Sphinx, this man cannot leave here without undergoing the test.

SPHINX. But...

ANUBIS. Question him.

OEDIPUS. But...

ANUBIS. Silence! Question this man.

(*A silence.* OEDIPUS *turns his back and remains motionless.*)

SPHINX.   I'll question him. . . . All right. . . . I'll question him.
. . . (*With a last look of surprise at* ANUBIS.) What animal is it
that walks on four legs in the morning, on two in the afternoon,
and on three in the evening?

OEDIPUS.   Why, man, of course! He crawls along on four legs when
he's little, and walks on two legs when he is big, and when he's
old he helps himself along with a stick as a third leg. (*The* SPHINX
sways on her pedestal. Making his way to the left.) Victory! (*He
rushes out left. The* SPHINX *slips down into the column, disappears behind the wall, and reappears wingless.*)

SPHINX.   Oedipus! Where is he? Where is he?

ANUBIS.   Gone, flown. He is running breathlessly to proclaim his
victory.

SPHINX.   Without so much as a look my way, without a movement
betraying feeling, without a sign of gratitude.

ANUBIS.   Did you expect anything else?

SPHINX.   Oh, you fool! Then he has not understood a single thing.

ANUBIS.   Not a single thing.

SPHINX.   Kss! Kss! Anubis. . . . Here, here, look, after him, quickly,
bite him, Anubis, bite him!

ANUBIS.   And now it's all going to begin afresh. You're a woman again
and I'm a dog.

SPHINX.   I'm sorry. I lost my head, I'm mad. My hands are trembling.
I'm like fire. I wish I could catch him again in one bound, I'd spit
in his face, claw him with my nails, disfigure him, trample on
him, castrate him, and flay him alive!

ANUBIS.   That's more like yourself.

SPHINX.   Help me! Avenge me! Don't stand there idle!

ANUBIS.   Do you really hate this man?

SPHINX.   I do.

ANUBIS.   The worst that could happen to him would seem too good
to you?

SPHINX.   It would.

ANUBIS.   (*Holding up the Sphinx's dress.*) Look at the folds in this
cloth. Crush them together. Now if you pierce this bundle with a
pin, remove the pin, smooth the cloth till all trace of the old
creases disappears, do you think a simple country loon would believe that the innumerable holes recurring at intervals result from
a single thrust of a pin?

SPHINX.   Certainly not.

ANUBIS.   Human time is a fold of eternity. For us time does not exist.
From his birth to his death the life of Oedipus is spread flat before
my eyes, with its series of episodes.

SPHINX.   Speak, speak, Anubis, I'm burning to hear. What d'you see?

ANUBIS.   In the past Jocasta and Laïus had a child. As the oracle gave
out that this child would be a scourge. . . .

SPHINX.   A scourge!

ANUBIS.   A monster, an unclean beast. . . .

SPHINX.   Quicker, quicker!

ANUBIS.   Jocasta bound it up and sent it into the mountains to get lost.
A shepherd of Polybius found it, took it away, and, as Polybius
and Merope were lamenting a sterile marriage . . .

SPHINX.   I can't contain myself for joy.

ANUBIS.   They adopted it. Oedipus, son of Laïus, killed Laïus where
the three roads cross.

SPHINX.   The old man.

ANUBIS.   Son of Jocasta, he will marry Jocasta.

SPHINX.   And to think I said to him: 'She might be your mother.' And
he replied: 'The main thing is that she is not.' Anubis! Anubis! It's
too good to be true. . . .

ANUBIS.   He will have two sons who will kill each other, and two
daughters, one of whom will hang herself. Jocasta will hang herself. . . .

SPHINX.   Stop! What more could I hope for? Think, Anubis: the
wedding of Jocasta and Oedipus! The union of mother and son.
. . . And will he know soon?

ANUBIS.   Soon enough.

SPHINX.   What a moment to live! I have a foretaste of its delights.
Oh, to be present!

ANUBIS.   You will be.

SPHINX.   Is that true? . . .

ANUBIS.   I think the moment has come to remind you who you are and
what a ridiculous distance separates you from the little body which
is listening to me. You who have assumed the role of Sphinx! You,
the Goddess of Goddesses! You, the greatest of the great! The
implacable! Vengeance! Nemesis! (ANUBIS *prostrates himself.*)

SPHINX.   Nemesis. . . . (*She turns her back to the audience and
remains a while erect, making a cross with her arms. Suddenly
she comes out of this hypnotic state and rushes upstage.*) Once
more, if he is in sight, I should like to feed my hatred, I want to
see him run from one trap to another like a stunned rat.

ANUBIS.   Is that the cry of the awakening goddess or of the jealous
woman?

SPHINX.   Of the goddess, Anubis, of the goddess. Our gods have cast
me for the part of the Sphinx, and I shall show myself worthy of it.

ANUBIS.   At last!

(*The* SPHINX *looks down on the plain, leaning over to examine it.
Suddenly she turns round. The last trace of the greatness and fury
which had transformed her has disappeared.*)

SPHINX.   Dog! you lied to me.

ANUBIS.   I?

SPHINX.   Yes, you! Liar! Liar! Look along the road. Oedipus is coming
back, he's running, he's flying, he loves me, he has understood!

ANUBIS.   You know very well of what goes with his success and why the Sphinx is not dead.

SPHINX.   Look how he jumps from rock to rock, just as my heart leaps in my breast.

ANUBIS.   Convinced of his triumphs and your death this young fool has just realized that in his haste he's forgotten the most important thing.

SPHINX.   Mean wretch! Do you mean to tell me he wants to find me dead?

ANUBIS.   Not you, my little fury: the Sphinx. He thinks he's killed the Sphinx; he will have to prove it. Thebes won't be satisfied with a fisherman's yarn.

SPHINX.   You're lying. I'll tell him everything. I'll warn him. I'll save him. I'll turn him away from Jocasta, from that miserable town. . . .

ANUBIS.   Take care.

SPHINX.   I shall speak.

ANUBIS.   He's coming. Let him speak first.

(OEDIPUS, *out of breath, comes in downstage left. He sees the* SPHINX *and* ANUBIS *standing side by side.*)

OEDIPUS.   (*Saluting.*) I'm glad to see what good health the immortals enjoy after their death.

SPHINX.   What brings you back here?

OEDIPUS.   The collecting of my due.

(*Angry movement on the part of* ANUBIS *towards* OEDIPUS, *who steps back.*)

SPHINX.   Anubis! (*With a gesture she orders him to leave her alone. He goes behind the ruins. To* OEDIPUS.) You shall have it. Stay where you are. The loser is a woman. She asks one last favor of her master.

OEDIPUS.   Excuse me for being on my guard, but you've taught me to distrust your feminine wiles.

SPHINX.   Ah! I was the Sphinx. No, Oedipus. . . . You will bear my mortal remains to Thebes and the future will reward you . . . according to your deserts. No . . . I ask you merely to let me disappear behind this wall so that I may take off this body in which, I must confess, I have, for some little while, felt rather . . . cramped.

OEDIPUS.   Very well. But be quick. At the last bugles . . .

(*The bugles are heard.*)

You see, I speak of them and they are sounded. I must waste no time.

SPHINX.   (*Hidden.*) Thebes will not leave a hero standing at her gates.

VOICE OF ANUBIS.   (*From behind the ruins.*) Hurry, hurry. It looks as though you're inventing excuses and dawdling on purpose.

SPHINX.   (*Hidden.*) Am I the first, God of the Dead, whom you've had to drag by the clothes?

OEDIPUS. You're trying to gain time, Sphinx.

SPHINX. (*Hidden.*) So much the better for you, Oedipus. My haste might have served you ill. A serious difficulty occurs to me. If you bear into Thebes the body of a girl instead of the monster which the people expect, the crowd will stone you.

OEDIPUS. That's true! Women are simply amazing; they think of everything.

SPHINX. (*Hidden.*) They call me: The virgin with the claws. . . . The singing bitch. . . . They will want to identify my fangs. Don't be alarmed. Anubis! My faithful dog! Listen, since our faces are only shadows, I want you to give me your jackal's head.

OEDIPUS. Splendid idea!

ANUBIS. (*Hidden.*) Do what you like, so long as this shameful play-acting may come to an end and you may become yourself once more.

SPHINX. (*Hidden.*) I shan't be long.

OEDIPUS. I shall count up to fifty as I did before. I'll have my own back.

ANUBIS. (*Hidden.*) Sphinx, Sphinx, what are you waiting for?

SPHINX. Now I'm ugly, Anubis. A monster! . . . Poor boy . . . supposing I frighten him. . . .

ANUBIS. Don't worry, he won't even see you.

SPHINX. Is he blind then?

ANUBIS. Many men are born blind and only realize it the day a home-truth hits them between the eyes.

OEDIPUS. Fifty!

ANUBIS. (*Hidden.*) Go on. . . . Go on. . . .

SPHINX. (*Hidden.*) Farewell, Sphinx.

(*From behind the wall comes the staggering figure of a girl with a jackal's head. She waves her arms in the air and falls.*)

OEDIPUS. About time too! (*He rushes forward, not stopping to look, lifts the body, and takes a stand downstage right. He carries the body before him on his outstretched arms.*) No, not like that! I should look like that tragedian I saw in Corinth playing the part of a king carrying the body of his son. The pose was pompous and moved no one. (*He tries holding the body under his left arm; behind the ruins on the mound appear two giant forms covered with rainbow veils: the gods.*) No! I should be ridiculous. Like a hunter going home empty-handed after killing his dog.

ANUBIS. (*The form on the right.*) To free your goddess's body of all contamination, perhaps it might be as well for this Oedipus to disinfect you by bestowing on himself at least a title of demigod.

NEMESIS. (*The form on the left.*) He is so young. . . .

OEDIPUS. Hercules! Hercules threw the lion over his shoulder! . . . (*He puts the body over his shoulder.*) Yes, over my shoulder. Over my shoulder! Like a demigod!

ANUBIS. (*Veiled.*) Isn't he simply *incredible*!

OEDIPUS.   (*Moving off towards the left, taking two steps after each of his thanksgivings.*) I have killed the unclean beast.

NEMESIS.   (*Veiled.*) Anubis . . . I feel very ill at ease.

ANUBIS.   We must go.

OEDIPUS.   I have saved the town!

ANUBIS.   Come along, mistress, let us go.

OEDIPUS.   I shall marry Queen Jocasta!

NEMESIS.   (*Veiled.*) Poor, poor, poor mankind! . . . I can stand no more, Anubis. . . . I can't breathe. Let us leave the earth.

OEDIPUS.   I shall be king!

(*A murmur envelops the two huge forms. The veils fly round them. Day breaks. Cocks crow.*)

END OF ACT II

ACT III
THE WEDDING NIGHT

THE VOICE.

The coronation and nuptial celebrations have been going on since dawn. The crowd has just acclaimed the queen and the conqueror of the Sphinx for the last time.

Everyone goes home. In the little square of the royal palace now rises only the slight murmur of a fountain. Oedipus and Jocasta find privacy at last in the nuptial chamber. They are very tired and heavy with sleep. In spite of a few hints and civilities on the part of destiny, sleep will prevent them from seeing the trap which is closing on them forever.

The platform represents Jocasta's bedroom, which is as red as a little butcher's shop amid the town buildings. A broad bed covered with white furs. At the foot of the bed an animal's skin. On the right of the bed a cradle.

On the right forestage a latticed bay window, looking into the square of Thebes. On the left forestage a movable mirror of human size.

OEDIPUS and JOCASTA are wearing their coronation costumes. From the moment the curtain rises they move about in the slow motion induced by extreme fatigue.

JOCASTA. Phew! I'm done! You are so full of life, dear! I am afraid, for you, this room will become a cage, a prison.

OEDIPUS. My dear love! A scented bedroom, a woman's room, yours! After this killing day, those processions, that ceremonial, that crowd which still clamored for us under our very windows. . . .

JOCASTA. Not clamored for us . . . for you, dear.

OEDIPUS. Same thing.

JOCASTA. You must be truthful, my young conqueror. They hate me. My dress annoys them, my accent annoys them, they are annoyed by my blackened eyelashes, my rouge, and my vivaciousness!

OEDIPUS. It's Creon who annoys them! The cold, hard, inhuman Creon! I shall make your star rise again. Ah! Jocasta! What a magnificent program!

JOCASTA. It was high time you came. I'm exhausted.

OEDIPUS. Your room a prison! Your room, dear . . . and our bed.

JOCASTA. Do you want me to remove the cradle? After the death of the child I had to have it near me, I couldn't sleep. . . . I was too lonely. . . . But now . . .

OEDIPUS. (*In an indistinct voice.*) But now . . .

233

JOCASTA.   What?

OEDIPUS.   I said . . . I said . . . that it's he . . . he . . . the dog
. . . I mean . . . the dog who won't . . . the dog . . . the
fountain dog. . . .

JOCASTA.   Oedipus! Oedipus!

OEDIPUS.   (*Awakens, startled.*) What?

JOCASTA.   You were falling asleep, dear!

OEDIPUS.   Me? Never.

JOCASTA.   Oh, yes, you were, dear. You were telling me about a dog
who won't . . . a fountain dog. And I was listening. (*She laughs
and herself seems to be becoming vague.*)

OEDIPUS.   Nonsense!

JOCASTA.   I was asking you if you wanted me to remove the cradle, if
it worries you.

OEDIPUS.   Am I such a kid as to fear this pretty muslin ghost? On
the contrary it will be the cradle of my luck. My luck will grow
in it beside our love until it can be used for our first son. So you
see! . . .

JOCASTA.   My poor love. . . . You're dropping with fatigue and here
we stand . . . (*Same business as with* OEDIPUS.) . . . stand on
this wall. . . .

OEDIPUS.   What wall?

JOCASTA.   This rampart wall. (*She starts.*) A wall. . . . What? I . . .
I . . . (*Haggard.*) What's happening?

OEDIPUS.   (*Laughing.*) Well, this time it's you dreaming. We're tired
out, my poor sweet.

JOCASTA.   I was asleep? Did I talk?

OEDIPUS.   We *are* a pretty pair! Here I go telling you about fountain-
dogs, and you tell me about rampart walls; and this is our wedding
night! Listen, Jocasta, if I happen to fall asleep again (Are you
listening?), do please awaken me, shake me, and if you fall asleep
I'll do the same for you. This one night of all must not founder in
sleep. That would be too sad.

JOCASTA.   You crazy darling you, why? We have all our life before us.

OEDIPUS.   Maybe, but I don't want sleep to spoil the miracle of passing
this joyous night alone, unutterably alone with you. I suggest we
remove these heavy clothes, and as we're not expecting anyone——

JOCASTA.   Listen, my darling boy, you'll be cross . . .

OEDIPUS.   Jocasta, don't tell me there's still some official duty on the
program!

JOCASTA.   While my women are doing my hair, etiquette demands that
you receive a visit.

OEDIPUS.   A visit? At this hour?

JOCASTA.   A visit . . . a visit . . . a purely formal visit.

OEDIPUS.   In this room?

JOCASTA.   In this room.

OEDIPUS.   From whom?

JOCASTA.   Now don't get cross. From Tiresias.

OEDIPUS.   Tiresias? I refuse!

JOCASTA.   Listen, dear. . . .

OEDIPUS.   That's the limit! Tiresias playing the part of the family pouring out their farewell advice. How comic! I shall refuse his visit.

JOCASTA.   You crazy dear, I am asking you to. It's an old custom in Thebes that the high priest must in some way bless the royal wedding bonds. And besides, Tiresias is our old uncle, our watchdog. I am very fond of him, Oedipus, and Laïus adored him. He is nearly blind. It would be unfortunate if you hurt his feelings and set him against our love.

OEDIPUS.   That's all very well . . . in the middle of the night. . . .

JOCASTA.   Do! Please, for our sake and the sake of the future. It's essential. See him for five minutes, but see him and listen to him. I ask you to. (*She kisses him.*)

OEDIPUS.   I warn you I shan't let him sit down.

JOCASTA.   I love you, dear. (*Long kiss.*) I shall not be long. (*At the right-hand exit.*) I am going to let him know he can come. Be patient. Do it for my sake. Think of me. (*She goes out.*)

(OEDIPUS, *alone, looks at himself in the mirror and tries attitudes.* TIRESIAS *comes in left, unheard.* OEDIPUS *sees him in the middle of the room and turns about face.*)

OEDIPUS.   I am listening.

TIRESIAS.   Steady, my lord. Who told you I had saved up a sermon for your especial benefit?

OEDIPUS.   No one, Tiresias, no one. But I don't suppose you find it pleasant acting as killjoy. I suggest you are waiting for me to pretend I have heard your words of counsel. I shall bow, and you will give me the accolade. That would be enough for us in our tired state and at the same time custom would be satisfied. Have I guessed right?

TIRESIAS.   It is perhaps correct that there is at the bottom of this procedure a sort of custom, but for that, it would be necessary to have a royal marriage with all the dynastic, mechanical, and, I admit, even irksome business which that entails. No, my lord. Unforeseen events bring us face to face with new problems and duties. And you will agree, I think, that your coronation, and your marriage, appear in a form which is difficult to classify, and does not fit into any code.

OEDIPUS.   No one could say more graciously that I have crashed on Thebes like a tile from a roof.

TIRESIAS.   My lord!

OEDIPUS.   Let me tell you that things fitting neatly into categories reek of death. What we want, Tiresias, is not to fit, but to make a new departure. That's the sign of masterpieces and heroes. And that's the way to astonish and to rule.

TIRESIAS.   Right! Then you will admit that I myself, by playing a part outside the ceremonial sphere, am also making a new departure.

OEDIPUS.   To the point, Tiresias, to the point.

TIRESIAS.   Very well. I shall come straight to the point and speak with all frankness. My lord, your auguries look black, very black. I must put you on your guard.

OEDIPUS.   There! Just as I expected! Anything else would have surprised me. This is not the first time the oracles have been violently against me and my audacity has thwarted them.

TIRESIAS.   Do you believe they can be thwarted?

OEDIPUS.   I am the living proof of it. And even if my marriage upsets the gods, what about your promises, your freeing of the town, and the death of the Sphinx? And why should the gods have pushed me on as far as this room if this marriage displeases them?

TIRESIAS.   Do you think you can solve the problem of free will in a minute! Ah, power, I fear, is going to your head!

OEDIPUS.   You mean, power is slipping from your hands.

TIRESIAS.   Take care! You are speaking to a high priest.

OEDIPUS.   Take care yourself, high priest. Must I remind you that you are speaking to your king?

TIRESIAS.   To the husband of my queen, my lord.

OEDIPUS.   Jocasta notified me a little while ago that her power is to pass into my hands, in full. Run and tell that to your master.

TIRESIAS.   I serve only the gods.

OEDIPUS.   Well, if you prefer that way of putting it, say that to the person who is awaiting your return.

TIRESIAS.   Headstrong youth! You don't understand me.

OEDIPUS.   I understand perfectly well: an adventurer is in your way. I expect you hope I found the Sphinx dead on my path. The real conqueror must have sold it to me, like those hunters who buy the hare from a poacher. And supposing I have paid for the mortal remains, whom will you find ultimately as the conqueror of the Sphinx? The same type of person who has been threatening you every minute and preventing Creon from sleeping: a poor private soldier whom the crowd will bear in triumph and who will claim his due . . . (*Shouting.*) *his due!*

TIRESIAS.   He would not dare.

OEDIPUS.   Ah, you see! I have made you say it. That's the secret of the intrigue. There go your beautiful promises. That is what you were counting on.

TIRESIAS.   The queen is more to me than my own daughter. I must watch over her and defend her. She is weak, credulous, romantic. . . .

OEDIPUS.   You are insulting her.

TIRESIAS.   I love her.

OEDIPUS.   She is in need of no one's love but mine.

TIRESIAS.   About this love, Oedipus, I demand an explanation. Do you love the queen?

OEDIPUS.   With all my being.

TIRESIAS.   I mean: do you love to take her in your arms?

OEDIPUS.   I love most of all to be taken in her arms.

TIRESIAS.   I appreciate that delicate distinction. You are young, Oedipus, very young. Jocasta might be your mother. I know, oh, I know, you are going to reply——

OEDIPUS.   I am going to reply that I have always dreamed of such a love, an almost motherly love.

TIRESIAS.   Oedipus, aren't you confusing love and love of glory? Would you love Jocasta if she were not on a throne?

OEDIPUS.   A stupid question which is always being asked. Would Jocasta love me if I was old, ugly, and had not appeared out of the unknown? Do you fancy you cannot be infected by love through touching purple and gold? Are not the privileges of which you speak of the very substance of Jocasta, an organic part of her? We have been each other's from all eternity. Within her body lie fold after fold of a purple mantle which is much more regal than the one she fastens on her shoulders. I love and adore her, Tiresias. At her side I seem to occupy at last my proper place. She is my wife, she is my queen. I possess her, I shall keep her, I shall find her again, and neither by prayers nor threats can you drag from me obedience to orders from heaven knows where.

TIRESIAS.   Think it over again, Oedipus. The omens and my own wisdom give me every reason to fear this wild marriage. Think it over.

OEDIPUS.   Rather late, don't you think?

TIRESIAS.   Have you had experience of women?

OEDIPUS.   Not the slightest. And to complete your astonishment and cover myself with ridicule in your eyes, I am a virgin.

TIRESIAS.   You!

OEDIPUS.   The high priest of a capital is astonished that a country boy should put all his pride in keeping himself pure for a single offering. You would, no doubt, have preferred a degenerate prince, a puppet, so that Creon and the priests could work the strings.

TIRESIAS.   You are going too far!

OEDIPUS.   Must I order you again? . . .

TIRESIAS.   Order? Has pride sent you mad?

OEDIPUS.   Don't put me into a rage! My patience is at an end, my temper is ungovernable, and I am capable of any unpremeditated act.

TIRESIAS.   What arrogance! . . . Weak and arrogant!

OEDIPUS.   You will have brought it on yourself. (*He throws himself upon* TIRESIAS, *seizing him by the neck.*)

TIRESIAS.   Let me go. . . . Have you no shame?

OEDIPUS.   You are afraid that I could, from your face, there, there, close up, and in your blind man's eyes, read the real truth about your behavior.

TIRESIAS.   Murderer! Sacrilege!

OEDIPUS.   Murderer! I ought to be. . . . One day I shall probably have to repent for this foolish respect, and if I dared . . . Oh, oh! Why!

Gods, look here . . . here . . . in his blind man's eyes, I had no idea it was possible.

TIRESIAS.   Let me go! Brute!

OEDIPUS.   The future! My future, as in a crystal bowl.

TIRESIAS.   You will repent. . . .

OEDIPUS.   I see, I see. . . . Soothsayer, you have lied! I shall marry Jocasta. . .. A happy life, rich, prosperous, two sons . . . daughters . . . and Jocasta still as beautiful, still the same, in love, a mother in a palace of happiness. . . . Now it's not so clear, not clear. I want to see! It's your fault, soothsayer. . . . I want to see! (*He shakes him.*)

TIRESIAS.   Accursed!

OEDIPUS.   (*Suddenly recoiling, letting* TIRESIAS *go, and putting his hands over his eyes.*) Oh filthy wretch! I am blind. He's thrown pepper at me. Jocasta! Help! Help! . . .

TIRESIAS.   I threw nothing, I swear. You are punished for your sacrilege.

OEDIPUS.   (*Writhing on the ground.*) You lie!

TIRESIAS.   You wanted to read by force the secrets my diseased eyes hold and that I myself have not yet interpreted; and you are punished.

OEDIPUS.   Water, water, quickly, it's burning me. . . .

TIRESIAS.   (*Laying his hands over* OEDIPUS's *face.*) There, there. . . . Keep quiet. . . . I forgive you. Your nerves are on edge. Come, keep still. Your sight will return, I swear. I expect you got to the point which the gods wish to keep in darkness, or they may be punishing you for your impudence.

OEDIPUS.   I can see a little . . . I think.

TIRESIAS.   Are you in pain?

OEDIPUS.   Less . . . the pain is going. Ah! . . . it was like fire, red pepper, a thousand pinpoints, a cat's paw scrabbling in my eye. Thank you. . . .

TIRESIAS.   Can you see?

OEDIPUS.   Not clearly, but I can see, I can see. Phew! I really thought I was blind for good and that it was one of your kind of tricks. In any case, I deserved it.

TIRESIAS.   We like to believe in miracles when miracles suit us, and when they don't we like to believe in them no longer, but say it is a trick on the part of the soothsayer.

OEDIPUS.   Forgive me. I am of a violent and vindictive disposition. I love Jocasta. I was waiting for her, impatiently, and this extraordinary phenomenon, all those images of the future in the pupil of your eyes bewitched me, fuddled me, as it were, and made me mad.

TIRESIAS.   Can you see better now? It is an almost blind man asking you.

OEDIPUS.   Quite, and I have no more pain. I'm really ashamed of my conduct towards you, a blind man and a priest. Will you accept my apologies?

TIRESIAS. I was only speaking for your own good and Jocasta's.

OEDIPUS. Tiresias, in a way I owe you something in return, a confession that is difficult to make, and which I had promised myself I would make to no one.

TIRESIAS. A confession?

OEDIPUS. I noticed during the coronation ceremony that you and Creon had some understanding between you. Do not deny it. Well, I wished to keep my identity secret; but I give it up. Listen carefully, Tiresias. I am not a wanderer. I come from Corinth. I am the only child of King Polybius and Queen Merope. A nobody will not soil this marriage bed. I am a king and son of a king.

TIRESIAS. My lord. (*He bows.*) A word from you would have cleared the atmosphere of the uneasiness created by your incognito. My little girl will be so glad. . . .

OEDIPUS. But wait! I ask you as a favor to safeguard at least this last night. Jocasta still loves in me the wanderer dropped out of the clouds, the young man stepping suddenly out of the shadows. It will unfortunately be only too easy to destroy this mirage tomorrow. In the meantime, I hope the queen will become sufficiently submissive for her to learn without disgust that Oedipus is not a prince fallen from the sky, but merely a prince.

I wish you good evening, Tiresias. Jocasta will be on her way back. I am dropping with fatigue . . . and we want to remain alone together. That is our desire.

TIRESIAS. My lord, excuse me. (OEDIPUS *makes a sign to him with his hand.* TIRESIAS *stops at the left-hand exit.*) One last word.

OEDIPUS. (*Loftily.*) What is it?

TIRESIAS. Forgive my boldness. This evening, after the closing of the temple, a beautiful young girl came into the private chapel where I work, and, without a word of excuse, handed me this belt and said: 'Give it to Lord Oedipus and repeat word for word this sentence: Take this belt: with that you will be able to get to me when I have killed the beast.' I had scarcely tucked away the belt when the girl burst out laughing and disappeared, I don't know how.

OEDIPUS. (*Snatching away the belt.*) And that's your trump card. You have already built up a whole system in order to destroy my hold on the queen's head and heart. How should I know? A previous promise of marriage. . . . A girl takes her revenge. . . . The temple scandal. . . . Telltale find. . . .

TIRESIAS. I was fulfilling my commission. That's all.

OEDIPUS. Miscalculation and bad policy. Go . . . and carry this bad news with all speed to Prince Creon. (TIRESIAS *stays on the threshold.*) He reckoned he was going to scare me! But in point of fact, it is I who scare you, Tiresias, I scare you. I can see it written in large letters on your face. It wasn't so easy to terrorize the child. Confess that the child terrifies you, grandpa! Confess, grandpa!

Confess I terrify you! Confess at least I make you afraid! (*OEDI-PUS is lying face down on the animal skin.* TIRESIAS *is standing like a bronze statue. Silence. Then thunder.*)

TIRESIAS. Yes. Very afraid. (*He leaves, walking backwards. His prophetic voice can be heard.*) Oedipus! Oedipus, listen to me! You are pursuing classic glory. There is another kind: obscure glory, the last resource of the arrogant person who persists in opposing the stars.

(OEDIPUS *remains looking at the belt. When* JOCASTA *comes in, in her nightdress, he quickly hides the belt under the animal skin.*)

JOCASTA. Well, now? What did the old ogre say? Did he torment you?

OEDIPUS. Yes . . . no. . . .

JOCASTA. He's a monster. Did he prove to you that you are too young for me?

OEDIPUS. You are beautiful, Jocasta! . . .

JOCASTA. That I am old?

OEDIPUS. He rather gave me to understand that I loved your pearls, and your diadem.

JOCASTA. Always spoiling everything! Ruining everything! Doing harm!

OEDIPUS. But you can take it from me, he didn't manage to scare me. On the contrary, I scared him. He admitted that.

JOCASTA. Well done! My love! You, dear, after my pearls and diadem!

OEDIPUS. I am happy to see you again without any pomp, without your jewels and orders, white, young, and beautiful, in our own room.

JOCASTA. Young! Oedipus! . . . You mustn't tell lies. . . .

OEDIPUS. Again! . . .

JOCASTA. Don't scold me.

OEDIPUS. Yes, I shall scold you! I shall scold you because a woman like you ought to be above such nonsense. A young girl's face is as boring as a white page on which my eyes can read nothing moving; whereas your face! . . . I must have the scars, the tattooing of destiny, a beauty which has weathered tempests. Why should you be afraid of crows' feet, Jocasta? What would a silly schoolgirl's look or smile be worth beside the remarkable sacred beauty of your face; slapped by fate, branded by the executioner, and tender, tender and . . . (*He notices that* JOCASTA *is weeping.*) Jocasta! my dear little girl, you're crying! Whatever's the matter? . . . All right, then. . . . What have I done now? Jocasta! . . .

JOCASTA. Am I so old . . . so very old?

OEDIPUS. My dear crazy girl! It's you who persist in——

JOCASTA. Women say things to be contradicted. They always hope it isn't true.

OEDIPUS. My dear Jocasta! . . . What a fool I am! What a great brute! . . . Darling. . . . Don't cry. Kiss me. . . . I meant——

JOCASTA.   Never mind. . . . I am being ridiculous. (*She dries her eyes.*)

OEDIPUS.   It's all my fault.

JOCASTA.   It isn't. . . . There . . . the black is running into my eye now. (OEDIPUS *coaxes her.*) It's all over.

OEDIPUS.   Quick, a smile. (*Slight rumbling of thunder.*) Listen.

JOCASTA.   My nerves are bad because of the storm.

OEDIPUS.   But look at the sky! It is full of stars, and clear.

JOCASTA.   Yes, but there is a storm brewing somewhere. When the fountain makes a still murmur like silence, and my shoulder aches, there is always a storm about and summer lightning. (*She leans against the bay window. Summer lightning.*)

OEDIPUS.   Come here, quickly. . . .

JOCASTA.   Oedipus! . . . come here a moment.

OEDIPUS.   What is it? . . .

JOCASTA.   The sentry . . . look, lean out. On the bench on the right, he's asleep. Don't you think he's handsome, that boy? with his mouth wide open.

OEDIPUS.   I'll throw some water in it. I'll teach him to sleep!

JOCASTA.   Oedipus!

OEDIPUS.   How dare he sleep when guarding the queen!

JOCASTA.   The Sphinx is dead and you're alive. Let him sleep in peace! May all the town sleep in peace! May they all sleep, every one!

OEDIPUS.   Lucky sentry!

JOCASTA.   Oedipus! Oedipus! I should like to make you jealous, but it isn't that. . . . This young guard——

OEDIPUS.   What is so extraordinary about this young guard then?

JOCASTA.   During that famous night, the night of the Sphinx, while you were encountering the beast, I had an escapade on the ramparts with Tiresias. I had heard that a young soldier had seen the ghost of Laïus, and that Laïus was calling for me to warn me of a threatening danger. Well . . . that soldier was the very sentry who is guarding us.

OEDIPUS.   Who is guarding us! . . . Anyway . . . Let him sleep in peace, my kind Jocasta. I can guard you all right on my own. Of course, not the slightest sign of the ghost of Laïus?

JOCASTA.   Not the slightest, I'm sorry to say. . . . Poor lad! I touched his shoulders and legs, and kept saying to Zizi, 'Touch, touch,' and I was in a state . . . because he was like you. And it's true, you know, Oedipus, he was like you.

OEDIPUS.   You say: 'This guard was like you.' But, Jocasta, you didn't know me then; it was impossible for you to know or to guess. . . .

JOCASTA.   Yes, indeed, that's true. I expect I meant to say my son would be about his age. (*Silence.*) Yes . . . I am getting muddled. It's only now that this likeness strikes me. (*She shakes off this uneasy feeling.*) You're a dear, you're good-looking, I love you. (*After a pause.*) Oedipus!

OEDIPUS. My goddess!

JOCASTA. I approve of your not telling the story of your victory to Creon or to Tiresias, or to everybody (*With her arms round his neck.*), but to me . . . to me!

OEDIPUS. (*Freeing himself.*) I had your promise! . . . And but for that boy——

JOCASTA. Is the Jocasta of yesterday the Jocasta of now? Haven't I a right to share your memories without anybody else knowing anything about it?

OEDIPUS. Of course.

JOCASTA. And do you remember you kept saying: 'No, no, Jocasta, later, later when we are in our own room.' Well, aren't we in our own room? . . .

OEDIPUS. Persistent monkey! Charmer! She always ends by getting what she wants. Now lie still. . . . I am beginning.

JOCASTA. Oh, Oedipus! Oedipus! What fun! What fun! I'm quite still. (JOCASTA *lies down, shuts her eyes, and keeps still.* OEDIPUS *begins lying, hesitating, inventing, accompanied by the storm.*)

OEDIPUS. Now. I was nearing Thebes. I was following the goat track which rounds the hill to the south of town. I was thinking of the future, of you whom I imagined less beautiful than you are in reality, but still, very beautiful, painted, and sitting on a throne in the center of a group of ladies-in-waiting. Supposing you do kill it, I said to myself, would you, Oedipus, dare to ask for the promised reward? Should I dare to go near the queen? . . . And I kept walking and worrying. All of a sudden I stopped dead. My heart was beating hard. I had just heard a sort of song. The voice that sang it was not of this world. Was it the Sphinx? My haversack contained a knife. I slipped the knife under my tunic and crept along. Do you know those ruins of a little temple on the hill, with a pedestal and the hind quarters of a chimera? (*Silence.*) Jocasta . . . Jocasta. . . . Are you asleep?

JOCASTA. (*Awakening with a start.*) What? Oedipus . . .

OEDIPUS. You were asleep.

JOCASTA. I wasn't.

OEDIPUS. Oh, yes, you were. There's a fickle little girl for you! She wants me to tell her a story and then goes and falls asleep in the middle of it, instead of listening.

JOCASTA. I heard it all. You're mistaken. You were speaking of a goat track.

OEDIPUS. I'd got a long way past the goat track! . . .

JOCASTA. Don't be angry, darling. Are you cross with me? . . .

OEDIPUS. Me?

JOCASTA. Yes, you are cross with me, and rightly. What a stupid silly I am! That's what age does for you.

OEDIPUS. Don't be sad. I'll start the story again, I promise you, but first of all you and I must lie down and sleep a little, side by side.

After that, we shall be clear of this sticky paste, this struggle against sleep which is spoiling everything. The first one to wake up will wake the other. Promise.

JOCASTA. Promised. Poor queens know how to snatch a moment's sleep where they sit, between two audiences. But give me your hand. I am too old. Tiresias was right.

OEDIPUS. Perhaps so for Thebes, where girls are marriageable at thirteen. But what about me? Am I an old man? My head keeps dropping and my chin hitting my chest wakes me up.

JOCASTA. You? That's quite different, it's the dustman, as children say! But as for me . . . You begin to tell the most marvelous story in the world, and I go and doze away like a grandma beside the fire. And you will punish me by never beginning it over again, and finding excuses. . . . Did I talk in my sleep?

OEDIPUS. Talk? No. I thought you were being very attentive. You naughty girl, have you some secrets you are afraid you might give away?

JOCASTA. No, only those foolish things we sometimes say when sleeping.

OEDIPUS. You were lying as good as gold. Till soon, my little queen.

JOCASTA. Very soon, my king, my love.

(*Hand in hand, side by side, they shut their eyes and fall into the heavy sleep of people who struggle against sleep. A pause. The fountain soliloquizes. Slight thunder. Suddenly the lighting becomes the lighting of dreams. The dream of* OEDIPUS. *The animal skin is pushed up. It is lifted by the head of* ANUBIS. *He shows the belt at the end of his outstretched arm.* OEDIPUS *tosses about and turns over.*)

ANUBIS. (*In a slow mocking voice.*) Thanks to my unhappy childhood, I have pursued studies which give me a great start over the riffraff of Thebes, and I don't think this simple-minded monster is expecting to be confronted by a pupil of the best scholars of Corinth. But if you have played a trick on me I shall drag you by the hair. (*Up to a howl.*) I shall drag you by the hair, I shall drag you by the hair, I shall grip you till the blood flows! . . . I shall grip you till the blood flows! . . .

JOCASTA. (*Dreaming.*) So, not that paste, not that foul paste! . . .

OEDIPUS. (*In a distant, muffled voice.*) I shall count up to fifty: one, two, three, four, eight, seven, nine, ten, ten, eleven, fourteen, five, two, four, seven, fifteen, fifteen, fifteen, fifteen, three, four. . . .

ANUBIS. And Anubis would bound forward. He would open his wolf-like jaws! (*He disappears under the platform. The animal skin resumes its normal appearance.*)

OEDIPUS. Help! Help! I'm here! Help me! Everybody! Come here!

JOCASTA. What? What is it? Oedipus, my darling! I was in a dead sleep! Wake up! (*She shakes him.*)

OEDIPUS.   (*Struggling and talking to the* SPHINX.) Oh, miss! No! no, miss! Please don't! No! Let me go, miss! No! No! No!

JOCASTA.   My pet, don't scare me so. It's a dream. This is me, me, Jocasta, your wife, Jocasta.

OEDIPUS.   No, no! (*He awakens.*) Where was I? How ghastly! Jocasta, is that you? . . . What a nightmare, what a horrible nightmare!

JOCASTA.   There, there, it's all over, you are in our room, dear, in my arms. . . .

OEDIPUS.   Didn't you see anything? Of course, how silly of me, it was that animal skin. . . . Phew, I must have talked. What did I say?

JOCASTA.   Now it's your turn. You were shouting: 'Oh no, miss! Please don't miss! Let me go, miss!' Who was that wicked young woman?

OEDIPUS.   I don't remember. What a night!

JOCASTA.   How about me? Your shouts saved me from an unspeakable nightmare. Look! You're soaked through, swimming in perspiration. It's my fault. I let you go to sleep in all those heavy clothes, golden chains, clasps, and those sandals which cut your heel. . . . (*She lifts him up. He falls back.*) Come along! What a big baby! I can't possibly leave you in this state. Don't make yourself so heavy, help me. . . . (*She lifts him up, takes off his tunic, and rubs him down.*)

OEDIPUS.   (*Still in a vague state.*) Yes, my little darling mother . . .

JOCASTA.   (*Mocking him.*) 'Yes, my little darling mother. . . .' What a child! Now he's taking me for his mother.

OEDIPUS.   (*Awake.*) Oh, forgive me, Jocasta, my love, I am being so silly. You see I'm half asleep, I mix up everything. I was thousands of miles away with my mother who always thinks I am too cold or too hot. You're not cross?

JOCASTA.   Silly boy! Let me see to you, and sleep away. All the time he's excusing himself and asking forgiveness. My word! What a polite young man! He must have been taken care of by a very kind mother, very kind, and then he goes and leaves her, yes. But I mustn't complain of that. I love with all the warmth of a woman in love that mother who petted you and kept you and brought you up for me, for us.

OEDIPUS.   Sweet.

JOCASTA.   I should say so! Your sandals. Raise your left leg. (*She takes off his sandals.*) And now the right. (*Same business; suddenly she utters a terrible cry.*)

OEDIPUS.   Hurt yourself?

JOCASTA.   No . . . no. . . . (*She recoils, and stares like a mad creature at Oedipus's feet.*)

OEDIPUS.   Ah, my scars! . . . I didn't know they were so ugly. My poor darling, did they upset you?

JOCASTA.   Those holes . . . how did you get them? . . . They must come from such serious injuries. . . .

OEDIPUS.   From the hunt, it seems. I was in the woods; my nurse was carrying me. Suddenly from a clump of trees a wild boar broke cover and charged her. She lost her head and let me go. I fell and a woodcutter killed the animal while it was belaboring me with its tusks. . . . But she is really as pale as a ghost! My darling! I ought to have warned you. I'm so used to them myself, those awful holes. I didn't know you were so sensitive. . . .

JOCASTA.   It's nothing. . . .

OEDIPUS.   Weariness and sleepiness put us into this state of vague terror . . . you had just come out of a bad dream. . . .

JOCASTA.   No, Oedipus. No. As a matter of fact, those scars remind me of something I am always trying to forget.

OEDIPUS.   I always strike unlucky.

JOCASTA.   You couldn't possibly know. It's to do with a woman, my foster-sister and linen-maid. She was with child at the same age as myself, at eighteen. She worshipped her husband despite the difference of age and wanted a son. But the oracles predicted so fearful a future for the child that, after giving birth to a son, she had not the courage to let it live.

OEDIPUS.   What?

JOCASTA.   Wait. . . . Imagine what strength of mind a poor woman must have to do away with the life of her life . . . the son from her womb, her ideal on earth and love of loves.

OEDIPUS.   And what did this . . . woman do?

JOCASTA.   With death in her heart, she bored holes in the feet of the nursling, tied them, carried it secretly to a mountainside, and left it to the mercy of the wolves and bears. (*She hides her face.*)

OEDIPUS.   And the husband?

JOCASTA.   Everyone thought the child had died a natural death, and that the mother had buried it with her own hands.

OEDIPUS.   And . . . this woman . . . still lives?

JOCASTA.   She is dead.

OEDIPUS.   So much the better for her, for my first example of royal authority would have been to inflict on her, publicly, the worst tortures, and afterwards, to have her put to death.

JOCASTA.   The oracles were clear and matter-of-fact. Before those things a woman always feels so stupid and helpless.

OEDIPUS.   To kill! (*Recalling Laïus.*) Of course, it isn't infamous to kill when carried away by the instinct of self-defense, and when bad luck is involved. But basely to kill in cold blood the flesh of one's flesh, to break the chain . . . to cheat in the game!

JOCASTA.   Oedipus, let's talk about something else . . . your furious little face upsets me too much.

OEDIPUS.   Yes, let us talk about something else. I should be in danger of loving you less if you tried to defend this miserable wretch.

JOCASTA.   You're a man, my love, a free man and a chief! Try and put yourself in the place of a child-mother who is credulous about the oracles, worn out, disgusted, confined, and terrified by the priests. . . .

OEDIPUS.   A linen-maid! That's her only excuse. Would you have done it?

JOCASTA.   (*With a gesture.*) No, of course not.

OEDIPUS.   And don't run away with the idea that to fight the oracles requires a herculean determination. I could boast and pose as a wonder; I should be lying. You know, to thwart the oracles I only had to turn my back on my family, my longings, and my country. But the farther I got from my native town, and the nearer I came to yours, the more I felt I was returning home.

JOCASTA.   Oedipus, Oedipus, that little mouth of yours which chatters away, that little wagging tongue, those frowning eyebrows and fiery eyes! Couldn't the eyebrows relax a little, Oedipus, and the eyes close gently for once, and that mouth be used for softer caresses than words?

OEDIPUS.   I tell you, I'm just a brute! A wretched, clumsy brute!

JOCASTA.   You are a child.

OEDIPUS.   I'm not a child!

JOCASTA.   Now he's off again! There, there, be a good boy.

OEDIPUS.   You're right. I'm behaving very badly. Calm this talkative mouth with yours, and these feverish eyes with your fingers.

JOCASTA.   One moment. I'll close the grille gate. I don't like that gate being open at night.

OEDIPUS.   I'll go.

JOCASTA.   You stay lying down. . . . I'll take a look in the mirror at the same time. Do you want to embrace a fright? After all this excitement the gods alone know what I look like. Don't make me nervous. Don't look at me. Turn the other way, Oedipus.

OEDIPUS.   I'm turning over. (*He lies across the bed with his head on the edge of the cradle.*) There, I'm shutting my eyes. I'm not here.

(JOCASTA *goes to the window.*)

JOCASTA.   (*To* OEDIPUS.) The little soldier is still asleep, he's half-naked . . . and it isn't warm tonight . . . poor lad! (*She goes to the movable mirror; suddenly she stops, listening in the direction of the square. A drunk is talking very loud with long pauses between his reflections.*)

VOICE OF THE DRUNK.   Politics! . . . Pol—i—tics! What a mess! They just tickle me to death! . . . Ho! Look, a dead 'un! . . . Sorry, a mistake: 's a soldier asleep. . . . Salute! Salute the sleeping army! (*Silence.* JOCASTA *stands on her toes, and tries to see outside.*) Politics! . . . (*Long silence.*) It's a disgrace . . . a disgrace. . . .

JOCASTA.   Oedipus, my dear!

OEDIPUS.   (*In his sleep.*) H'm!

JOCASTA.   Oedipus! Oedipus! There's a drunk and the sentry doesn't hear him. I hate drunks. I want him sent away, and the soldier woken up. Oedipus! Oedipus! Please! (*She shakes him.*)

OEDIPUS. I wind, I unwind, I calculate, I meditate, I weave, I win-
   now, I knit, I plait, I cross . . .
JOCASTA. What's he saying? How soundly he sleeps! I might die, he
   wouldn't notice it.
DRUNK. Politics! (*He sings. As soon as the first lines are sung
   JOCASTA leaves OEDIPUS, putting his head back on the edge of
   the cradle, and goes to the middle of the room. She listens.*)
   'Majesty, whatever are you at?
   Majesty, whatever are you at?
   Your husband's much too young,
   Much too young for you, that's flat . . . Flat. . . .'
   Et cetera. . . .
JOCASTA. Oh! The beasts . . .
DRUNK. 'Majesty, whatever are you at
   With this holy marriage?'

   (*During what follows JOCASTA, bewildered, goes to the window
   on tiptoe. Then she returns to the bed, and leaning over OEDIPUS,
   watches his face, but still looking from time to time in the direction of the window, where the voice of the Drunk alternates with
   the murmur of the fountain and the cockcrows. She lulls the sleep
   of OEDIPUS by gently rocking the cradle.*)

   Now, if I were in politics . . . I'd say to the queen: Majesty! . . .
   a minor can't be your man. . . . Take a husband who's serious,
   sober, and strong . . . a husband like me. . . .
VOICE OF THE GUARD. (*Who has just awakened. He gradually re-
   covers his self-assurance.*) Get along, there!
VOICE OF THE DRUNK. Salute the waking army! . . .
GUARD. Get a move on!
DRUNK. You might at least be polite. . . .

   (*As soon as the GUARD is heard JOCASTA leaves the cradle, having first muffled Oedipus's head in the muslin.*)

GUARD. D'you want a taste of the cooler?
DRUNK. 'Always politics! What a mess!
   Majesty, whatever are you at? . . .'
GUARD. Come on, hop it! Clear off! . . .
DRUNK. I'm clearing off, I'm clearing off, but you might be polite
   about it.

   (*During these remarks JOCASTA goes to the mirror. She cannot
   see herself owing to the moonlight conflicting with the dawn. She
   takes the mirror by its supports and moves it away from the wall.
   The mirror itself stays fastened to the scenery. JOCASTA drags the
   frame along, trying to get some light, glancing at OEDIPUS who
   sleeps on. She brings the piece of furniture carefully into the fore-
   ground, opposite the prompter's box, so that the public becomes
   her mirror and JOCASTA looks at herself in full view of all.*)

DRUNK.   (*Very distant.*)
     'Your husband's much too young,
     Much too young for you, that's flat! . . . Flat! . . .'
     (*Sound of the sentry's footsteps, bugle calls, cockcrows, a kind of
     snoring noise from the rhythmic, youthful breathing of* OEDIPUS.
     JOCASTA, *with her face up against the empty mirror, lifts her
     cheeks by handfuls.*)

END OF ACT III

ACT IV

OEDIPUS REX

(SEVENTEEN YEARS LATER)

THE VOICE.

Seventeen years soon pass. The great plague in Thebes seems to be the first setback to that renowned good luck of Oedipus. For their infernal machine to work properly the gods wanted all ill luck to appear in the guise of good luck. After delusive good fortune the king is to know true misfortune, the supreme consecration, which, in the hands of the cruel gods, makes of this playing-card king, in the end, a man.

Cleared of the bedroom, the red hangings of which are pulled away into the flies, the platform seems to be surrounded by walls which grow in size. It finally represents an inner courtyard. By a balcony high up Jocasta's room is made to communicate with this court. One gets to it through an open door below, in the center.

When the curtain rises OEDIPUS, *aged, and wearing a little beard, stands near the door.* TIRESIAS *and* CREON *are standing on the right and left of the court. Center right, a young boy rests one knee on the ground: he is the* MESSENGER *from Corinth.*

OEDIPUS. What have I done to shock people now, Tiresias?

TIRESIAS. You are enlarging on things, as usual. I think, and I'll say again, it might be more decent to learn of a father's death with less joy.

OEDIPUS. Indeed. (*To the* MESSENGER.) Don't be afraid, boy. Tell me, what was the cause of Polybius's death? Is Merope so very terribly unhappy?

MESSENGER. King Polybius died of old age, my lord, and . . . the queen, his wife, is barely conscious. She is so old she can't fully realize even her misfortune.

OEDIPUS. (*His hand to his mouth.*) Jocasta! Jocasta!

(JOCASTA *appears on the balcony; she parts the curtain. She is wearing her red scarf.*)

JOCASTA. What is it?

OEDIPUS. How pale you are! Don't you feel well?

JOCASTA. Oh, you know, the plague, the heat, and visits to hospitals —I'm absolutely exhausted. I was resting on my bed.

OEDIPUS. This messenger has brought me great news, worth disturbing you for.

JOCASTA. (*Astonished.*) Good news? . . .

OEDIPUS. Tiresias blames me for finding it good: My father is dead.

JOCASTA. Oedipus!

249

OEDIPUS.   The oracle told me I should be his murderer, and that I should be the husband of my mother. Poor Merope! she is very old, and my father, Polybius, has died a good natural death!

JOCASTA.   I never knew the death of a father was a subject for rejoicing!

OEDIPUS.   I hate play-acting and conventional tears. To tell the truth, I was so young when I left my father and mother that I no longer have any particular feelings for them.

MESSENGER.   Lord Oedipus, if I may . . .

OEDIPUS.   You may, my boy.

MESSENGER.   Your indifference is not really indifference. I can explain it to you.

OEDIPUS.   Something new.

MESSENGER.   I ought to have begun at the end of the story. On his deathbed the King of Corinth asked me to tell you that you are only his adopted son.

OEDIPUS.   What?

MESSENGER.   My father, one of Polybius's shepherds, found you on a hill, at the mercy of wild beasts. He was a poor man; he carried his find to the queen who used to weep because she had no children. This is how the honor of performing such an extraordinary mission at the Theban court has fallen to me.

TIRESIAS.   This young man must be exhausted after his journey, and he has crossed our town which is full of noxious vapors. Perhaps it would be better if he took some refreshment and rested before being questioned.

OEDIPUS.   No doubt, Tiresias, you would like the torture to last. You think my world is tottering. You don't know me well enough. Don't you rejoice too soon. Perhaps I am happy to be a child of fortune.

TIRESIAS.   I was only putting you on your guard against your sinister habit of questioning, seeking to know and understand everything.

OEDIPUS.   Whether I am a child of the muses or of a common tramp, I shall question without fear; I will know things.

JOCASTA.   Oedipus, my love, he is right. You get excited. . . . You get excited . . . and you believe everything you're told, and then afterwards——

OEDIPUS.   What! That's the last straw! Unflinchingly I withstand the hardest knocks, and you all plot to make me put up with these things and not try to find out where I come from.

JOCASTA.   Nobody is plotting . . . my love . . . but I know you. . . .

OEDIPUS.   You're wrong, Jocasta. Nobody knows me at present, neither you, nor I, nor anyone else. (*To the* MESSENGER.) Don't tremble, my lad. Speak up. Tell us more.

MESSENGER.   That's all I know, Lord Oedipus, except that my father untied you when you were half dead, hanging by your wounded feet from a short branch.

OEDIPUS.   Oh, so that's how we come by those fine scars!

JOCASTA. Oedipus, Oedipus, dear . . . come up here. . . . Anybody would think you enjoy opening old wounds.

OEDIPUS. And so those were my swaddling clothes! . . . My story of the hunt is . . . false, like so many others. Well, if that's the way things are . . . I may come of a god of the woods and a dryad, and have been nourished by wolves. Don't you rejoice too soon, Tiresias!

TIRESIAS. You do me an injustice. . . .

OEDIPUS. At any rate I haven't killed Polybius, but . . . now I come to think of it . . . I have killed a man.

JOCASTA. You!

OEDIPUS. Yes! I! Oh, you needn't be alarmed! It was accidental, and sheer bad luck! Yes, I have killed, soothsayer, but as for parricide, you'd better officially give it up. During a brawl with the serving-men I killed an old man at the crossroads of Delphi and Daulis.

JOCASTA. At the crossroads of Delphi and Daulis! . . . (*She disappears as if drowning.*)

OEDIPUS. There's marvelous material for you to build up a really fine catastrophe. That traveler must have been my father. 'Heavens, my father!' But incest won't be easy, gentlemen. What do *you* think, Jocasta? . . . (*He turns round and sees* JOCASTA *has disappeared.*) Splendid! Seventeen years of happiness, and a perfect reign, two sons, two daughters, and then this noble lady only has to learn that I am the stranger whom, by the way, she first loved, and she turns her back on me. Let her sulk! Let her sulk! I shall be left alone with my fate.

CREON. Your wife, Oedipus, is ill. The plague is demoralizing us all. The gods are punishing the town and desire a victim. A monster is hiding in our midst. They demand he shall be driven out. Day after day the police have failed and the streets are littered with corpses. Do you realize what an effort you are asking of Jocasta? Do you realize that you are a man and she is a woman, an ageing woman at that, and a mother who is worried about the plague? Instead of blaming Jocasta for a movement of impatience, you might have found some excuse for her.

OEDIPUS. I see what you are getting at, brother-in-law. The ideal victim, the monster in hiding. . . . From one coincidence to another . . . wouldn't it be a pretty job, with the help of the priests and the police, to succeed in muddling the people of Thebes and make them believe *I* am that monster!

CREON. Don't be absurd!

OEDIPUS. I think you're capable of anything, my friend. But Jocasta, that's another matter. . . . I am astonished at her attitude. (*He calls her.*) Jocasta! Jocasta! Where are you?

TIRESIAS. She looked all to pieces. She is resting . . . let her be.

OEDIPUS. I am going. . . . (*He goes toward the* MESSENGER.) Now, let us come to the point. . . .

MESSENGER. My lord!

OEDIPUS.   Holes in my feet . . . bound . . . on the mountainside. . . .
How did I fail to understand at once? . . . And then I wondered
why Jocasta . . .
   It's very hard to give up enigmas. . . . Gentlemen, I was not the
son of a dryad. Allow me to introduce you to the son of a linen-
maid, a child of the people, a native product.

CREON.   What's this all about?

OEDIPUS.   Poor Jocasta! One day I unwittingly told her what I thought
of my mother. . . . I understand everything now. She must be
terrified, and utterly desperate. In short . . . wait for me. I must
question her at all costs. Nothing must be left in the dark. This
horrible farce must come to an end. (*He leaves by the middle door.*
CREON *immediately rushes to the* MESSENGER, *whom he pushes
out through the door on the right.*)

CREON.   He is mad. What does all this mean?

TIRESIAS.   Don't move. A storm is approaching from out of the ages.
A thunderbolt is aimed at this man, and I ask you, Creon, to let
this thunderbolt follow its capricious course, to wait motionless
and not to interfere in the slightest.

(*Suddenly,* OEDIPUS *is seen on the balcony, stranded and aghast.
He leans on the wall with one hand.*)

OEDIPUS.   You have killed her for me.

CREON.   What do you mean, killed?

OEDIPUS.   You have killed her for me. . . . There she is, hanging . . .
hanging by her scarf. . . . She is dead . . . gentlemen, she is dead.
. . . It's all over . . . all over.

CREON.   Dead? I'm coming. . . .

TIRESIAS.   Stay here. . . . As a priest I order you to. It's inhuman, I
know; but the circle is closing; we must keep silent and remain
here. . . .

CREON.   You wouldn't stop a brother from——

TIRESIAS.   I would! Let the story be. Don't interfere.

OEDIPUS.   (*At the door.*) You have killed her for me . . . she was
romantic . . . weak . . . ill . . . you forced me to say I was a murderer. . . . Whom did I murder, gentlemen, I ask you? . . . through
clumsiness, mere clumsiness . . . just an old man on the road . . .
a stranger.

TIRESIAS.   Oedipus: through mere clumsiness you have murdered
Jocasta's husband, King Laïus.

OEDIPUS.   You scoundrels! . . . I can see it now! You are carrying on
your plot! . . . It was even worse than I thought. . . . You have
made my poor Jocasta believe that I was the murderer of Laïus
. . . that I killed the king to set her free and so that I could marry
her.

TIRESIAS.   Oedipus, you have murdered Jocasta's husband, King
Laïus. I have known it for a long time, and you are telling lies. I

haven't said a word about it either to you or to her or to Creon or to anyone else. This is how you reward me for my silence.

OEDIPUS. Laïus! . . . So that's it. . . . I am the son of Laïus and of the linen-maid. The son of Jocasta's foster-sister and Laïus.

TIRESIAS. (*To* CREON.) If you want to act, now's the time. Quickly. There are limits even to harshness.

CREON. Oedipus, through you, my sister is dead. I kept silence only to protect Jocasta. I think it is useless to prolong unduly the false mystery and the unraveling of a sordid drama whose intrigue I have finally succeeded in discovering.

OEDIPUS. Intrigue?

CREON. The most secret of secrets are betrayed one day or another to the determined seeker. The honest man, sworn to silence, talks to his wife, who talks to an intimate friend, and so on. (*Into the wings.*) Come in, shepherd.

(*An old* SHEPHERD *comes in, trembling.*)

OEDIPUS. Who is this man?

CREON. The man who carried you bleeding and bound onto the mountainside, in obedience to your mother's orders. Let him confess.

SHEPHERD. To speak means death to me. Princes, why haven't I died before so as not to live through this minute?

OEDIPUS. Whose son am I, old man? Strike, strike quickly!

SHEPHERD. Alas!

OEDIPUS. I am near to the sound of something that should not be heard.

SHEPHERD. And I . . . to the saying of something that should not be said.

CREON. You must say it. I wish you to.

SHEPHERD. You are the son of Jocasta, your wife, and of Laïus, killed by you where the three roads cross. Incest and parricide, may the gods forgive you!

OEDIPUS. I have killed whom I should not. I have married whom I should not. I have perpetuated what I should not. All is clear. . . .

(*He goes out.* CREON *drives out the* SHEPHERD.)

CREON. Who was the linen-maid and foster-sister he was talking about?

TIRESIAS. Women cannot hold their tongues. Jocasta must have made out that her crime had been committed by a servant to see what effect it had on Oedipus. (*He holds his arm and listens with bent head. The little* ANTIGONE, *with hair dishevelled, appears on the balcony.*)

ANTIGONE. Uncle! Tiresias! Come up, quickly! Hurry, it's horrible! I heard shrieks inside; mother, my darling mother, doesn't move anymore, she has fallen like a log, and my dear, dear father is writhing over her body and stabbing at his eyes with her big golden brooch. There's blood everywhere. I'm frightened! I'm too frightened, come up . . . come up, quickly. . . . (*She goes in.*)

CREON.   This time nothing shall prevent me. . . .

TIRESIAS.   Yes, I shall. I tell you, Creon, the finishing touches are being put to a masterpiece of horror. Not a word, not a gesture. It would be improper for us to cast over it so much as a shadow of ourselves.

CREON.   Sheer insanity!

TIRESIAS.   Sheer wisdom. . . . You must admit——

CREON.   No! Besides, power falls once more into my hands. (*He frees himself, and at the very moment when he bounds forward the door opens.* OEDIPUS *appears, blind.* ANTIGONE *is clinging to his clothes.*)

TIRESIAS.   Stop!

CREON.   I shall go mad! Why, but why has he done that? Better have killed himself.

TIRESIAS.   His pride does not desert him. He wanted to be the happiest of men, now he wants to be the most unhappy.

OEDIPUS.   Let them drive me out, let them finish me off, stone me, strike down the foul beast!

ANTIGONE.   Father!

TIRESIAS.   Antigone! My soothsaying staff! Offer it to him from me. It will bring him some luck.

(ANTIGONE *kisses the hand of* TIRESIAS *and carries the staff to* OEDIPUS.)

ANTIGONE.   Tiresias offers you his staff.

OEDIPUS.   Is he there? . . . I accept it, Tiresias. . . . I accept it. . . . Do you remember, seventeen years ago, I saw in your eyes that I should become blind, and I couldn't understand it? I see it all clearly now, Tiresias, but I am in pain. . . . I suffer. . . . The journey will be hard.

CREON.   We must not let him cross the town, it would cause an awful scandal.

TIRESIAS.   (*In a low voice.*) In a town of plague? And besides, you know, they saw the king Oedipus wished to be; they won't see the king he is now.

CREON.   Do you mean he will be invisible because he is blind?

TIRESIAS.   Almost.

CREON.   Well, I can tell you I have had enough of your riddles and symbols. *My* head is firmly fixed on my shoulders and my feet planted firmly on the ground. I shall give my orders.

TIRESIAS.   Your police may be well organized, Creon; but where this man goes they will not have the slightest power.

CREON.   I——

(TIRESIAS *seizes his arm and puts his hand over his mouth. . . . For* JOCASTA *appears in the doorway.* JOCASTA, *dead, white, beautiful, with closed eyes. Her long scarf is wound round her neck.*)

OEDIPUS.   Jocasta! You, dear! You alive!

JOCASTA.   No, Oedipus. I am dead. You can see me because you are blind; the others cannot see me.

OEDIPUS.   Tiresias is blind. . . .

JOCASTA.   Perhaps he can see me faintly . . . but he loves me, he won't say anything. . . .

OEDIPUS.   Wife, do not touch me! . . .

JOCASTA.   Your wife is dead, hanged, Oedipus. I am your mother. It's your mother who is coming to help you. . . . How would you even get down these steps alone, my poor child?

OEDIPUS.   Mother!

JOCASTA.   Yes, my child, my little boy. . . . Things which appear abominable to human beings, if only you knew, from the place where I live, if only you knew how unimportant they are!

OEDIPUS.   I am still on this earth.

JOCASTA.   Only just. . . .

CREON.   He is talking with phantoms, he's delirious. I shall not allow that little girl——

TIRESIAS.   They are in good care.

CREON.   Antigone! Antigone! I am calling you. . . .

ANTIGONE.   I don't want to stay with my uncle! I don't want to, I don't want to stay in the house. Dear father, dear father, don't leave me! I will show you the way, I will lead you. . . .

CREON.   Thankless creature.

OEDIPUS.   Impossible, Antigone. You must be a good girl. . . . I cannot take you with me.

ANTIGONE.   Yes, you can!

OEDIPUS.   Are you going to desert your sister Ismene?

ANTIGONE.   She must stay with Eteocles and Polynices. Take me away, please! Please! Don't leave me alone! Don't leave me with uncle! Don't leave me at home!

JOCASTA.   The child is so pleased with herself. She imagines she is your guide. Let her think she is. Take her. Leave everything to me.

OEDIPUS.   Oh! . . . (*He puts his hand to his head.*)

JOCASTA.   Are you in pain, dear?

OEDIPUS.   Yes, my head, my neck and arms. . . . It's fearful.

JOCASTA.   I'll give you a dressing at the fountain.

OEDIPUS.   (*Breaking down.*) Mother . . .

JOCASTA.   Who would have believed it? That wicked old scarf and that terrible brooch! Didn't I say so time and again?

CREON.   It's utterly impossible. I shall not allow a madman to go out free with Antigone. It is my duty to——

TIRESIAS.   Duty! They no longer belong to you; they no longer come under your authority.

CREON.   And pray whom should they belong to?

TIRESIAS.   To the people, poets, and unspoiled souls.

JOCASTA.   Forward! Grip my dress firmly . . . don't be afraid. (*They start off.*)

ANTIGONE.   Come along, father dear . . . let's go. . . .

OEDIPUS.   Where do the steps begin?

JOCASTA and ANTIGONE.   There is the whole of the platform yet. . . .
(*They disappear* . . . JOCASTA *and* ANTIGONE *speak in perfect unison.*) Careful . . . count the steps . . . One, two, three, four, five. . . .

CREON.   And even supposing they leave the town, who will look after them, who will admit them?

TIRESIAS.   Glory.

CREON.   You mean rather dishonor, shame. . . .

TIRESIAS.   Who knows?

CURTAIN

QUESTIONS

[*Act I*]

1. Cocteau could certainly assume that any audience would know the Oedipus myth, and yet he has The Voice retell it. Why? Consider that it tells the story, but also tells a great deal more. The tone of the retelling is brusque, caustic, tough-minded. How is this tone created? What does it tell us about the way we should take the play? What attributes are ascribed to Oedipus and what is their relevance to what unfolds? What is the attitude toward "the gods"? Why the reference to Siegfried? How does the final paragraph sum up the attitude of The Voice? (What do "infernal" and "machine" mean in this context? Why is *The Infernal Machine* a better title than *The Infernal Gods* would be?)

2. How does the brief description of the basic stage setting and lighting support the attitude which The Voice has suggested we take toward the story as it will unfold?

3. The first "scene" in Act I, the confrontation of the young and old soldiers, serves several purposes. What background information comes out in their talk? Characterize them: in what ways are they similar and in what ways different? Show that they talk in terms suggestive of modern times despite the references to ghosts, sphinxes, and vampires.

4. What purpose does the Captain serve? (Jocasta and Tiresias could have come upon the two soldiers without his presence.) Why does he show up? What is his attitude toward the soldiers and their "ghost" story? What advantage is there in having the details of the ghost's appearance told first to the Captain instead of to Jocasta and Tiresias?

5. Consider Jocasta's role in Act I:
   (a) Why does she go to the ramparts to find the young soldier?
   (b) Does she learn anything that she will pay any attention to? If not, why not?
   (c) How does she treat Tiresias and he her?
   (d) Is there anything "queenly" about her? Explain.

6. The comments Jocasta makes about being "surrounded by objects which hate me" and about Zizi's stepping on her scarf would be merely childish if we were not aware of what she does to herself at the end. How does the light-handed treatment add a lurid flavor to this piece of foreshadowing? In the same vein, discuss (a) her statement, "I feel [things] there" (putting "her hand on her belly"), and (b) her dream.

7. What is ironic about the way Jocasta carries on with the young soldier? Why is it significant that she is more interested in him than in his story?

8. Why is it that the ghost can appear to the soldiers but not to Jocasta or Tiresias? (At one point she says, "I think I hear my name." Why is that significant?) The act heading is "The Ghost of Laïus."

Why? What purpose is served by this act as one of four that dramatize the "machine . . . constructed . . . for the mathematical destruction of a mortal"? Consider what the ghost is and what it is trying to do, how successful it is, and what attitudes different people have toward it. If the ghost's appearance is a warning, why is it significant that people pay little attention?

9. Just before its final disappearance the ghost says, "Alas! Do these simple souls then know what the priests cannot divine?" Besides the direct reference to the soldier's common-sense comments about not fetching the Queen and Tiresias, what other meaning does the ghost's remark have? In what other ways have the simple soldiers known what the priests "cannot divine"?

10. Discuss the blending of realism and fantasy in Act I. Point out as many references as you can to modern concerns and attitudes.

[*Act II*]

1. Act II takes place in time simultaneously with Act I: while the ghost is unsuccessfully trying to warn Jocasta, the "infernal gods" are successfully operating the infernal machine. What is Cocteau's reason for such a juxtaposition? How does each act comment on the other? Since the acts occur simultaneously, could they be switched in performance? Discuss.

2. What do we know about the "infernal gods" after the brief opening confrontation between the Sphinx and Anubis? What does Anubis mean by ". . . logic forces us to appear to men in the shape in which they imagine us; otherwise, they could see only emptiness"? Why does Anubis have to explain to the Sphinx what she certainly ought to know? (Remember that she is Nemesis—Vengeance— and is well aware of that fact.)

3. What purposes are served by the scene between the Sphinx and the Matron? What is the Matron's attitude toward the existence of such things as the Sphinx and vampires? What conflicting attitudes are revealed here and in Act I? (Notice that her sons have a perfectly rational explanation for the vampire story, as the Captain has a perfectly rational explanation for the Sphinx and ghost stories.)

4. The Matron's complaints about the state of affairs in Thebes are the stock complaints about any city at any time. Her desire for a "dictator . . . a man of action" to "make an end of corruption . . . and care for the people and save us" is a stock response to frustration. Show how Cocteau has individualized her sufficiently to keep her from being simply a mouther of complaints.

5. Anubis has mentioned "victims" who touch the "girl-figure," but the little boy stumbles into the "girl-figure" with no ill effects. Why? The little boy also unwittingly speaks the truth about the Sphinx. (His mother says, "At that age they don't know what they're saying.") What is comparable to this in Act I?

6. Why does the Sphinx "hope that this massacre would come to an end"? Anubis has said that "these victims . . . are no more than noughts wiped off a slate" to the gods. What does her human form do to her? (How would you have an actor read Anubis's line: "It's nice to see that human form doesn't make a great goddess become a little woman.") Why is it necessary and effective to have the Sphinx foretell what she intends to do when the right young man comes along? (At the beginning of the play The Voice says, "The meeting takes place. What was the nature of this meeting? Mystery." But there is no mystery about it, except to the people of Thebes.)

7. Show that the confrontation between Oedipus and the Sphinx proceeds just like that of two young people attracted to each other and testing each other, which is how Cocteau wants us to see their meeting.

8. Characterize Oedipus as he reveals himself in this confrontation. What is important to him? What attractive qualities does he have? What unattractive ones? Why does the Sphinx find him "pleasing"? There are a number of fascinating ironies in his comments. One is, "The thing is to clear all obstacles, to wear blinkers, and not to give way to self-pity." Show why that is ironic. Point out other examples.

9. The Sphinx's recital of how she works is more than a clever incantation, although it has its incantatory effect. What qualities does she attribute to herself, and what qualities does the "thread" have with which she immobilizes her victims? (Is she speaking as the Sphinx here, or as Nemesis? Or isn't there any difference? Why is she at Thebes in the first place? How is it that Anubis knows Oedipus's background and fate and the Sphinx doesn't?)

10. What had the Sphinx hoped Oedipus would do after his prearranged "victory"? What does she mean by ". . . he has not understood a single thing"? What should he have understood? Why is it significant that she reverts quickly to her womanly attitude when she sees him returning, and that she suggests that he will be stoned if he goes to Thebes with her girl-figure and not the monster the people expect the Sphinx to be?

11. For the second time in the play we are reminded in detail of Oedipus's fate, this time by Anubis. How is this foretelling related in tone to The Voice's foretelling?

12. When the Sphinx puts on Anubis's jackal's head, she says of Oedipus: "Poor boy . . . supposing I frighten him . . ." Anubis answers, "Don't worry, he won't even see you." Why is it significant that Oedipus *doesn't* look at the remains, so intent is he on savoring his triumphal entrance into Thebes "Like a demigod" and that he never even mentions the change?

13. Characterize Oedipus's behavior after the Sphinx falls. Why does Anubis say, "Isn't he *incredible*?" How are the last comments of

Nemesis and Anubis to be taken as observations on Oedipus in particular and mankind in general? Do *these* gods, at least, seem infernal, despite their assigned tasks? Discuss.

14. What happens at the end of Act I at the same time that Oedipus marches toward Thebes with the Sphinx slung over his shoulder? How do the events of each act dovetail?

[*Act III*]

1. The Voice says, "In spite of a few hints and civilities on the part of destiny, sleep will prevent them from seeing the trap which is closing on them forever." What "hints and civilities" does destiny give? The cradle is the most obvious one; what uses of it does Cocteau make throughout the act? How is Tiresias successfully ignored and rebuffed? What do Oedipus and Jocasta dream about in the brief moments when fatigue overcomes them?

2. What is the significance of the bedroom's being "as red as a little butcher's shop amid the town buildings"? How does the stage direction that during the act Oedipus and Jocasta are to "move about in the slow motion induced by extreme fatigue" enhance symbolically and visually the effect of a trap's "closing on them forever"?

3. For Cocteau's purposes why is it essential to have one act take place on the wedding night before the marriage is consummated?

4. Soon after their confrontation opens, Tiresias refers to Oedipus as "Headstrong youth!" How does Oedipus show himself to be headstrong, callow, arrogant? Why does he react so violently to Tiresias's warnings? What does he think disturbs Tiresias about the marriage? What in truth does disturb him?

5. Seeing the truth in Tiresias's eyes is another bit of fantasy—like the ghost of Laïus and the appearance of the gods—mixed in straightforwardly with a realistic, heated exchange between Oedipus and Tiresias. Why are we willing to accept the impossible as entirely reasonable?

6. What is the irony of Oedipus's repeated "I want to see!" as he searches the blind man's eyes?

7. What is the purpose of the return of the belt through Tiresias? What should it remind Oedipus of, besides the incident of giving it to the young girl who turns out to be the Sphinx? What is Oedipus's reaction to Tiresias's disclosure? How long does he remember the belt? Where is it during the rest of the act? Is the "scourge" dead? Discuss.

8. Explain Jocasta's reference to "foul paste." Where else has she described a nightmare experience in such terms?

9. The Matron had said of Jocasta that "at a distance you would say she was twenty-nine or thirty." How old does she act? How regal does she act? She is obviously vain and flirtatious; she bullies Tiresias and pampers Oedipus. Both men find her fascinating. Why? What is there in them or in her that ties them to her? How

is Oedipus, in particular, partially characterized by his relationship to Jocasta as Queen and woman? (Notice the terms she continually uses in addressing him.)

10. What is the young soldier's role in the act? Consider his falling asleep on guard duty, his handling of the drunk, and his earlier relationship to Jocasta, which she has mentioned to Oedipus.

11. What is the drunk's role? What does he say about the marriage? Is there supposedly a kind of wisdom (truth?) in drunks, much like that in simple-minded people and children, who previously in the play have shown themselves wiser than they know?

[*Act IV*]

1. The Voice says that "in the end . . . this playing-card king . . ." will become "a man." Clearly, then, Act IV is meant to dramatize this. In what sense has Oedipus been a "playing-card king"? In what sense has he been less than "a man"? What changes come in him as he learns the truth about his past and present? Review the words that have been used to characterize him? How many are relevant in Act IV? What does it mean to become "a man"?

2. What is Tiresias's role in restraining Creon and letting Oedipus work out the action to its bitter end? He calls the "story" a "masterpiece of horror"; and to Creon's "Sheer insanity!" he responds, "Sheer wisdom." What does he mean by that, and why will he not let Creon interfere? Why is he wiser than Creon?

3. Why does Jocasta return as mother and not as wife?

4. What do the closing lines between Tiresias and Creon mean? What is the "glory" Tiresias refers to? How can it be the same as "dishonor, shame"—Creon's words for it? If Oedipus is moving off the literal platform of the stage back into myth, how can his fate be considered as "glory" to some ("the people, poets, and unspoiled souls") and "dishonor, shame" to others?

ESSAY QUESTIONS

1. Discuss the number of ways in which the details of the Oedipus myth are given seemingly rational explanations. (For instance, Cocteau has Oedipus say that he left Corinth because he wanted to "satisfy [his] thirst for the unknown," and the oracle's prophecy gave him a good excuse to get out of town, even though he didn't believe a word of it.) Why is it that the "clever" people in the play —Oedipus, Creon, the Matron's sixteen-year-old son—have answers for all the superstitious nonsense? Why are their answers just as nonsensical? What is Cocteau saying about the connection between the mythic and the actual?

2. If you haven't read Sophocles's *Oedipus Rex* (*Oedipus the King*) with which Cocteau's play has more than a casual connection, find a copy and read it. Sophocles's play concerns itself wholly with Oedipus's quest for self-knowledge. It opens at the edge of the abyss, as it were; and Oedipus's relentless insistence on knowing who he is finally plunges him into it. How is Cocteau's play different in structure and therefore in emphasis? Consider the four scenes chosen to dramatize the working of the "infernal machine." Notice that the last act, "Oedipus Rex," is much shorter than the first three. Why? If the play does not focus on a quest for self-knowledge, what is its focus? How is Cocteau's Oedipus like Sophocles's Oedipus and how is he different?

3. After the lengthy commentary at the beginning of Act I, The Voice has little to say, even though it provides the bridge between the acts. Why do you suppose Cocteau uses it at all? Show why it is certainly not a modern substitute for Sophocles's Chorus. What would be lost if it were eliminated? (Consider that for Cocteau's play as well as for Sophocles's the audience must know that Oedipus is marked for "destruction" from the beginning.)